Dessert

More Than 200 Recipes for Delicious Cakes, Pies, Pastries and More

Dessert

More Than 200 Recipes for Delicious Cakes, Pies, Pastries and More

Fireside
A Division of Simon & Schuster, Inc.
1230 Avenue of the Americas
New York, NY 10020

Published originally under the title *I Segreti del Dolce*

Copyright © 2007 Food Editore srl
Via Bordoni, 8 - 20124 MILAN
Via Mazzini, 6 - 43100 PARMA
www.foodeditore.it

English translation by
Traduzioni Culinarie

English layout by
TGM

Photographs by
Davide Di Prato, Alberto Rossi

Recipes by
Simone Rugiati, Licia Cagnoni

First Fireside edition April 2009
FIRESIDE and colophon are registered trademarks of Simon & Schuster, Inc.

For information about special discounts for bulk purchases, please contact Simon & Schuster Special Sales
at 1-800-456-6798 or business@simonandschuster.com.

Printed in China
10 9 8 7 6 5 4 3 2 1

ISBN-13: 978-1-4391-1001-0
ISBN-10:   1-4391-1001-8

Dessert

More Than 200 Recipes for Delicious Cakes, Pies, Pastries and More

A Fireside Book
Published by Simon & Schuster
New York   London   Toronto   Sydney

Table of Contents

Have you ever walked past a bakery window and wished you could make those glazed tortes, fruit-filled tartlets and colorful mousses at home? What about soufflés, sorbets and layered semifreddos? Or the beautiful decorations of sugar, caramelized fruit and chocolate that garnish restaurant desserts?

This book contains all the secrets, advice and invaluable tips you need to make delicious desserts, from the most classic recipes to modern, innovative variations.

The introduction contains a short overview of the main ingredients used in confectionery and baking, a section dedicated to the tools of the trade and a glossary with common pastry-making terminology.

With the help of expert pastry chefs, we have created a "dessert school" that will help you find your way through the varied world of sweet cooking. The "school" is divided into six sections: Cakes and Pies, Small Pastries, Mousses and Creams, Frozen Desserts, Risen Breads and Fried Sweets and Decorations.

In each chapter, you'll find step-by-step procedures illustrated with clear color photographs, explanations of techniques, recipes for basic elements and suggestions and advice for getting the best results every time. Each chapter concludes with a selection of creative and elaborate recipes that our pastry chefs have chosen especially for you.

This symbol marks the recipes created by pastry chefs at the end of each chapter.

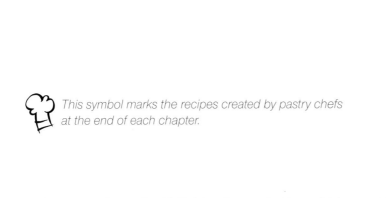

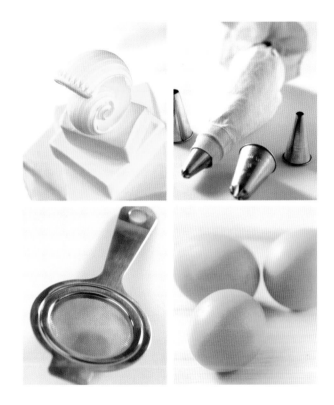

Ingredients & Tools

An overview of the indispensable ingredients for making desserts
and the kitchen tools helpful for the recipes in this book,
followed by a glossary of useful terms.

Flour There are several types of wheat flour and, for optimal results, each recipe calls for a specific variety of flour. When making cakes with baking powder and for thickening sauces, it is best to use flours high in starch and low in protein. Baking powder is activated by heat during cooking, but too much gluten reduces rising power, causing uneven-looking cakes. In many cases extra starch is added to the batter or dough to avoid such problems. When making sauces, flour is often used as a thickening agent. Liquids are absorbed by starch molecules, causing them to expand and thicken the sauce.

When preparing risen desserts, the strength of the flour is one of the most important factors. Strength is mainly determined by the amount of protein in the flour, specifically the qualities of gliadin and glutenin, the components of gluten. A strong flour will absorb more liquid, making the batter or dough more resistant, especially during the rising phase. This prevents desserts from "falling" and helps the batter or dough to absorb moisture.

All-purpose flour is suitable for cookies, wafers and pastries such as beignets, as well as cakes like sponge cake or shortcrust dough. Manitoba flour, made from hard wheat, has a fairly high protein content and should be used for batters and doughs that contain more liquid such as babà, croissants and brioche.

Sweeteners Any substance that creates a sweet flavor can be included in this category. Sugar is the most common sweetener and is usually made from sugar cane or sugar beets. Sugar, or sucrose, is made up of one glucose and one fructose molecule. Raw sugar has larger crystals and ranges in color from pale to dark brown. During the refining process, the color of the sugar changes from brown to white and the sugar crystal becomes smaller. Many types of sugar are available for purchase, and some of the most common include granulated sugar, confectioners' sugar, sugar cubes and raw cane sugar.

Confectioners' sugar is refined sugar that has been ground to obtain a flour-like consistency. It is used for preparations like royal icing, delicate cookies and marzipan, and in desserts with short cooking times.

ingredients

Honey is used to flavor certain types of cookies and is an essential ingredient of candy like torrone and nougat.

Glucose is a natural cereal-based sweetener, usually made from the wheat, which like fructose is usually sold in a 40-45% density and is available in specialty baking stores.

Eggs Eggs are used in many desserts. They are classified into three categories in the United States: AA, A and B, in descending quality order. For desserts using raw or briefly cooked eggs it is best to use the freshest, highest quality eggs available. However these desserts are best avoided by anyone in a high-risk category for salmonella, such as pregnant women.

Eggs are also divided into size categories: XL (extra large) for eggs weighing around 2.6 oz (75 g), L (large) for eggs around 2.3 oz (65 g), M (medium) for eggs around 2 oz (55 g) and S (small) for eggs weighing less than 2 oz (53 g). The recipes in this book are based on large eggs.

To determine how fresh an egg is, fill a container with 4 cups (1 liter) of water and 1 ½ tablespoons of salt. Carefully lower the egg into the water. If it sinks to the bottom and remains there the egg is very fresh; if the egg tends to float upwards it is anywhere from 1-5 days old; if the egg reaches the surface of the water it is more than 2 weeks old.

When making desserts, remember not to let a mixture of eggs and sugar sit for too long. Sugar is often used to preserve foods and could "cook" the fats and proteins in the egg yolk, giving the finished dessert a slight cooked-egg flavor.

Butter is an animal fat made from the cream of cow's milk. When making milk products, the milk is separated into a solid part and a liquid part. The solid part is further processed to make butter. By law, butter is made from the cream or whey from cow's milk and has specific chemical, physical and taste properties. Butter should have a uniform shape and color and should be compact and shiny; it should not have excessive quantities of water, which can be detected if drops of condensation form when sliced. Artisanal butter made from grass-fed cow's milk tends to have a whiter color in the winter months, while the summer butter tends to have a pale yellow color; this is due to the cows' changing diet.

Salted Butter is used for cookies, brisée dough and savory pastry.

Cream Before homogenization, the thick fatty layer is skimmed off the milk; this is called cream. Cream is divided into various grades, which are determined by the percentage of fat. In the U.S. the grades are as follows: half and half (10.5% to 18% fat), light or table cream (18-30% fat), heavy cream or whipping cream (above 36% fat). Pasteurized cream may be stored in the refrigerator for 10-12 days. For bests results when whipping cream, make sure that both the unwhipped cream and bowl are chilled in the refrigerator before whipping the cream. 4 cups (1 l) of cream should take about 2 ½ minutes to whip; small lumps of butter will form if the cream is beaten for too long.

Yeast and Baking Powder Several types of rising agents are used in baking; some of the most common are described here.

Baking powder is a chemical rising agent made from tartaric acid and sodium bicarbonate mixed together with a little flour. It is used for making cookies, muffins, cakes, quick breads and some shortcrust doughs. It has two rises, one when it comes into contact with liquid and a second when the batter heated or baked.

Starter This is a small amount of risen dough that is saved and added to new doughs. Starters can made and used almost immediately or may be kept for years if they are correctly stored. Starters are used when making pandoro, panettone or croissants.

Yeast There are many types of yeast. In this book, recipes call for active dry yeast as it is easiest to work with and most readily available. Active dry yeast, cake yeast and starters are all activated when they reach 98.6°F (37°C) and are combined with a little liquid and sugar.

Chocolate comes from the cocoa beans. The cocoa butter is extracted and soluble cocoa is produced. Chocolate is made by mixing cocoa

ingredients

butter with varying quantities of sugar or other aromatic substances. The quality of any chocolate is determined by the percentage of cocoa butter it contains.

There are various types of chocolate: dark, milk, gianduia (made from a mixture of cocoa and hazelnut paste) and white (which contains no cocoa solids). Some confectionery recipes call for chocolate couverture, which has a higher cocoa butter content and is often used by professional chefs because it melts smoothly and hardens to a glossy shine. It is often used for coatings and confectionery.

Vanilla This is the seed pod from an orchid native to Central America. Today vanilla beans are cultivated in many tropical countries. The vanilla bean has a dark brown color and can be up to 10 inches (25 cm) long and 1/2 inch (1 ½ cm) thick. The seed pod contains an oily pulp that holds the tiny, aromatic vanilla seeds. The whole beans are fermented and dried before commercialization.

Today, due to cost and convenience, vanilla beans are often substituted with vanilla extract, which gives a similar though less intense flavor. Vanilla extract can be easily mixed into batters and doughs, making it a quick and easy alternative to vanilla beans. Vanilla is an important flavoring in many pastry creams, sauces, cakes and cookies.

AGAR AGAR: An algae extract used to thicken ice creams, puddings or jellies. An excellent alternative to animal-based gelatins.

BAIN-MARIE: Cooking technique in which baking dishes, bowls or pans are immersed in or placed just above another baking dish or saucepan containing hot water. This technique allows for ingredients to be gently cooked (custards or flans) or heated without burning (pastry creams, sabayon, chocolate).

BATTER: A batter is a thick liquid, usually made of water, milk, eggs and flour; depending on the use it can be made either sweet or savory by adding sugar or salt.

BEAT: To whip air into a mixture, giving it added volume and softness.

BUTTER: To lightly coat pans, molds, or baking dishes with butter before pouring in or topping with batter or pastry.

CANDYING: A method of preservation most often used for fruit. Fresh fruits are cooked in a series of sugar syrups of increasing concentration.

CARAMEL: A thick sugar syrup that is cooked to above 320°F (160°C). It can be used as a sauce or to coat the inside of a mold for puddings or tarts.

CARAMELIZE: To heat sugar until it melts and colors. This term is often used for vegetables and meat when cooking them over high heat until a brown crust forms.

CHINOIS SIEVE: A fine, conical sieve for straining juices or other thin liquids. The shape means the liquid can be sieved directly into a small bowl or pan.

CHOUX PASTRY: Used to make beignets and other filled desserts.

CLARIFY: To make a cloudy liquid clear. Butter can be clarified by heating it in a double boiler to 175°F (80°C), without boiling, for about 1 hour. Refrigerate until solid and a white layer has formed over the surface. Remove the white layer and carefully pour off the watery liquid to obtain the pure fat. Clarified butter is used in recipes with prolonged cooking times or in place of lard when frying.

COULIS: A sauce made from pureed, strained fruit. Often the fruit is first cooked to remove some of its water content.

CREAM OF TARTAR: A naturally forming acidic salt that acts as a rising agent. It is found in grapes and in wine. When mixed with a little baking soda it can replace baking powder.

DUST: To uniformly coat a dessert or surface with a dry ingredient such as confectioners' sugar, sugar, flour or cornstarch.

EMULSIFY: To combine two or more liquids with differing densities by whisking them together until a single homogenous liquid forms.

EXTRACTS AND ESSENCES: Used in pastry to flavor creams, cakes and fillings. Common flavors including orange, mint, ginger, vanilla and almond. Extracts are made of an infusion preserved in alcohol and then diluted.

FERMENTATION: The process by which sugars are transformed by various microorganisms. Wine and yogurt are both fermented.

FLOUR: To coat a pan or baking dish with flour before pouring in a batter, or to dust a work surface with flour before rolling out or mixing a dough.

FOLD: To carefully add beaten mixtures, like egg whites or whipped cream, to thicker batters. The folding motion, from bottom to top, incorporates ingredients without losing an airy consistency.

FONDANT: A white paste used to decorate cakes, petit fours or beignets. In its simplest form it is made from confectioners' sugar and water.

GELATIN: Odorless and pale in color, gelatin is used to set desserts or make jellies. It comes in both sheet or granular form. Sheet gelatin should be soaked in cold water, drained and squeezed out before dissolving in a liquid.

GLAZE: To cover a dessert with a thin layer of jelly, sugar syrup or chocolate to give a dessert added sheen.

LINE: To cover the inside of a mold or baking dish with a sheet of dough, parchment paper or plastic wrap.

LUMP: A small ball of flour or any other insoluble ingredient which can form in batters or sauces. To avoid lumps it is best to sift dry ingredients and to incorporate them slowly into batters.

glossary

MARINATE: To soak ingredients in a sugar syrup, wine or other aromatic infusion to give added flavor.

MELT: Heating a solid substance until it becomes liquid, like butter or chocolate. In pastry, it is best to melt on low heat in the microwave or over a double boiler so as to avoid overheating and burning.

PASTRY BAG TIPS: Removable tips that fit into the opening of a pastry bag. Various sizes and shapes are available and help to create beautiful decorations when making desserts.

PASTEURIZATION: A heating process used to sterilize and preserve foods, eliminating potentially dangerous bacteria.

PECTIN: A natural gelling agent contained in acidic fruit. It can be purchased in powder form and is used to thicken jams and jellies. Pectin is heat and cold resistant.

PRALINE: Nuts covered with sugar or chocolate or a paste made of nuts and sugar used to fill chocolates, cakes or other desserts.

QUENELLE: Oval shapes made using two spoons. May be sweet or savory, cooked or raw.

REDUCE: To cook off excess liquid, resulting in a denser consistency and more concentrated flavor.

ROLL OUT: To flatten a dough to a specific thickness using a rolling pin or a pasta machine.

ROYAL ICING: Made from confectioners' sugar and egg whites and often colored or flavored, royal icing is used to decorate cakes and cupcakes.

SIFT: To pass a dry ingredient (flour, confectioners' sugar, baking powder) through a wire-mesh sieve to break up any lumps and give a lighter consistency.

SOFTENED BUTTER: To quickly soften butter without melting it, microwave for 10 seconds on low power and then work with a spatula until creamy. The same result may be obtained by leaving the butter at room temperature until it is spreadable.

SOUR CREAM: Cream that is thickened and slightly fermented. It has a more acidic flavor due to the addition of lemon juice or citric acid.

STIFF PEAKS: Refers to beating egg whites or whipping cream. When the mixture is stiff enough to hold the peaks that form while beating, it has reached the stiff peak stage.

SUGAR SYRUP: A cooked syrup made of sugar and water. Used to moisten sponge cakes, make infusions and sweeten sorbets. With the addition of glucose and citric acid this syrup becomes the base for sugar decorations.

SUPREME: Technique for segmenting citrus in which the peel, pith, membrane and seeds are removed.

TEMPER: A technique of heating and cooling chocolate so that it hardens to a glossy shine. The chocolate is melted over a double boiler and heated to 122°F (50°C). It is then removed from the heat and cooled to 82°F (28°C). Additional unmelted chocolate is added to the chocolate and it is brought to 98°F (37°C), then removed from the heat and cooled to 88°F (31°C).

THICKEN: Adding a thickening agent (flour, cornstarch, gelatin) to a sauce, soup, mousse, etc.

THICKENING AGENT: Cornstarch (for further information see p. 55), potato starch or flour added to sauces to thicken or maintain consistency. Most thickening agents come in a powder form and should be dissolved in a little cold water before adding to a sauce.

TOAST: Generally used to describe the heating of dry ingredients such as bread. Also refers to the quick browning of nuts, either in a frying pan or in the oven.

WAX PAPER: A waterproof kitchen paper that is resistant to steam. It is used to preserve cooked foods, to cover surfaces in the kitchen or to make pastry cones.

WELL: Term used to describe the depression or hole made at the center of a mound of flour where liquid ingredients are added before mixing.

WHISK: Used to blend ingredients until smooth or incorporate air into creams, sauces or other liquids, usually made from stainless steel or plastic.

glossary

1 Silicon spatula The ideal utensil for scraping chocolate, cream or batter out of bowls or pans. Made from silicon, this spatula has a flexible shape that will fit into almost any size of container.

2 Cocoa shaker A practical dispenser that makes decorating cakes and desserts with cocoa powder and confectioners' sugar fun and easy.

3 Double-boiler ceramic bowl A ceramic bowl made to fit inside a double boiler, useful for melting chocolate. The thick ceramic bowl keeps the temperature even and the chocolate liquid.

4 Brushes The ideal tool for spreading chocolate or for brushing egg wash over cakes and desserts before baking. Also useful for coating cake pans and ramekins with melted butter.

5 Whisks Available in many shapes and sizes and indispensable in the kitchen when mixing batters. Whisks can also be used to beat egg whites and creams.

6 Pastry bag Plastic or cloth triangular bag with removable metal tips. A pastry bag is used to decoratively pipe out cream or frosting or to fill beignets or doughnuts.

7 Tartlet tin Used for making miniature tarts and individual desserts, these small tins are made from aluminum. Varying sizes and shapes are available.

8 Chinois A fine-mesh conical sieve used for making soups or sauces that must be very smooth. In pastry it is often used to strain sauces made with egg or fruit purees.

9 Trifle bowl A glass bowl set on a pedestal is an ideal way to elegantly serve mousses and creams and layered desserts like trifle.

kitchen tools

10 Fine-mesh sieve To avoid the formation of lumps, this is used to sift confectioners' sugar, flour or cocoa powder.

11 Stainless-steel mixing bowl The perfect container for preparing almost any type of dessert. Stainless steel doesn't absorb any flavors or leave residues.

12 Silicon molds Available in many shapes and sizes. These molds are especially useful for shaping creams and mousses and make them easy to unmold.

13 Cake knife A triangular-shaped knife used to slice and serve cakes, tortes and pies.

14 Candy thermometer A glass thermometer with a special hook that allows it to be attached to the side of a pan. A candy thermometer must be used when making certain syrups, sauces, meringues and mousses.

15 Spatula This common utensil is one of the most useful when baking. It may be used to spread and level creams and glazes.

16 Spring-form pan A two-piece pan with detachable, round base with an interlocking band 2-3 inches (5-8 centimeters) high forming the rim, with a latch for opening and closing.

17 Chocolate molds Available in a variety of sizes and shapes and made from silicon or plastic. Used for shaping chocolates and pralines.

18 Cookie cutter Made in steel or stainless steel, they come in various shapes and sizes. In Italian cooking the coppapasta (pasta cutter) is round, smooth or fluted, and is used to cut out pasta and other types of dough. It can also be used as a mold to shape a finished dish for an elegant presentation.

10

11

12

13

14

15

16

17

18

19 Cannoli molds Straight, seamless tubes made of stainless steel, for making cylindrical pastry shells.

20 Rolling cutter For cutting dough. Rolling cutters can have one or more wheels. Multi-wheeled cutters can be regulated and serve to make uniform strips of dough.

21 Pastry scorer Used for scoring pastry so that it bakes evenly.

22 Pastry tongs Used for serving small pastries like beignets or miniature tartlets.

23 Decorative cookie cutters Ideal for shaping shortcrust cookies into fun and decorative shapes.

24 Siphon Bottle-shaped container with nitrous oxide cartridges, used for aerating and whipping cream.

25 Ice cream scoop Perfect tool for neatly serving ice cream or sorbet. Available in several shapes or sizes, such as oval or round.

26 Electric beaters Electric whisks for quickly whipping cream, eggs or batters. This time-saving tool makes dessert preparation fast and easy.

27 Foils and papers Those useful in baking and dessert-making include parchment paper, wax paper, plastic wrap and aluminum foil. They can be used for lining molds and baking dishes or for covering ingredients.

kitchen tools

28 Melon baller Used to cut fruits and vegetables into decorative balls.

29 Plastic molds Individual molds can be of different shapes, sizes and materials and are used for sweet and savory tarts, flans and cakes.

30 Non-stick ramekins Small round baking cups are used to make individual tarts, creams and soufflés. Non-stick ramekins are common and can be purchased in many sizes.

31 Aluminum ramekins Light-weight aluminum ensures quick and even cooking times and allows for easy unmolding. Desserts may also be served directly from the ramekins.

32 Cutting board Ideal for cutting and chopping chocolate, fruit and nuts. Cutting boards are available in a variety of sizes and in materials such as wood, plastic or silicon.

33 Spring whisk Made of stainless steel and used to eliminate lumps from sauces or other liquids.

34 Flat whisk For mixing small quantities, this whisk is perfect for emulsifying vinaigrettes or for omelets.

35 Grater and mandoline Utensils used to thinly slice fruit, grate chocolate or zest citrus.

36 Serving spatula Indispensable for flipping or serving cakes and tortes, these spatulas are made in many shapes and sizes and from a variety of materials, most commonly metal and plastic.

28

29

30

31

32

33

34

35

36

techniques&recipes

Cakes and Pies

Ideas, suggestions and recipes for quick and delicious
cakes and tarts, including sponge cakes
and shortcrust tarts filled with chocolate and fruit.

1 Sift the flour into a mound on a clean work surface. Make a well in the center and add the softened butter, eggs, sugar and lemon zest.

2 Mix the ingredients together using two plastic spatulas, making sure that the dough is worked evenly, lifting it off of the work surface with one spatula. When the dough begins to come together, finish combining it using the palms of the hands.

3 Form the dough into a flat ball and wrap in plastic wrap. Refrigerate for 30 minutes at 43°F (6°C).

4 Remove the dough from the refrigerator and using a rolling pin, roll it out into a 1/4-inch (1/2 cm) sheet on lightly floured work surface.

5 Using a spatula if necessary, lift the dough off of the work surface.

6 Roll the dough around a rolling pin and transfer it to a buttered and floured baking dish or tart tin.

Ingredients

Serves 6

2 cups (9 oz or 250 g) all-purpose flour

9 Tbsps (4 ½ oz or 125 g) butter, softened

3 egg yolks

1/2 cup (3 ½ oz or 100 g) sugar

zest from **1** organic lemon

SHORTCRUST DOUGH

PASTRY CHEF'S TIP

For best results when making shortcrust dough, it is important to make sure that the temperature of the butter is never more than 100°F (40°C). Working the butter and flour with the hands heats the dough and, if overheated, the butter can separate and the dough will not come together properly. If this happens the dough may be saved by adding a little cream.

Recipe on p. 50

1 Mix together the cold water, sifted flour and a pinch of salt to form a smooth dough.

2 Roll out the dough on a lightly floured work surface. Place the softened butter in the center of the dough and fold the dough back over the butter to form a square package.

3 Using a rolling pin, roll out the square of dough, taking care to always roll in the same direction, to form a single sheet.

4 Fold the dough over itself into thirds to form a rectangle.

5 Turn the rectangle 90°, fold in thirds again and refrigerate for 30 minutes.

6 Roll out the square of dough on a lightly floured work surface and repeat this process three more times. Puff pastry should be cooked on a baking sheet lined with parchment paper for 15-20 minutes in an oven preheated to 400-425°F (200-220°C or Gas Mark 6-7).

Ingredients
Serves 6
7 Tbsps (100 ml) cold water
1 ⅔ cups (7 oz or 200 g) all-purpose flour, sifted
salt
14 Tbsps (7 oz or 200 g) butter, softened

PUFF PASTRY

Pastry Chef's Tip

Making puff pastry is a long and complicated process. To make a good puff pastry the layers of pastry and butter must be surrounded by air so that the pastry will puff during baking, creating a light texture and delicious flavor. For best results when making the dough, all of the ingredients should be at the same temperature.

Recipe on p. 68

1 Pour the flour, egg, warm water and lemon juice into a large bowl and begin to mix.

2 Melt the butter in a double boiler and add to the mixture.

3 Continue mixing to form a very smooth and elastic dough.

Ingredients
Serves 6
2 cups (9 oz or 250 g) all-purpose flour
1 egg
1/3 cup plus 1 Tbsp (90 ml) warm water
1/2 tsp lemon juice
6 Tbsps (3 oz or 90 g) butter

4 Roll the dough into a ball, cover with plastic wrap and refrigerate for 15 minutes at 39°F (4°C).

5 Place a clean dry kitchen towel on a work surface and lightly flour it. Place the dough on the towel and sprinkle with flour. Roll the dough into a 1/4-inch (1/2 cm) sheet with a rolling pin.

6 Working carefully with both fists and the backs of the hands, stretch the sheet of dough until it is transparent. Proceed with the recipe to finish the strudel.

STRUDEL DOUGH

Pastry Chef's Tip
Remember to make diagonal incisions along the top of the strudel before baking. This releases excess moisture from the strudel and allows for even cooking.

Recipe on p. 70

1 Using a whisk or electric beaters, beat the eggs and sugar together over a double boiler.

2 Sift the flour and baking powder into the eggs and mix gently using a spatula, using bottom to top folding motions to incorporate air into the batter.

3 Lightly butter and flour a spring-form pan.

4 Pour the batter into the prepared pan and for 30 minutes at 350°F (180°C or Gas Mark 4) until the cake has risen and is golden-brown in color.

Ingredients
Serves 4
1 cup plus 3 Tbsps
(5 ½ oz or 150 g)
all-purpose flour
3/4 cup (5 ½ oz or 150 g)
sugar
4 eggs
2 tsps baking powder
butter and flour for the
baking dish

SPONGE CAKE

Recipe on p. 74

Pastry Chef's Tip

For a softer sponge cake, reduce the amount of flour used and add 2/3 cup (2 ½ oz or 75 g) of cornstarch to the batter. For a lighter cake, use confectioners' sugar in place of granulated sugar. For another variation, omit the baking powder, separate the eggs and mix only the yolks with the sugar. Stiffly beat the egg whites and fold into the batter after the flour.

1 Heat the milk and the vanilla bean halves in a saucepan.

2 Beat the sugar and egg yolks together until thick. Sift in the flour and stir until smooth.

3 Pour the egg and sugar mixture into the hot milk. Whisk the mixture until smooth.

4 Cook the cream over medium heat until it begins to thicken. When the cream comes to a simmer remove from the heat and remove the vanilla bean.

5 Transfer the cream to a bowl, sprinkle with confectioners' sugar and cover tightly with plastic wrap so that a film doesn't form over the top of the cream. Refrigerate until use.

Ingredients
Serves 6
4 cups (1 l) milk
1 vanilla bean,
halved lengthwise
1 cup (7 oz or 200 g)
sugar
6 egg yolks
1 cup (4 oz or 120 g)
all-purpose flour
confectioners' sugar

PASTRY CREAM

PASTRY CHEF'S TIP
For a lighter cream,
add a few tablespoons
of whipped cream to
the mixture or replace
1/3 of the flour with
the same quantity
of cornstarch.

Recipe on p. 116

1 Melt the butter and chocolate in a double boiler and then stir in the cream.

2 Spread the ganache evenly over the cake using a spatula.

1 Melt the chocolate in a double boiler, add the rum and stir to combine.

2 Place the cake on a baking rack and pour the glaze over the cake. Let set before serving.

Ingredients for covering one 11-inch (28 cm) cake

Ganache
7 oz (200 g) chocolate
4 Tbsps (2 oz or 50 g) butter
2 Tbsps whipping cream

Chocolate Glaze
14 oz (400 g) dark chocolate
2 Tbsps rum

GANACHE AND CHOCOLATE GLAZE

Lemon Cream Tart

Serves 6

Crust

4 ¾ cups plus 1 Tbsp (1 lb 5 oz or 600 g) all-purpose flour

3 eggs

2 ¼ cups (9 oz or 250 g) sugar

11 Tbsps (5 ½ oz or 150 g) butter, softened

1 tsp baking powder

1 tsp vanilla extract

Lemon Cream

3 organic lemons

1 Tbsp cornstarch

3/4 cup plus 1 Tbsp (3 ½ oz or 100 g) all-purpose flour

2 cups (500 ml) water

1 cup (7 oz or 200 g) sugar

1 tsp vanilla extract

2 eggs

4 Tbsps (2 oz or 50 g) butter

Preparation time 40 minutes
Cooking time 40 minutes
Level medium

1 Pour the flour onto a work surface and make a well in the center. Break the eggs into the center. Add the sugar, softened butter, baking powder and vanilla extract. Mix to form a smooth and compact dough. Cover with a damp towel and refrigerate for at least 30 minutes. Preheat the oven to 350°F (180°C or Gas Mark 4).

2 Zest the lemons and then juice them. In a mixing bowl stir together the cornstarch and flour for the cream and slowly pour in the water, stirring constantly with a wooden spoon. Add the sugar and vanilla extract. Beat the eggs separately and then add them to the batter along with the lemon juice and zest. Mix well and transfer the batter to a saucepan. Bring to a simmer over low heat and cook, stirring constantly, until the cream thickens. Remove from heat, stir in the butter and cover.

3 Remove the pastry from the refrigerator and knead briefly. Roll three-quarters of the dough into an even sheet and use it to line a buttered tart tin. Fill the tart with the lemon cream. Use the remaining dough to make a lattice to decorate the top of the tart. Bake until the lattice is golden-brown and cool before serving.

Chocolate Cream Tart

Serves 6

Crust

2 cups (9 oz or 250 g)
all-purpose flour

3/4 cup (5 ½ oz or 150 g) sugar

1 egg plus 1 egg yolk

11 Tbsps (5 ½ oz or 150 g)
butter, softened

1 tsp baking powder

1 tsp vanilla extract

zest of 1 organic lemon

Chocolate Cream

5 ½ oz (150 g) dark chocolate

1 egg

2/3 cup (4 oz or 120 g) sugar

3 Tbsps whipping cream

1 tsp vanilla extract

Preparation time 40 minutes
Cooking time 35 minutes
Level medium

1 Mix the flour and sugar; add the egg and egg yolk, softened butter, baking powder and vanilla. Quickly stir together to form a smooth dough. Add the lemon zest, cover with plastic wrap and let rest in a cool place for at least 30 minutes. Preheat the oven to 325°F (170°C or Gas Mark 3).

2 Melt the chocolate in a double boiler, remove from the heat and let cool slightly. Meanwhile, beat the egg and sugar until they become thick and foamy. Add the whipping cream and vanilla. Add the chocolate to the egg mixture and stir until smooth.

3 Roll out three-quarters of the shortcrust dough into a sheet of medium thickness and use it to line a tart tin. Pour in the chocolate cream. Use the remaining dough to make a lattice and place it over the top of the tart, tucking in the sides and folding over any excess dough. Bake for 30 minutes. Remove from the oven and cool completely.

Ricotta Tart
with Alchermes Liqueur

Serves 6

Crust

2 ¾ cups (12 ½ oz or 350 g)
all-purpose flour

2 eggs

3/4 cup (5 ½ oz or 150 g) sugar

7 Tbsps (3 ½ oz or 100 g)
butter, softened

1 tsp baking powder

zest of 1 organic lemon

Filling

1 lb (500 g) mixed sheep's
and cow's milk ricotta

4 Tbsps sugar

3 Tbsps Alchermes liqueur

1/2 tsp freshly grated nutmeg

1/2 tsp ground cinnamon

Preparation time 30 minutes
Cooking time 35 minutes
Level medium

1 Sift the flour into a mound and make a well at the center. Add the eggs, sugar, softened butter, baking powder and lemon zest. Mix well to form a smooth dough and let rest. Preheat the oven to 350°F (180°C or Gas Mark 4).

2 Meanwhile, mix the ricotta and the sugar together with the Alchermes, nutmeg and cinnamon.

3 Roll out most of the pastry dough into a thin sheet and line into a 12-inch (32 cm) buttered and floured tart tin. Pour the ricotta mixture into the tart and spread to form an even layer. Decorate the top of the tart with the remaining dough. Bake for 30 minutes and let cool completely before serving.

Mixed Berry Tart

Serves 8

Crust

10 Tbsps (5 oz or 135 g) butter

2 cups (9 oz or 250 g)
all-purpose flour

2/3 cup (4 ½ oz or 125 g) sugar

1 egg plus 1 egg yolk

zest of 1 organic lemon

salt

Filling

4 oz (120 g) mascarpone

3 Tbsps confectioners' sugar

1 tsp vanilla extract

1/3 cup (80 ml)
whipping cream

Decoration

7 oz (200 g) mixed berries

1/2 tsp vanilla-flavored
confectioners' sugar

Preparation time 30 minutes
Cooking time 25 minutes
Level easy

1 Cut the butter into small pieces and let it soften. Mound the flour on a work surface and make a well at the center. Place the sugar, egg and egg yolk, butter, lemon zest and a pinch of salt in the well. Using the fingertips, quickly mix to form a dough. Wrap the dough in plastic wrap and refrigerate for 30 minutes. Preheat the oven to 350°F (180°C or Gas Mark 4).

2 Sprinkle the work surface with flour, roll the dough into a 1/4-inch (1/2 cm) thick sheet and use it to line a buttered and floured tart tin. Bake for 20-25 minutes and remove from the oven. Let cool completely.

3 Meanwhile, mix together the mascarpone, confectioners' sugar and vanilla extract. Whip the whipping cream to stiff peaks and fold it into the mascarpone mixture. Fill the cooked tart base with the mascarpone filling and top with the mixed berries. Sprinkle the tart with vanilla-flavored confectioners' sugar and refrigerate. Serve the tart cold.

Chocolate-Almond Tart

Serves 6

Crust

1 ⅔ cups (7 oz or 200 g)
all-purpose flour

1/4 cup (2 oz or 50 g) sugar

8 Tbsps (4 oz or 120 g)
butter, cold

2 egg yolks

1 tsp baking powder

Filling

7 oz (200 g) dark chocolate

1/2 cup (100 ml) milk

1/3 cup (2 ½ oz or 75 g) sugar

3-4 graham crackers, crushed

1/4 cup (1 oz or 30 g) almonds,
coarsely chopped

Preparation time 15 minutes
Cooking time 40 minutes
Level easy

1 Preheat the oven to 325°F (160°C or Gas Mark 3). Place the flour and sugar into a bowl and quickly cut in the cold butter. When the mixture resembles a coarse meal, add the egg yolks and baking powder and mix to form a compact dough.

2 Roll out the dough into a thin sheet. Line a 10 ½-inch (26 cm) round tart tin with the dough, making a slightly thicker layer around the edge. Refrigerate the crust for 30 minutes.

3 Meanwhile, melt the chocolate with the milk over a double boiler. Add the sugar and mix well to incorporate.

4 Pour the chocolate mixture into the pastry crust and sprinkle with the crushed graham crackers and chopped almonds. Bake the tart for 30 minutes. Remove from the oven and cool completely before serving.

PASTRY CHEF'S TIP

The graham crackers can be replaced with amaretto cookies; their sweet flavor and fragrance pairs well with the almonds.

Pear Tart
with Amaretto Cream

Serves 6

Crust

2 cups (9 oz or 250 g)
all-purpose flour

1/2 cup (3 ½ oz or 100 g)
sugar

8 Tbsps (4 oz or 120 g) butter

3 egg yolks

1 tsp vanilla extract

salt

Pears

2 ¼ lb (1 kg) Kaiser pears
(or Martin pears)

1 pat of butter

1/4 cup (2 oz or 50 g) sugar

3 Tbsps white wine

Filling

5 egg yolks

3/4 cup (5 ½ oz or 150 g)
sugar

2/3 cup (3 oz or 80 g)
cornstarch

3 cups (750 ml) warm milk

3 ½ oz (100 g)
amaretto cookies, crushed

1/4 cup (60 ml)
amaretto liqueur

Preparation time 20 minutes
Cooking time 50 minutes
Level easy

1 Preheat the oven to 350°F (180°C or Gas Mark 4). To make the crust, quickly mix the flour, sugar, butter, egg yolks, vanilla and salt together to form an elastic dough. Cover with plastic wrap and refrigerate for 30 minutes.

2 Peel, core and dice the pears. Melt the butter and sugar in a saucepan, add the pears and cook for a few minutes. Add the wine and cook over high heat for 5 minutes. To make the filling, beat the egg yolks with the sugar in a saucepan, then add the cornstarch and warm milk. Cook over low heat until the mixture thickens. Remove from heat and add the amaretto cookies and liqueur.

3 Butter a tart tin. Roll out the dough and line the tart tin with the dough. Pour the amaretto cream over the crust and then place the pears on top of the cream. Bake for 40 minutes. Remove from the oven, cool completely and serve.

Classic Fruit Tart

Serves 6

Crust

10 Tbsps (5 oz or 135 g) butter

2 cups (9 oz or 250 g)
all-purpose flour

2/3 cup (4 ½ oz or 125 g) sugar

1 egg plus 1 egg yolk

zest of 1 organic lemon

salt

Cream

2 cups (500 ml) milk

4 egg yolks

2/3 cup (4 oz or 120 g) sugar

1 tsp vanilla extract

6 ½ Tbsps all-purpose flour

Decoration

mixed fruit

Preparation time 40 minutes
Cooking time 35 minutes
Level easy

1 Dice the butter and let soften. Mound the flour on a clean work surface and make a well in the center. Place the sugar, butter, egg and yolk, lemon zest and salt in the center and mix quickly using the fingertips. When the dough comes together, roll it into a ball and cover with plastic wrap. Refrigerate for 30 minutes. Preheat the oven to 350°F (180°C or Gas Mark 4).

2 Bring the milk to a simmer. Beat the egg yolks with the sugar and vanilla and add the flour. Whisk in the hot milk and return the mixture to the saucepan. Cook over low heat, stirring constantly, until the cream thickens. Remove from heat, transfer to a bowl and let cool.

3 Butter and flour a round tart tin. Roll out the pastry and line the tin with the dough. Cut off any excess dough and pierce the surface of the dough with a fork. Bake for 25 minutes and let cool. Wash and slice the fresh fruit. Pour the pastry cream into the baked crust and decorate with fresh fruit. Chill until serving.

PASTRY CHEF'S TIP

To keep fresh fruit from discoloring, brush the top of the tart with a neutral-flavored jelly.

Blueberry
Cheesecake

Serves 6

Crust

6 ½ oz (180 g)
graham crackers

7 Tbsps (3 ½ oz or 100 g)
butter, melted

Filling

3 eggs, separated

2/3 cup (4 oz or 120 g) sugar

9 oz (250 g) mascarpone

9 oz (250 g) ricotta

1 Tbsp all-purpose flour

1 tsp vanilla extract

zest of 1 organic lemon

Decoration

1 jar of blueberry jam

Preparation 40 minutes
Cooking time 5 minutes
Level easy

1 Preheat the oven to 350°F (180°C or Gas Mark 4). Blend the graham crackers in a food processor and add the melted butter. Press the mixture into a tart tin lined with parchment paper and refrigerate for at least 15 minutes.

2 Meanwhile, beat the egg yolks with the sugar and beat the egg whites to stiff peaks. Stir the mascarpone, ricotta, sugar, flour, vanilla extract and lemon zest into the egg yolk mixture. Fold in the egg whites.

3 Carefully spread the filling over the prepared crust and bake for about 30 minutes. Remove from the oven and spread the blueberry jam over the top of the cheesecake.

Lemon Tart
with Blueberries and White Chocolate

Serves 6

Crust

9 oz (350 g) shortcrust dough
(see p. 32)

Filling

3 eggs

2/3 cup (4 ½ oz or 125 g) sugar

2 organic lemons

4 Tbsps whipping cream

1 Tbsp cornstarch

Topping

2 oz (50 g) white chocolate

2 Tbsps whipping cream

3 ½ oz (100 g) blueberries

Preparation time 30 minutes
Cooking time 35 minutes
Level medium

PASTRY CHEF'S TIP

Cornstarch is a thickening agent used to flour foods before cooking or to thicken sauces and creams. Potato starch may be used in place of cornstarch.

1 Preheat the oven to 350°F (180°C or Gas Mark 4). Roll out the shortcrust dough on a lightly floured work surface. Butter and flour a tart tin and line it with the dough. Pierce the bottom of the dough with a fork and refrigerate for 20 minutes.

2 Place a sheet of aluminum foil over the dough and cover with dried beans or pie weights. Bake for 10 minutes. Remove from the oven and cool completely. Using an electric mixer, beat the eggs with the sugar, the juice of 1 lemon and the grated zest from both lemons. Add the whipping cream and cornstarch and continue beating until thick. Pour the filling into the cooled tart crust and bake for 15 minutes. Lower the oven temperature to 325°F (160°C or Gas Mark 3) and bake for another 20 minutes. Remove from the oven and let cool.

3 Melt the white chocolate, stir in the whipping cream, and spread the mixture over the top of the tart. Top with the blueberries and serve.

Almond Tart
with Chocolate Chips

Serves 6

Crust

1 lb 5 oz (600 g) shortcrust dough (see p. 32)

Filling

cocoa powder

1 ¾ cups (250 g) blanched almonds

13 Tbsps (6 ½ oz or 180 g) butter, softened

3/4 cup (5 ½ oz or 150 g) sugar

chocolate chips

butter

Decoration

3/4 cup (180 ml) dry Marsala wine

Preparation time 20 minutes
Cooking time 40 minutes
Level medium

1 Preheat the oven to 350°F (180°C or Gas Mark 4). Roll out the dough on a lightly floured work surface, reserving a small amount. Line a tart tin with the dough. Sprinkle cocoa powder over the dough.

2 Grind the almonds and place them in a warm oven to remove any moisture. Transfer the almonds to a mixing bowl and add the butter and sugar. Mix well. Spread the mixture on a baking sheet and bake for 10 minutes, or until golden-brown. Let cool.

3 Place the baked filling in the crust and top with the chocolate chips and a few pats of butter. Roll out the remaining pastry and cut it into strips. Make a lattice top for the tart.

4 Bake for about 30 minutes. Remove the tart from the oven and let cool slightly. Brush the top of the tart with Marsala and let cool completely.

PASTRY CHEF'S TIP

Almonds have been used for centuries in pastry-making. Historical documents show that almonds were used to make primitive sweets prepared with honey, milk and fresh fruit.

Chocolate Pear Tart

Serves 4

Crust

1 ¾ cups (8 oz or 225 g)
all-purpose flour

2 Tbsps sugar

1/4 cup (1 oz or 30 g)
ground almonds

3-4 Tbsps water

salt

7 Tbsps (3 ½ oz or 100 g) butter

Filling

4-5 ripe pears

1 cup (7 oz or 200 g)
raw cane sugar

4 Tbsps (2 oz or 50 g) butter

1/2 cup (1 ½ oz or 45 g)
cocoa powder

1 egg

1/3 cup (1 ½ oz or 45 g)
all-purpose flour

1 tsp vanilla extract

Decoration

confectioners' sugar

Preparation time 40 minutes
Cooking time 30 minutes
Level medium

1 Place the flour, sugar, ground almonds, water and salt in a large mixing bowl. Work in the butter with the fingertips until the mixture resembles a coarse meal. Continue to mix with a fork and then transfer the dough to a work surface and knead with the hands. Form the dough into a ball and cover with plastic wrap. Refrigerate for 30 minutes. Preheat the oven to 350°F (180°C or Gas Mark 4).

2 Roll out the dough into a thin sheet. Line a round tart pan with the dough and refrigerate. Peel, quarter and core the pears. Remove the tart crust from the refrigerator and pierce it with a fork. Sprinkle with 2 tablespoons of sugar and top with the pears. Bake for 15 minutes. Remove from the oven and let cool.

3 Meanwhile, melt the butter with the cocoa powder in a saucepan. Stir until smooth. Beat the egg with the remaining sugar, add the butter mixture and sift in the flour. Add the vanilla and mix well. Pour the mixture over the pear tart and smooth with a spatula. Bake for another 15 minutes. Remove from the oven and cool completely. Sprinkle with confectioners' sugar and serve.

Ricotta Tart
with Grape Jam

Serves 6

Crust

3 cups plus 3 Tbsps (14 oz or 400 g) all-purpose flour

6 egg yolks

3/4 cup (7 oz or 200 g) butter, softened

1 cup (7 oz or 200 g) sugar

zest of 1 organic lemon

Filling

6 eggs

1 ½ cups (10 ½ oz or 300 g) sugar

2 ¼ lb (1 kg) fresh ricotta

zest of 2 organic lemons

12 oz (350 g) grape jam

Preparation time 40 minutes
Cooking time 20 minutes
Level medium

1 Mound the flour in a work surface and make a well at the center. Place the egg yolks, softened butter, sugar and lemon zest in the center and work with fingertips to obtain a compact and even dough. Cover with plastic wrap and refrigerate for 30 minutes.

2 Meanwhile, beat the eggs and sugar for the filling in a large mixing bowl. Pass the ricotta through a fine mesh sieve and add it to the mixture together with the lemon zest. Preheat the oven to 325°F (160°c or Gas Mark 3).

3 Roll out the pastry dough and use it to line a round tart tin. Pierce the bottom of the crust with a fork and then spread over the grape jam to form an even layer. Top with the ricotta mixture and bake for 20 minutes. Remove from the oven and cool slightly before serving.

PASTRY CHEF'S TIP

The grape jam can be replaced with any flavor of fruit preserves or jam including lemon or orange marmalade.

Gianduia and Ricotta Tart

Serves 8

Crust

3/4 cup (7 oz or 200 g) butter

1 cup (7 oz or 200 g) sugar

3 cups plus 3 Tbsps (14 oz or 400 g) all-purpose flour

2 eggs

1 tsp vanilla extract

salt

Filling

2 cups (500 ml) milk

4 egg yolks

2/3 cup (4 ½ oz or 125 g) sugar

6 ½ Tbsps all-purpose flour

3 drops of hazelnut extract

3 oz (80 g) gianduia chocolate, chopped (see p. 64)

3 ½ oz (100 g) fresh ricotta

Preparation time 40 minutes

Cooking time 40 minutes

Level easy

1 Mix together the ingredients for the crust. When the dough comes together, knead it with the palm of the hand for a few minutes and then form into a disk. Cover with plastic wrap and refrigerate. Preheat the oven to 350°F (180°C or Gas Mark 4).

2 Heat the milk in a saucepan. Beat the egg yolks and sugar in a mixing bowl and stir in the flour and hazelnut extract. Whisk the boiling hot milk into the egg mixture and return to the saucepan. Cook over low heat, stirring with a whisk, until the cream thickens. Remove from the heat and add the chocolate. Stir until the chocolate is melted and the cream is smooth. Let cool, then stir in the ricotta.

3 Roll out three-quarters of the dough on a lightly floured work surface. Butter and flour a tart pan and line it with the dough. Pierce the dough with a fork and fill with the gianduia-ricotta mixture. Roll out the remaining dough and cut it into strips. Make a criss-cross lattice over the top of the tart. Bake for about 30 minutes. Let cool and refrigerate for 1 hour before serving.

Plum Tart

Serves 6

Crust

1 ⅔ cups (7 oz or 200 g) all-purpose flour

1/4 cup (2 oz or 50 g) sugar

7 Tbsps (3 ½ oz or 100 g) butter, softened

2 egg yolks

1 jar of plum jam

Preparation time 20 minutes
Cooking time 20 minutes
Level easy

1 Preheat the oven to 350°F (180°C or Gas Mark 4). Mix together the flour, sugar, butter and egg yolks. When the dough comes together, knead to form a smooth and elastic ball. Cover with plastic wrap and refrigerate for 30 minutes.

2 Butter and flour a 8-inch (22 cm) tart pan. Roll out the dough into a thin sheet and line the tart pan with the dough, reserving some strips for the top. Spread a thick layer of plum jam over the dough. Top with the reserved strips in a lattice pattern.

3 Bake for 20 minutes. Remove from the oven and place the tart on a wire rack to cool completely before serving.

Pastry Chef's Tip
For an elegant variation spread a layer of melted white chocolate over the crust of the tart before adding the plum jam.

Chestnut Tart
with Dark Chocolate

Serves 8

Crust

2 ¾ cups (12 ½ oz or 350 g) all-purpose flour

1 egg

4 Tbsps (3 oz or 80 g) butter, softened

3/4 cup (5 ½ oz or 150 g) sugar

1 tsp vanilla extract

Filling

1 ¾ lb (800 g) chestnuts

1 ¼ cups (300 ml) milk

1/2 cup (3 ½ oz or 100 g) sugar

9 oz (250 g) dark chocolate, chopped

4 Tbsps mascarpone

Preparation time 30 minutes
Cooking time 3 hours
Level easy

1 Preheat the oven to 350°F (180°C or Gas Mark 4). Boil the chestnuts until soft. Drain, peel and mash with a potato ricer. Mix the mashed chestnut with the milk and sugar in a saucepan and cook for 10 minutes. Add the chocolate and cook for another 10 minutes. Add mascarpone and cook for 2 more minutes. Remove from heat and let cool.

2 Mound the flour on a work surface and make a well in the center. Add the egg, softened butter, sugar and vanilla. Mix to form an elastic dough. If the dough seems dry add a few teaspoons of warm water. Divide the dough in half. Roll out half the dough into a sheet and place in a pie dish. Fill with the chestnut cream and roll out the remaining dough. Cover the filling with the second sheet of dough; tuck the top sheet over the filling and fold the edges of the bottom sheet over to seal. Prick the top of the tart with a fork and bake for 45 minutes. Remove from the oven and let cool.

Milk-Chocolate Sabayon Tart
with Caramelized Strawberries

Serves 8

Crust

9 Tbsps (4 ½ oz or 125 g) butter, softened

3 Tbsps sugar

1 tsp vanilla extract

1 egg, salt

1 ⅔ cups (7 oz or 200 g) all-purpose flour

Sabayon

9 oz (250 g) milk chocolate

2 eggs plus 4 egg yolks

3 Tbsps sugar

3/4 cup (7 oz or 200 g) butter

Decoration

3 ½ oz (100 g) strawberries, hulled and halved

2 Tbsps raw cane sugar

1/2 cup (120 ml) whipping cream, whipped

dark chocolate, shaved

Preparation time 30 minutes
Cooking time 30 minutes
Level medium

Pastry Chef's Tip

Adding 1/2 teaspoon of cornstarch to the sabayon will ensure that it doesn't fall or separate while cooking.

1 Preheat the oven to 350°F (180°C or Gas Mark 4). Make the crust: Cream the softened butter with the sugar and vanilla. Add the egg, a pinch of salt and the flour. When the dough is smooth form it into a ball and cover with plastic wrap. Place in the refrigerator. Meanwhile, butter and flour 2 small to medium-sized fluted tart tins. Roll out the dough and line the tart tins with it. Place a sheet of parchment paper over the tarts and fill with dried beans or pie weights. Bake for 8 minutes, remove the paper and beans or weights and continue baking for another 5 minutes.

2 Make the sabayon: Melt the milk chocolate over a double boiler. In a round-bottomed pan beat the eggs and egg yolks with the sugar. Place the pan over the already hot water used for the chocolate and continue whisking until quadrupled in volume. Stir the butter into the melted chocolate and then whisk the mixture into the egg mixture. Remove from the heat and pour the sabayon into the tart crusts. Bake the tarts for 10 minutes. Remove from the oven, let cool and then refrigerate.

3 Place the strawberries in a frying pan and sprinkle with the raw cane sugar. Cook over medium heat until the sugar begins to caramelize. Top the tarts with the strawberries, a dollop of whipped cream and the chocolate shavings.

Coffee Cream Mille-feuilles

Serves 4

Crust

14 oz (400 g) shortcrust pastry
(see p. 32)

Coffee Cream

5 oz (140 g) gianduia
chocolate

4 oz (130 g) dark chocolate

1 cup plus 1 Tbsp (280 ml)
whipping cream

2 Tbsps instant coffee

Decoration

vanilla sugar

2 vanilla beans, halved

Preparation time 20 minutes
Cooking time 30 minutes
Level easy

1 Preheat the oven to 350°F (180°C or Gas Mark 4). Place both types of chocolate, the coffee and 1/3 cup (80 ml) of the whipping cream over a double boiler and heat until the chocolate is melted. Remove from heat and cool slightly.

2 Meanwhile, roll out the pastry into a thin sheet and cut it into 12 rectangles. Bake the pastry rectangles for 12 minutes. Remove from the oven and cool completely.

3 Beat the remaining whipping cream into stiff peaks and slowly pour over the chocolate mixture. Carefully fold the chocolate into the whipped cream. Transfer the chocolate cream to a pastry bag with a ridged tip.

4 Pipe 3 puffs of cream onto 4 pastry rectangles and top with more pastry rectangles. Repeat to create a three-layered mille-feuille. Dust the mille-feuilles with vanilla sugar and decorate with half a vanilla bean. Serve immediately.

PASTRY CHEF'S TIP

If you can't find gianduia chocolate, mix together equal parts of melted milk chocolate and hazelnut paste.

Chestnut and Ricotta Roll

Serves 6

Crust

2 cups (250 ml) water

3 Tbsps sugar

2 Tbsps rum

1 sheet of sponge cake
(see p. 38)

8 oz (230 g) ricotta

2 Tbsps confectioners' sugar

1 tsp vanilla extract

6 ½ oz (180 g)
canned chestnuts

1/2 cup (100 ml)
whipping cream

2 oz (50 g) dark chocolate
chips

Decoration

cocoa powder

Preparation time 20 minutes

Level easy

1 Bring the water and sugar to a boil to make a syrup then add the rum. Let cool. Place the sponge cake on a foil-lined baking sheet. Brush one side of the sponge cake with the sugar syrup, turn over and brush the other side.

2 Mix together the ricotta, confectioners' sugar and vanilla. Drain the chestnuts and puree them with the whipping cream. Add the chestnut mixture to the ricotta and then stir in the chocolate chips. Spread the filling onto the sponge cake and even out the layer with a spatula.

3 Tightly roll up the sponge cake like a jelly roll. Close the foil around the roll and refrigerate for 2 hours. Slice the roll and dust with cocoa powder.

Sicilian Cassata

Serves 6

Base

1 lb (500 g) round of sponge cake (see p. 38)

Filling

14 oz (400 g) ricotta

1 ⅔ cups (7 oz or 200 g) confectioners' sugar

7 oz (200 g) candied fruit, chopped

3 ½ oz (100 g) dark chocolate, chopped

1 tsp vanilla extract

4 Tbsps rum

Glaze

1 ⅔ cups (7 oz or 200 g) confectioners' sugar

pistachio paste (see p.170)

juice of 1/2 lemon

Preparation time 40 minutes
Level medium

1 Sieve the ricotta into a bowl. Add the confectioners' sugar, half of the candied fruit and all the chocolate. Add the vanilla and the rum and mix well. Cut the sponge cake into 2 rounds. Slice 1 round into strips and line the edges of a deep cake pan with the strips. Fill the pan with the ricotta mixture and place the remaining sponge cake round over the top of the filling. Refrigerate for a few hours.

2 Prepare the glaze by mixing the confectioners' sugar, a small amount of pistachio paste, the lemon juice and enough hot water to form a thick syrup.

3 Unmold the cassata on a serving dish and cover with the glaze. Decorate with the remaining candied fruit.

Fresh Cheese Mille-feuille

Serves 6

Crust

2 Tbsps (1 oz or 30 g) butter

1 lb (500 g) puff pastry dough (see p. 34)

3 Tbsps confectioners' sugar

Cream

7 oz (200 g) sheep's milk ricotta

5 ½ oz (150 g) robiola or other soft cow's milk cheese

3 ½ oz (100 g) cream cheese

3 Tbsps confectioners' sugar

1/3 cup (80 ml) whipping cream

1 Tbsp mixed candied fruit, finely chopped

zest of 1 organic orange

Preparation time 20 minutes
Cooking time 20 minutes
Level easy

1 Preheat the oven to 375°F (190°C or Gas Mark 5). Roll out the puff pastry into a large sheet. Melt the butter and brush it over the sheet of puff pastry. Sprinkle with the confectioners' sugar and bake for 20 minutes, until golden-brown and crunchy.

2 Sieve the ricotta into a mixing bowl and add the robiola, cream cheese and confectioners' sugar. Beat the mixture with a wooden spoon until it is soft and fluffy.

3 Whip the whipping cream to stiff peaks and fold it into the ricotta mixture. Stir in the candied fruit and orange zest.

4 Cut the puff pastry into 8 equally sized rectangles. Transfer the cheese cream to a pastry bag. Pipe the cream onto 4 of the pastry rectangles and then top with the remaining pastry. Sprinkle with confectioners' sugar and top with fresh fruit if desired.

Mimosa Cake

Serves 8

Cake

16 egg yolks (9 ½ oz
or 270 g in total)

5 eggs

1 ¾ cups plus 1 Tbsp
(13 oz or 370 g) sugar

1 ¾ cups (8 oz or 220 g)
all-purpose flour

1 ½ cups (6 ½ oz or 180 g)
cornstarch

6 Tbsps (3 oz or 90 g)
butter, melted

Chantilly Cream

15 egg yolks (9 oz
or 250 g in total)

1 ¾ cups (12 oz or 340 g) sugar

1/4 cup (1 oz or 25 g)
cornstarch

2 cups (500 ml) Marsala wine

1 ¾ cups (400 ml)
whipping cream

Syrup

1 cup (7 oz or 200 g) sugar

1 ¼ cups (300 ml) water

7 Tbsps (100 ml)
Maraschino liqueur

Filling

mixed fruit (berries,
strawberries, peaches in syrup)

Preparation time 1 hour
Cooking time 30 minutes
Level medium

1 Preheat the oven to 400°F (200°C or Gas Mark 6). Make the cake: Over a double boiler, beat the egg yolks, eggs and sugar until thick and foamy. Sift the flour and cornstarch together and carefully fold it into the egg mixture. Add the butter and stir to combine. Pour the batter into a buttered and floured round cake pan. Bake for 20 minutes.

2 Meanwhile, make the Chantilly cream: Beat the egg yolks with the sugar and cornstarch over a double boiler. Add the Marsala and bring to a simmer, stirring constantly with a whisk. Remove from the heat and let cool. When cool, whip the whipped cream and fold it into the mixture.

3 Make the syrup: Bring the sugar and water to a boil in a small saucepan until a thin syrup forms. Remove from heat and let cool. Add the Maraschino. Cut the cake into 3 rounds. Brush the first round with the syrup, top with the Chantilly cream and cover with the fruit.

4 Repeat with the remaining cake rounds and finish with a layer of Chantilly cream. Decorate with strawberries, berries or cape gooseberries.

Apple Strudel

Serves 6

Crust

3/4 cup plus 1 Tbsp
(200 ml) milk

3 Tbsps water

2 cups (9 oz or 250 g)
all-purpose flour

1 Tbsp honey

1 tsp cinnamon

salt

Filling

2 apples

2 Tbsps raisins

zest and juice of
1 organic lemon

1 Tbsp honey

1 Tbsp sugar

1 tsp cinnamon

2 Tbsps breadcrumbs

2 Tbsps (1 oz or 20 g)
butter, melted

Decoration

confectioners' sugar

Preparation time 20 minutes
Cooking time 30 minutes
Level easy

1 Heat the milk and the water until warm. Pour the flour into a bowl, add the honey and then the milk mixture. Add the cinnamon, a pinch of salt and stir to form a smooth and elastic dough. Wrap the dough in plastic wrap and refrigerate for 30 minutes.

2 Meanwhile peel and core the apples and chop into small pieces. Soak the raisins in warm water. Toss the apple pieces with the lemon juice and zest. Add the honey, sugar, cinnamon and drained raisins. Stir to combine. Preheat the oven to 375°F (190°C or Gas Mark 5).

3 On a lightly floured work surface, roll out the pastry into a very thin sheet. Cut into a rectangle and sprinkle with the breadcrumbs. Pour over the apple filling, roll the strudel up and seal both ends. Brush the strudel with the melted butter and make two small cuts along the top of the strudel. Bake for 30 minutes, remove from the oven and let cool. Slice and sprinkle with confectioners' sugar before serving.

Chocolate and Ricotta Cream Cake

Serves 6

Sponge Cake

2 oz (50 g) dark chocolate

3 Tbsps (1 ½ oz or 40 g) butter

1/2 cup (3 ½ oz or 100 g) sugar

salt

3 eggs, separated

1/2 cup (2 oz or 60 g)
all-purpose flour

1/3 cup (1 ½ oz or 40 g)
cornstarch

Cream

7 oz (200 g) ricotta

2 ½ oz (70 g) hazelnut cream
(like Nutella)

2 oz (50 g) dark chocolate,
melted

1/3 cup (80 ml) whipping
cream, whipped

Decoration

Maraschino cherries

dark chocolate shavings

Preparation time 40 minutes
Cooking time 50 minutes
Level medium

1 Preheat the oven to 325°F (160°C or Gas Mark 3). Melt the chocolate in a double boiler. Meanwhile, cream the butter and sugar together with a pinch of salt. Add the chocolate and the egg yolks one at a time, stirring to incorporate each yolk before adding the next. Beat the egg whites to stiff peaks and fold them into the batter with a wooden spoon. Sift the flour and cornstarch and sprinkle them into the batter, stirring constantly.

2 Butter a 10-inch (24 cm) spring-form pan and line it with waxed paper. Pour in the cake batter and bake for 50 minutes. Meanwhile, make the cream. Sieve the ricotta into a bowl and stir it until smooth and creamy. Add the hazelnut cream and the melted chocolate and fold in the whipped cream.

3 Unmold the cake and slice it into 4 rounds. Frost each layer, reserving 4 tablespoons of filling, and place them on top of one another. Fill a pastry bag with the reserved filling and decorate the top of the cake with little puffs of filling. Place a Maraschino cherry on top of each puff and sprinkle the cake with chocolate shavings. Refrigerate for 20 minutes before serving.

Milk Chocolate
and Citrus Cake

Serves 6

Cake

5 ½ oz (150 g) milk chocolate

grated zest of
1 organic orange

grated zest of 1 organic lemon

1/2 cup (2 oz or 60 g)
all-purpose flour

1/2 tsp baking powder

3/4 cup (3 ½ oz or 95 g)
almonds

4 eggs, separated

2/3 cup (4 ½ oz or 125 g) sugar

2 Tbsps warm milk

salt

Decoration

2/3 cup plus 1 Tbsp (170 ml)
whipping cream

confectioners' sugar

milk chocolate, shaved
(optional)

Preparation time 30 minutes
Cooking time 45 minutes
Level medium

1 Preheat the oven to 350°F (180°C or Gas Mark 4). Butter a spring-form pan and line the bottom with parchment paper. Pulse two-thirds of the chocolate in a food processor with the orange and lemon zest. Add the flour, baking powder and almonds and pulse until blended.

2 Using an electric mixer, beat the egg yolks with the sugar and add to the chocolate-almond mixture. Stir in the milk. Beat the egg whites with a pinch of salt and fold them into the batter. Pour the batter into the prepared pan. Bake for 45 minutes, remove from the oven and cool completely. Slice the cake in half horizontally.

3 Whip the whipping cream and use it to frost the bottom layer of the cake. Cover with the top layer and refrigerate for 20 minutes. Dust with confectioners' sugar and decorate with milk chocolate shavings if desired.

Blackberry Cake
with Milk-Chocolate Sauce

Serves 4

Cake

3 ½ oz (100 g) blackberries

2 Tbsps sugar

2/3 cup (150 ml) water

4 sponge cake rounds
(see p. 38)

5 ½ oz (150 g) mascarpone

5 ½ oz (150 g) ricotta

2 Tbsps confectioners' sugar

grated zest of 1 organic lemon

1 tsp vanilla extract

1/4 cup (60 ml)
whipping cream

Garnish

20 blackberries

Chocolate Sauce

3 ½ oz (100 g) milk chocolate

1/4 cup (60 ml)
whipping cream

Preparation time 25 minutes
Cooking time 10 minutes
Level easy

1. Place the blackberries in a saucepan with the sugar and water. Bring to a boil and cook for 8 minutes. Remove from the heat and puree in a food processor.

2. Slice each sponge cake round in half horizontally. Brush the 8 sponge cake rounds with the berry puree. Beat the mascarpone and ricotta with the confectioners' sugar, lemon zest and vanilla extract. Whip the whipping cream to stiff peaks and fold into the mascarpone mixture.

3. Fill a pastry bag with the mascarpone filling. Pipe the filling between each layer, finishing with a layer of filling. Decorate with blackberries.

4. Heat the chocolate and whipping cream over a double boiler. Stir until melted and remove from heat. Serve the cake with the chocolate sauce.

PASTRY CHEF'S TIP

Brioche may be used instead of sponge cake for the base of this dessert.

Carrot, Chocolate
and Coconut Cake

Serves 6

Cake

3 eggs

1 ⅔ cups (7 oz or 200 g)
all-purpose flour

3/4 cups (3 ½ oz or 100 g)
shredded coconut

3/4 cups (5 ½ oz or 150 g)
sugar

5 Tbsps sunflower oil

3 Tbsps milk

2 tsps vanilla extract

3/4 cups (5 ½ oz or 150 g)
grated carrots

1 tsp baking powder

3 ½ oz (100 g) coconut-flavored
chocolate, chopped

Decoration

confectioners' sugar (optional)

shredded coconut (optional)

Preparation time 20 minutes
Cooking time 30 minutes
Level easy

1 Preheat the oven to 350°F (180°C or Gas Mark 4). Mix together the eggs, flour, shredded coconut, sugar, sunflower oil, milk, vanilla, grated carrots and baking powder. Pour the batter into a buttered and floured cake pan.

2 Add the chocolate pieces and stir in with a wooden spoon.

3 Bake for 30 minutes. Serve warm, decorated, if desired with confectioners' sugar and shredded coconut.

PASTRY CHEF'S TIP

For best results, spread the grated carrots in an even layer over a clean kitchen towel. Cover with another towel and let dry for about 1 hour.

Chocolate-Glazed Walnut Cake

Serves 6

Cake

13 Tbsps (6 ½ oz 185 g) butter

1/2 cup (3 ½ oz or 95 g) raw cane sugar

2 eggs, lightly beaten

1 ½ cups (6 ½ oz or 185 g) all-purpose flour

1 tsp baking powder

6 Tbsps milk, salt

1 cup (3 ½ oz or 100 g) walnut halves

Chocolate Glaze

4 oz (120 g) milk chocolate

1 pat of butter

Preparation time 30 minutes
Cooking time 40 minutes
Level medium

1 Preheat the oven to 350°F (180°C or Gas Mark 4). Cream the butter and sugar in a mixer. Add the beaten eggs gradually. Sift in the flour and baking powder and add a pinch of salt. Slowly pour in the milk and continue mixing until it has been completely incorporated.

2 Chop the walnuts and add 2/3 cup (2 oz or 60 g) to the batter. Butter and flour a round cake tin and pour in the batter. Bake for about 35 minutes. Meanwhile, melt the chocolate and butter in a double boiler or in the microwave and then let cool until tepid, stirring constantly. Remove the cake from the oven and let cool slightly. Unmold the cake onto a wire rack and let cool completely.

3 Pour the chocolate glaze over the cake and using a spatula, smooth the glaze evenly over the cake. Sprinkle over the remaining chopped walnuts.

Pumpkin Tart

Serves 4

Crust

2 cups (9 oz or 250 g) all-purpose flour

3 Tbsps sesame oil

2 Tbsps raw cane sugar

1 tsp baking powder

1 Tbsp almond cream

salt

zest of 1 organic lemon

rice milk

Filling

14 oz (400 g) cooked pumpkin puree

2 Tbsps malt extract

1 tsp vanilla extract

1/2 cup raisins, soaked and drained

2 Tbsps almond flour

Preparation time 40 minutes
Cooking time 30 minutes
Level easy

1 Preheat the oven to 350°F (180°C or Gas Mark 4). Mix together the flour, sesame oil, raw cane sugar, baking powder, almond cream, a pinch of salt and the lemon zest to form a dough.

2 Add enough rice milk to form a soft but firm dough. Cover and let rest for 30 minutes. Roll out the dough into a thin sheet and use it to line a tart tin.

3 Make the pumpkin filling: Mix together the pumpkin puree, malt extract, vanilla extract, raisins, and the almond flour. Pour the pumpkin filling into the prepared tart crust and bake for 40 minutes. Let the tart cool before serving.

Mocha Cake

Serves 4

Cake

8 Tbsps (4 oz or 120 g) butter, softened

1/2 cup (3 ½ oz or 100 g) sugar

2 eggs, lightly beaten

3/4 cup plus 1 Tbsp (3 ½ oz or 100 g) all-purpose flour

3 Tbsps cocoa powder

salt

2 Tbsps milk

1 tsp baking powder

1 demitasse cup of lightly sweetened espresso coffee

Preparation time 25 minutes
Cooking time 35 minutes
Level easy

1 Preheat the oven to 350°F (180°C or Gas Mark 4). Cream the butter and all but 1 tablespoon of the sugar using an electric mixer on low speed. Add the lightly beaten eggs, flour, 2 Tbsps of cocoa powder and a pinch of salt and mix well. Add 2 Tbsps of milk and the baking powder and stir to combine.

2 Pour the batter into a buttered cake pan and sprinkle with 1 Tbsp of cocoa together with 1 Tbsp of sugar. Pour the cooled espresso over the batter. Bake for 30-35 minutes.

3 Serve the cake warm with a little of the coffee cream that will have formed at the bottom of the pan.

PASTRY CHEF'S TIP

For an elegant presentation, bake the cake in individual ramekins or miniature silicon molds.

Buckwheat Cake

Serves 6

Cake

1 ⅓ cups (10 ½ oz or 300 g) butter, softened

1 ½ cups (10 ½ oz or 300 g) sugar

6 eggs, separated

2 tsps vanilla extract

2 ½ cups (10 ½ oz or 300 g) buckwheat flour

3 Tbsps all-purpose flour

2 tsps baking powder

Filling

blackcurrant or blueberry jam

Decoration

confectioners' sugar

Preparation time 40 minutes
Cooking time 45 minutes
Level medium

1 Preheat the oven to 350°F (180°C or Gas Mark 4). Cream the butter and sugar together. Add the egg yolks one at a time and then the vanilla and mix until creamy. Sift in the flours and baking powder.

2 Beat the egg whites to stiff peaks and fold into the batter.

3 Butter and flour a cake pan and pour in the batter. Bake for 45 minutes. Remove from the oven and let cool. Cut the cake in half horizontally to form 2 rounds. Spread the jam over one round and top with the remaining round. Sprinkle with confectioners' sugar and serve with whipped cream if desired.

Marble Cake

Serves 6

Cake

4 cups (1 lb 2 oz or 500 g) all-purpose flour

3 eggs

3/4 cup (5 ½ oz or 150 g) sugar

1/4 cup (60 ml) anise liqueur

1 cup (250 ml) milk

2 tsps baking powder

3/4 cup (6 oz or 170 g) butter

grated zest of 1/2 organic lemon

1/4 cup (1 oz or 25 g) cocoa powder

Preparation time 20 minutes

Cooking time 30 minutes

Level easy

1 Preheat the oven to 350°F (180°C or Gas Mark 4). Place the flour in a large mixing bowl. Make a well in the center. Add the eggs, sugar, anise liqueur, milk, 10 ½ tablespoons (5 ½ oz or 150 g) butter, baking powder and the lemon zest in the center of the well.

2 Mix well to form a smooth batter. Pour 1/3 of the batter into a smaller bowl and mix in the cocoa powder.

3 Butter and flour a cake pan and pour in half of the plain batter. Top with the cocoa batter and then pour over the remaining plain batter. Bake until the cake is golden-brown on top, about 30 minutes. Cool and serve.

PASTRY CHEF'S TIP

To verify the doneness of the cake, insert a toothpick into the center of the cake. If the toothpick comes out clean, the cake is done.

Carrot and Walnut Cake
with Chocolate Frosting

Serves 8

Cake

5 eggs

3/4 cup (5 ½ oz or 150 g) sugar

1 cup plus 3 Tbsps (5 1/2 oz or 150 g) all-purpose flour

1/2 cup (1 ½ oz or 40 g) cocoa powder

2 large carrots, peeled and grated

1/3 cup plus 1 Tbsp (2 oz or 50 g) chopped walnuts

3 Tbsps sunflower oil

Frosting

12 ½ oz (350 g) mascarpone

1 1/2 cups (6 oz or 175 g) confectioners' sugar

6 oz (175 g) milk chocolate

Preparation time 30 minutes
Cooking time 45 minutes
Level easy

1 Preheat the oven to 350°F (180°C or Gas Mark 4). Oil an 8-inch (20 cm) cake pan and line with parchment paper. Beat the eggs with the sugar over a double boiler. Cook the mixture, stirring constantly, until it thickens, forming a dense cream. Remove from heat and sift in the flour and cocoa powder. Add the carrots, walnuts and sunflower oil and mix well. Pour the batter into the prepared cake pan and bake for 45 minutes. Remove from the oven and cool completely on a wire rack.

2 Meanwhile, beat the mascarpone with the confectioners' sugar. Melt the chocolate over a double boiler or the microwave, then let cool until tepid. Stir the chocolate into the mascarpone mixture.

3 Slice the cake in half horizontally. Frost the bottom layer, cover with the top layer and frost the top as well. Refrigerate for 20 minutes before serving.

PASTRY CHEF'S TIP

For a delicious variation, substitute the walnuts with the same quantity of almonds and proceed with the recipe. Enrich this cake by adding pears caramelized with honey and a pinch of fresh grated ginger to the batter before baking.

Apricot and Pine-Nut Cake
with Chocolate Sauce

Serves 6

Cake

3/4 cup (3 ½ oz or 100 g) pine nuts

1 cup plus 2 Tbsps (9 oz or 250 g) butter, softened

1 ¼ cups (9 oz or 250 g) sugar

grated zest and juice of 2 organic oranges

3 eggs

2 ½ cups (11 oz or 310 g) all-purpose flour

1 tsp baking powder

3/4 cup (7 oz or 200 g) dried apricots, chopped

Sauce

3 ½ oz (100 g) dark chocolate

5 Tbsps heavy cream

Preparation time 30 minutes
Cooking time 1 hour 25 minutes
Level easy

1 Preheat the oven to 325°F (170°C or Gas Mark 3). Toast the pine nuts in the oven or in a non-stick frying pan for a few minutes. Let cool and coarsely chop.

2 Cream the softened butter with the sugar and orange zest. Beat in the eggs one by one, then sift in the flour and baking powder little by little, stirring constantly with a wooden spoon or spatula. Add the pine nuts, dried apricots and orange juice. Stir to combine, forming a smooth batter.

3 Pour the batter into a cake pan lined with parchment paper and bake for 1 hour 20 minutes. Let cool for 15 minutes before unmolding the cake. Melt the chocolate with the cream. Pour the hot chocolate sauce over slices of cake before serving.

Caprese Cake

Serves 6

Cake

2 cups (10 ½ oz or 300 g) almonds

1 cup (7 oz or 200 g) sugar

5 eggs

10 oz (280 g) dark chocolate

7 Tbsps (3 1/2 oz or 100 g) butter

1/4 cup (60 ml) amaretto liqueur

1 tsp almond extract

2 tsps vanilla extract

3 Tbsps cornstarch

salt

2 tsps baking powder

Decoration

confectioners' sugar

Preparation time 20 minutes

Cooking time 55 minutes

Level easy

Preheat the oven to 350°F (180°C or Gas Mark 4). Blend the almonds in a food processor with the sugar to the consistency of a coarse meal. Transfer to a mixing bowl and stir in the eggs.

Melt the chocolate and butter together and let cool slightly. Add the amaretto liqueur, vanilla and almond extracts, cornstarch and a pinch of salt to the egg mixture. Add the chocolate to the egg mixture and stir to combine. Sift in the baking powder and mix to incorporate.

Butter and flour the sides of a 9-inch (22 cm) spring-form pan. Cut out a 9-inch (22 cm) round of parchment paper and line the bottom of the pan. Pour the cake batter into the pan and bake for 45 minutes. Sprinkle the cake with confectioners' sugar and serve warm.

Dark Chocolate Torte

Serves 6

Cake

7 oz (200 g) dark chocolate
7 Tbsps (3 ½ oz or 100 g) butter
3 eggs, separated
1/2 cup (3 ½ oz or 100 g) sugar
2 Tbsps all-purpose flour
confectioners' sugar (optional)

Preparation time 30 minutes
Cooking time 50 minutes
Level easy

1 Preheat the oven to 350°F (180°C or Gas Mark 4). Melt the chocolate and butter over a double boiler. Meanwhile, beat the egg yolks and sugar until thick. Carefully stir in the melted chocolate mixture and add the flour.

2 Beat the egg whites to stiff peaks and fold them into the batter.

3 Butter and flour a cake pan. Pour the batter into the prepared pan and bake for 50 minutes. Let the cake cool and serve, if desired, sprinkled with confectioners' sugar.

PASTRY CHEF'S TIP

This simple chocolate cake is delicious on its own or accompanied by whipped cream or crème anglaise (see p. 98).

Sacher Torte

Serves 6

Cake

7 oz (200 g) dark chocolate

8 egg yolks

9 Tbsps (4 ½ oz or 125 g)
butter, softened

1 tsp vanilla extract

1 ¼ cups (5 ½ oz or 150 g)
confectioners' sugar

10 egg whites

salt

1 cup (4 oz or 120 g)
all-purpose flour

1/2 tsp baking powder

Filling

1/2 jar of apricot jam

Glaze

3 oz (90 g) dark chocolate

1/2 cup (120 ml)
whipping cream

1 ¼ cups (5 ½ oz or 150 g)
confectioners' sugar

Preparation time 30 minutes
Cooking time 40 minutes
Level medium

1 Preheat the oven to 325°F (170°C or Gas Mark 3). Break up the chocolate for the cake and melt it in a double boiler. Beat the egg yolks until thick and add the cooled melted chocolate. Add 7 tablespoons (3 ½ oz or 100 g) of butter, the vanilla and confectioners' sugar. Stir to combine completely.

2 Beat the egg whites and a pinch of salt to stiff peaks. Add 1/3 of the egg whites to the chocolate mixture and carefully fold in using bottom to top motions. Add the flour and the remaining egg whites and the baking powder and fold together.

3 Butter and flour two 9-inch (22 cm) round cake pans and pour half of the batter into each pan. Bake the cakes for 35 minutes. Remove from the oven and let cool completely. Unmold the cakes and spread the apricot jam over one round. Top with the remaining cake round.

4 Prepare the glaze: Cook the chocolate and the whipping cream together over low heat for 5 minutes and then stir in the confectioners' sugar. To test the consistency of the glaze, tip one teaspoonful of glaze in a glass of cold water. If the glaze hardens it is ready to use. Pour the glaze over the cake and refrigerate for at least 3 hours before serving.

Milk Chocolate
and Almond Cake

Serves 8

Cake

3/4 cup (7 oz or 200 g) butter
at room temperature

1 ¼ cups (9 oz or 250 g) sugar

1 tsp vanilla extract

4 eggs, separated

1/2 cup (2 oz or 60 g)
all-purpose flour

4 Tbsps cocoa powder

2 Tbsps cornstarch

2 ½ cups (9 oz or 250 g)
ground almonds

salt

Frosting

6 Tbsps whipping cream

7 oz (200 g) milk chocolate,
chopped

Preparation time 20 minutes
Cooking time 40 minutes
Level easy

Preheat the oven to 350°F (180°C or Gas Mark 4). Cream the butter with the sugar and vanilla. Add the egg yolks one at a time. Sift in the flour, cocoa powder and cornstarch. Add the ground almonds and stir to combine.

Beat the egg whites and a pinch of salt to stiff peaks and carefully fold them into the batter. Butter and flour a spring-form pan and pour in the batter. Bake for 40 minutes. Remove the cake from the oven, let cool completely and unmold.

Meanwhile, heat the cream and whisk in the chocolate, stirring until the cream is smooth and fluid. Let the frosting harden slightly. Frost the cooled cake and refrigerate for 20 minutes before serving.

PASTRY CHEF'S TIP

If the frosting becomes too hard, beat it with a wooden spoon until it softens and reaches the correct consistency.

Chocolate-Mascarpone Cake

Serves 8

Cake

2/3 cup (3 ½ oz or 100 g) whole almonds

2 oz (50 g) brioche bread

7 oz (200 g) milk chocolate

3 ½ oz (100 g) dark chocolate

2 Tbsps brandy

11 Tbsps (5 ½ oz or 150 g) butter, softened

3/4 cup (5 ½ oz or 150 g) sugar

4 eggs

1 tsp vanilla extract

7 oz (200 g) mascarpone

cocoa powder

Preparation time 35 minutes
Cooking time 40 minutes
Level easy

PASTRY CHEF'S TIP

The brioche bread may be substituted with left over panettone or pandoro.

1 Preheat the oven to 325°F (170°C or Gas Mark 3). Toast the almonds in the oven until they begin to brown. Let cool completely and then blend them in a food processor together with the brioche bread.

2 Butter two 4-inch (10 cm) cake pans and press some of the almond mixture into the pans to line them. Melt the milk chocolate on a low setting in the microwave. Stir in the brandy until the mixture is cool and slightly firm. Using an electric mixer, cream the softened butter together with the sugar. Add the melted chocolate, eggs, vanilla and mascarpone. Add the remaining almond mixture to the batter and transfer it to the prepared pans.

3 Bake for 30 minutes. Let cool for 10 minutes and before unmolding, sprinkle the cakes with cocoa powder. Serve with a little whipped cream if desired.

Chocolate-Glazed Carrot Cake
with Almonds and Coconut

Serves 4

Cake

5 medium carrots, peeled

1 cup (5 ½ oz or 150 g) almonds

3/4 cup (5 ½ oz or 150 g) sugar

1 ¼ cups (5 ½ oz or 150 g) shredded coconut

3 eggs

1 tsp baking powder

Glaze

7 oz (200 g) milk chocolate

shredded coconut (optional)

Preparation time 30 minutes
Cooking time 50 minutes
Level easy

1 Preheat the oven to 325°F (160°C or Gas Mark 3). Puree the carrots in a food processor and transfer to a mixing bowl. Grind the almonds with the sugar in a food processor and add them to the carrots. Stir in the shredded coconut, eggs and baking powder. Stir with a wooden spoon to combine.

2 Pour the mixture into a 10-inch (24 cm) cake pan and bake for 10 minutes. Raise the oven temperature to 350°F (180°C or Gas Mark 4) and continue baking for 40 minutes. Remove from the oven and let cool completely.

3 Meanwhile, melt the chocolate over a double boiler. Pour the glaze over the cake, smoothing with a spatula. Let the glaze harden before serving and decorate, if desired, with shredded coconut.

PASTRY CHEF'S TIP
This cake may also be made in a loaf pan.

Spicy Chocolate Cake

Serves 8

Cake

4 oz (110 g) chili-flavored dark chocolate, chopped

8 Tbsps (4 oz or 110 g) butter, softened

1/2 cup plus 1 Tbsp (4 oz or 110 g) raw cane sugar

3 eggs, separated

2 Tbsps golden rum

1/2 cup (2 oz or 60 g) all-purpose flour

2 oz (60 g) graham crackers, crumbled

salt

Decoration

whipped cream or Chantilly cream

fresh chili peppers (optional)

Preparation time 20 minutes
Cooking time 40 minutes
Level easy

1 Preheat the oven to 350°F (180°C or Gas Mark 4). Melt the chocolate over a double boiler or in the microwave. Cream the softened butter with the sugar until light and fluffy. Add the egg yolks one at a time and then pour in the melted chocolate.

2 Mix well and add the rum. Add the flour and crumble in the graham crackers. Stir to combine. Beat the egg whites and a pinch of salt to stiff peaks and fold them into the chocolate batter.

3 Line a spring-form pan with parchment paper and pour in the batter. Bake for 30 minutes. Let the cake cool completely. Serve with whipped cream or Chantilly cream and decorate with fresh chili peppers if desired.

Pastry Chef's Tip

Chili-flavored chocolate can be found in specialty stores, or add about 1/2 teaspoon ground chili pepper, depending on taste, to 200 g (7 oz) melted dark chocolate.

White Chocolate Cake

with Pears

Serves 8

Cake

2 ripe pears

3/4 cup plus 2 Tbsps (6 oz or 165 g) raw cane sugar

3 Tbsps grappa

3 eggs, lightly beaten

2 cups (9 oz or 250 g) all-purpose flour

1 tsp baking powder

1/2 cup (4 oz or 120 g) melted butter

1/2 cup (120 ml) whipping cream at room temperature

3 ½ oz (100 g) white chocolate

Caramel Glaze

1/2 cup (3 ½ oz or 100 g) sugar

5 Tbsps water

Preparation time 40 minutes
Cooking time 1 hour 5 minutes
Level medium

1 Preheat the oven to 350°F (180°C or Gas Mark 4). Heat the sugar and water for the glaze in a small saucepan. Bring to a boil and cook until it forms a golden syrup, without becoming too thick. Pour the glaze into the bottom of a high-rimmed round cake tin, spreading it evenly with a spoon.

2 Peel, core and slice the pears. Place them in a bowl and sprinkle over the raw cane sugar and the grappa. Add the beaten eggs and sift over the flour and baking powder. Stir to incorporate all of the ingredients. Add the melted butter and whipping cream. Melt the white chocolate in a double boiler. Add the chocolate to the cake batter and mix well.

3 Pour the batter into the prepared cake pan and bake for about 1 hour. Let cool completely and serve.

Pastry Chef's Tip

If there is any caramel glaze left over, use it to decorate the serving plates for the cake.

Glazed Chocolate-Almond Torte

Serves 8

Cake

10 ½ oz (300 g) dark chocolate

1 cup (9 oz or 250 g) butter

5 eggs

4 Tbsps sugar

1 cup (3 ½ oz or 100 g) ground almonds

1 cup plus 3 Tbsps (5 1/2 oz or 150 g) all-purpose flour

1 tsp baking powder

Glaze

7 Tbsps (100 ml) whipping cream

4 ½ oz (125 g) dark chocolate

Preparation time 15 minutes

Cooking time 45 minutes

Level easy

1 Preheat the oven to 325°F (160°C or Gas Mark 3). Melt the chocolate and the butter in a saucepan until smooth. Let cool.

2 Beat the eggs with the sugar until foamy. Add the ground almonds, flour, baking powder and the melted chocolate. Butter and flour a spring-form pan and pour in the batter. Bake for 45 minutes. Let the cake cool in the pan and then unmold.

3 Heat the cream in a saucepan over low heat and add the chocolate. Stir until melted and smooth. Pour the glaze over the cake and serve.

PASTRY CHEF'S TIP

For a richer glaze, boil 3 tablespoons water with 3 tablespoons sugar. After 1 minute, pour in 3 tablespoons cream. Return to a boil and add 2 ½ oz (70 g) dark chocolate.

Duchess Cake

Serves 6

Cake

1 cup plus 1 Tbsp (5 ½ oz or 150 g) hazelnuts, toasted and finely chopped

1 cup (5 ½ oz or 150 g) almonds, finely chopped

2 cups (9 oz or 250 g) confectioners' sugar

1 cup plus 2 Tbsps (9 oz or 250 g) butter

2 cups plus 2 Tbsps (10 ½ oz or 300 g) cake flour

Sabayon

4 egg yolks

4 Tbsps sugar

1/3 cup (80 ml) dry Marsala

3 ½ Tbsps (50 ml) white wine

Chocolate Cream

4 egg yolks

4 Tbsps sugar

2 Tbsps all-purpose flour

½ cup plus 1 tsp (125 ml) milk

5 ½ oz (150 g) dark chocolate, chopped

Decoration

confectioners' sugar

candied cherries

Preparation time 30 minutes
Cooking time 40 minutes
Level medium

1 Mix together the chopped nuts with the sugar, add the butter and stir until smooth. Add the flour and stir to obtain an even dough. Refrigerate for 2-3 hours. Preheat the oven to 400°F (200°C or Gas Mark 6). Roll out the dough and cut out three rounds. Transfer the rounds to a buttered baking sheet and bake for 5 minutes.

2 Make the sabayon: Beat the egg yolks with the sugar until creamy and add the Marsala and white wine. Cook over a double boiler over medium heat, whisking constantly, until the mixture is creamy and has doubled in volume.

3 Make the chocolate cream: Beat the egg yolks with the sugar until thick and creamy. Sift in the flour and beat until smooth. Bring the milk to a boil and remove from heat. Drizzle the milk into the egg mixture, whisking constantly. Return the mixture to the saucepan and cook over low heat until thick. Remove from heat, add the chocolate and stir until smooth. Refrigerate until cool.

4 Place 1 cake round on a serving plate and spread over a layer of chocolate cream. Top with the second layer of cake and spread over the sabayon. Place the remaining cake layer on top and frost with the remaining chocolate cream. Decorate the cake with confectioners' sugar and candied cherries.

Flourless Chocolate Torte

Serves 6

Cake

9 oz (250 g) dark chocolate
(70% cocoa content)

14 Tbsps (7 oz or 200 g) butter

1 cup (3 ½ oz or 100 g)
confectioners' sugar

4 eggs

Preparation time 15 minutes
Cooking time 30 minutes
Level easy

PASTRY CHEF'S TIP

Serve this cake, if desired,
with crème anglaise: Boil 2 cups
(500 ml) milk with the grated zest
of 1 orange. Remove from the heat.
Beat 4 eggs and 2/3 cup (4 oz or
125 g) sugar until thick and creamy.
Whisk into the hot milk and return
to the stove. Cook the cream
over low heat until thick. Strain
the cream into a cold bowl.

1 Preheat the oven to 350°F (180°C or Gas Mark 4). Break the chocolate into pieces and place them over a double boiler. Melt the chocolate over low heat and then add the butter, stirring constantly.

2 Add the confectioners' sugar and stir until smooth. Add the eggs one by one and mix well.

3 Butter and flour a loaf pan and pour the batter into the pan.

4 Bake for 25-30 minutes. Let the cake cool and then invert it onto a serving plate.

Carrot and Pistachio Cake
with White Chocolate-Limoncello Frosting

Serves 8

Cake

5 ½ oz (150 g) unsalted pistachios

3/4 cup (5 ½ oz or 150 g) sugar

grated zest of 1 organic lemon

5 medium carrots, peeled

4 eggs

salt

1/3 cup (1 ½ oz or 40 g) all-purpose flour

1 tsp baking powder

Frosting

3 ½ oz (100 g) white chocolate

1 Tbsp butter

grated zest of 1 organic lemon

1 Tbsp limoncello liqueur

Preparation time 30 minutes
Cooking time 45 minutes
Level easy

1. Preheat the oven to 325°F (160°C or Gas Mark 3). Finely grind the pistachios with the sugar and the zest of 1 lemon in a food processor. Transfer to a mixing bowl.

2. Slice the carrots into rounds and then puree them in a food processor or blender with the eggs and a pinch of salt. Add the carrot mixture to the pistachio mixture and stir to combine. Sift in the flour and baking powder and stir to combine.

3. Pour the batter into a 9-inch (22 cm) cake pan and bake for 10 minutes. Raise the oven temperature to 350°F (180°C or Gas Mark 4) and bake for another 35 minutes. Remove from the oven and cool on a wire rack. Meanwhile, melt the white chocolate and butter over a double boiler or in the microwave. Add the lemon zest. When the cake is completely cooled, add the limoncello to the chocolate mixture and stir to combine. Pour the frosting over the cake and spread evenly with a spatula. Let the frosting set in the refrigerator before serving.

Chocolate-Hazelnut Bundt Cake

Serves 6

Cake

4 eggs, separated

1/2 cup (3 ½ oz or 100 g) sugar

6 ½ oz (180 g) dark chocolate

3 Tbsps (1 ½ oz or 50 g) butter

3/4 cup (1 ½ oz or 50 g)
ground hazelnuts
or hazelnut paste

3 Tbsps all-purpose flour

3 Tbsps cornstarch

salt

Decoration

1/2 cup (120 ml)
whipping cream

1/2 Tbsp confectioners' sugar

5 mint leaves

raspberry puree (optional)

Preparation time 15 minutes
Cooking time 45 minutes
Level easy

1 Preheat the oven to 350°F (180°C or Gas Mark 4). Beat the egg yolks with the sugar until foamy. Melt the chocolate and the butter over a double boiler or in the microwave. Stir the chocolate into the egg mixture. Add the hazelnuts and sift in the flour and cornstarch. Stir to combine.

2 Beat the egg whites and a pinch of salt to stiff peaks and fold them into the batter. Butter and flour a fluted Bundt pan and fill with the batter. Bake for 45 minutes. Let cool and invert onto a serving plate. Whip the cream.

3 Decorate the cake with the whipped cream, confectioners' sugar, mint leaves and a puree of fresh raspberries (see below) if desired.

Pastry Chef's Tip

For the raspberry puree: Puree 2 ½ cups (10 ½ oz or 300 g) of raspberries with 1 tablespoon of raw cane sugar and a few drops of lemon juice. Strain the mixture after pureeing to create a smooth, seedless sauce.

Ricotta-Raisin Cake

Serves 6

Cake

1 cup (4 ½ oz or 125 g) raisins

3 Tbsps all-purpose flour

9 Tbsps (4 ½ oz or 125 g) butter

1 ½ cups plus 2 Tbsps (375 ml) fructose syrup

4 eggs

2 ¼ lb (1 kg) ricotta

2 Tbsps semolina flour

2 tsps baking powder

zest of 1 organic lemon

2 Tbsps breadcrumbs

Decoration

confectioners' sugar

raisins, soaked and drained

Preparation time 30 minutes
Cooking time 1 hour
Level medium

1. Preheat the oven to 350°F (180°C or Gas Mark 4). Soak the raisins in a little warm water. Drain, squeeze out the excess water and dust the raisins with flour. In a mixing bowl beat together the butter and fructose syrup. Add the eggs one at a time and then the ricotta, semolina flour, baking powder and lemon zest.

2. Butter a round cake pan and sprinkle with the breadcrumbs. Stir the raisins into the batter, then transfer the batter to the prepared cake pan. Bake for 1 hour.

3. Remove from the oven, let cool slightly and sprinkle with confectioners' sugar and raisins.

Orange Cream Cake

Serves 6

Cake

3 eggs, separated

3/4 cup (5 ½ oz or 150 g) sugar

7 Tbsps (3 ½ oz or 100 g) butter, softened

1 cup (250 ml) milk

zest of 3 organic oranges

1/3 cup plus 1 Tbsp (2 oz or 50 g) cornstarch

1 cup plus 3 Tbsps (5 1/2 oz or 150 g) all-purpose flour

2 tsps baking powder

Orange Cream

3 Tbsps all-purpose flour

juice of 3 oranges

6 ½ Tbsps sugar

3 Tbsps (1 ½ oz or 40 g) butter

Preparation time 50 minutes
Cooking time 50 minutes
Level medium

1 Preheat the oven to 350°F (180°C or Gas Mark 4). Beat the egg yolks and the sugar together in a large mixing bowl; add the butter, milk, orange zest and the cornstarch. Beat the egg whites to stiff peaks and fold them into the batter. Sift in the flour, stir carefully to combine and then add the baking powder. Transfer the batter to a buttered and floured cake pan and cook for 40 minutes.

2 Meanwhile, make the orange cream: Stir together the flour and orange juice and then add the sugar and butter. Transfer the mixture to a small saucepan and cook over low heat, stirring constantly, until a thick cream forms.

3 Remove the cake from the oven and let cool. Unmold and slice into 2 rounds. Frost the bottom layer with the orange cream and top with the remaining layer. Sprinkle the top of the cake with confectioners' sugar if desired.

Carrot-Almond Cake

Serves 6

Cake

1 ⅓ cups (7 oz or 200 g) almonds

2 ¼ cups (9 oz or 250 g) sugar

8 small carrots (about 14 oz or 400 g), peeled

4 eggs

3/4 cup plus 2 Tbsps (3 ½ oz or 110 g) all-purpose flour

1 ½ tsps baking powder

zest of 1 organic lemon

salt

Preparation time 20 minutes
Cooking time 40 minutes
Level easy

1 Preheat the oven to 325°F (160°C or Gas Mark 3). Blend the almonds and the sugar in a food processor until the mixture resembles coarse meal. Prolonged blending will create a flour that will soften the cake while pulsing the mixture will form a coarse flour making a thicker, more rustic cake.

2 Grate the carrots in the food processor and add them to the almond mixture. Stir in the eggs, sift in the flour and baking powder and add the lemon zest and a pinch of salt. Using a whisk, mix the batter until smooth.

3 Butter and flour a 10-inch (24 cm) cake pan. Pour the batter into the pan and bake for 12 minutes. Raise the oven temperature to 350°F (180°C or Gas Mark 4) and continue baking for another 30 minutes. Remove from the oven and cool slightly before serving.

Cinnamon Cake
with Milk-Chocolate Glaze

Serves 8

Cake

2 cups (9 oz or 250 g)
all-purpose flour

2 tsps baking powder

1 Tbsp ground cinnamon

1 ¼ cups (9 oz or 250 g) sugar

1 cup (250 ml) milk

2 eggs

salt

9 Tbsps (4 ½ oz or 125 g)
butter, melted

Glaze

3 ½ oz (100 g) milk chocolate

2 Tbsps whipping cream

Preparation time 40 minutes
Cooking time 35 minutes
Level medium

1. Sift the flour, baking powder and cinnamon into a bowl and add the sugar. Whisk together the milk, eggs and a pinch of salt and add to the flour mixture. Quickly stir with a wooden spoon to combine.

2. Drizzle in the melted butter while stirring. Butter and flour a rectangular baking dish, or line it with parchment paper, and pour in the batter. Bake for 30 minutes and let cool before unmolding.

3. Meanwhile, melt the chocolate in the microwave or over a double boiler and let cool slightly. Whisk in the cream and continue whisking until the glaze thickens slightly. Unmold the cake and cut it into squares. Glaze each square and set aside until the glaze hardens. Serve sprinkled with a little cinnamon if desired.

Pastry Chef's Tip

For an unusual variation, pour 2/3 of the batter into the pan and sprinkle with 3 tablespoons of raw sugar and 1/2 tablespoon of ground cinnamon. Top with the remaining batter and continue with the recipe. While baking, the sugar and cinnamon will caramelize, forming a crunchy layer at the center of the cake.

Yogurt Cake
with Plums and Red Wine

Serves 8

Cake

13 Tbsps (6 ½ oz or 180 g) butter

1 ¼ cups (9 oz or 250 g) sugar

5 eggs, separated

1 cup (9 oz or 250 g) yogurt

zest of 2 organic lemons

2 ¼ cups (10 oz or 280 g)
all-purpose flour

2 tsps baking powder

salt

Plums

4 red plums

3/4 cup plus 1 Tbsp (200 ml)
full-bodied red wine

1/2 cup (3 ½ oz or 100 g) sugar

1/4 cup (2 oz or 50 g)
raw sugar

1 star anise

1 juniper berry

1 clove

Preparation time 1 hour
Cooking time 1 hour 10 minutes
Level medium

1 Slice the plums into wedges, remove the pits and set aside. In a small saucepan bring the wine, sugar, raw sugar, and spices to a boil. Let cook until the liquid is reduced to 1/3 of the original volume. Add the plums, remove from the heat and let sit for 30 minutes. Preheat the oven to 350°F (180°C or Gas Mark 4).

2 Cream the butter and sugar until light and fluffy. Add the egg yolks one at a time and then the yogurt and lemon zest. Sift in the flour and baking powder and mix carefully using a spatula. Beat the egg whites with a pinch of salt to form stiff peaks. Fold in the egg whites.

3 Line a spring-form pan with parchment paper and pour in the batter. Drain the plums, reserving the marinade, and dust them with a little flour. Place the plums on top of the cake and bake for 45-50 minutes. Remove from the oven when golden-brown and let cool completely. Serve the cake drizzled with the strained, reduced marinade.

Nectarine-Hazelnut Cake

Serves 8

Cake

1/3 cup (2 oz or 50 g) hazelnuts

1 cup (7 oz or 200 g) sugar

zest of 1 organic lemon

5 amaretto cookies

3 eggs

5 Tbsps (2 ½ oz or 70 g) butter

1/2 cup (4 ½ oz or 125 g)
plain yogurt

2 cups (9 oz or 250 g)
all-purpose flour

2 tsps baking powder

4 medium nectarines
(1 lb 5 oz or 600 g in total)

Preparation time 20 minutes
Cooking time 50 minutes
Level medium

1. Preheat the oven to 350°F (180°C or Gas Mark 4). Blend the hazelnuts, sugar and lemon zest in a food processor. Transfer to a mixing bowl and crumble in the amaretto cookies.

2. Add the eggs, butter and yogurt. Whisk the mixture until a smooth batter forms. Sift in the flour and baking powder, stirring with a wooden spoon or spatula.

3. Cut the nectarines into very thin slices. Butter and flour a rectangular baking dish. Pour in the batter and then place the nectarine slices along the top of the batter. Bake for 50 minutes.

Paradise Cake

Serves 8

Cake

4 eggs

1 cup (7 oz or 200 g) raw sugar

1 Tbsp malt extract

salt

3/4 cup (7 oz or 200 g) yogurt with whole grains (or sweetened plain yogurt)

2 cups (9 oz or 250 g) all-purpose flour

2 tsps baking powder

6 Tbsps (3 oz or 80 g) butter, melted

zest of 1 organic lemon

Decoration

confectioners' sugar

Preparation time 25 minutes
Cooking time 45 minutes
Level easy

1. Preheat the oven to 325°F (170°C or Gas Mark 3). Beat the eggs and the raw sugar together and add the malt extract and a pinch of salt.

2. Add the yogurt and sift in the flour and baking powder. Drizzle in the melted butter and stir to combine. Add the lemon zest and stir gently.

3. Butter and flour a loaf pan and pour in the batter. Bake for 45 minutes. Let cool before unmolding the cake. Sprinkle with confectioners' sugar before serving.

Bundt Cake
with Pine Nuts, Raisins and Candied Fruit

Serves 4

Cake

4 cups (1 lb 2 oz or 500 g)
all-purpose flour

3 eggs, separated

3/4 cup (5 ½ oz or 150 g) sugar

7 Tbsps (3 ½ oz or 100 g)
butter, melted

1/2 cup (125 ml) milk

1/3 cup (1 ½ oz or 40 g) raisins,
soaked and drained

1/3 cup (1 ½ oz or 40 g)
pine nuts

2 oz (60 g) mixed
candied fruit, diced

2 Tbsps (1 oz or 20 g) aniseeds

zest of 1/2 organic lemon

2 tsps baking powder

1 egg yolk

Preparation time 30 minutes
Cooking time 40 minutes
Level easy

1 Preheat the oven to 400°F (200°C or Gas Mark 5). Pour the flour into a large mixing bowl and make a well at the center. Add the 3 egg yolks, sugar, melted butter and milk and mix well. Add the raisins, pine nuts, candied fruit and aniseeds and stir to combine.

2 Meanwhile, beat the egg whites to stiff peaks and fold into the batter along with the lemon zest and the baking powder.

3 Pour the batter into a Bundt pan and brush the top with the lightly beaten egg yolk. Bake for 40 minutes or until golden-brown. Let cool before serving.

PASTRY CHEF'S TIP
Serve this cake with a Marsala-mascarpone cream made by beating 2 egg yolks together with 1/2 cup (3 ½ oz or 100 g) sugar, 5 ½ oz (150 g) mascarpone and 4 tablespoons of Marsala wine.

Dark Chocolate Bundt Cake

Serves 4

Cake

4 medium potatoes
(1 ¾ lb or 800 g in total)

7 Tbsps (3 ½ oz or 100 g) butter

1 cup plus 2 Tbsps
(8 oz or 225 g) sugar

1 tsp vanilla extract

1 cup (3 ½ oz or 100 g)
ground almonds

grated zest of 1 organic
orange

4 eggs, separated

4 ½ oz (125 g) dark chocolate

salt

Preparation time 20 minutes
Cooking time 1 hour 20 minutes
Level easy

1 Preheat the oven to 350°F (180°C or Gas Mark 4). Boil the potatoes until tender. Drain, peel and mash them with a ricer. Let cool. Melt the butter and add it to the potatoes. Mix well. Add the sugar, vanilla, ground almonds and grated orange zest. Mix well. Add the egg yolks. Shave the chocolate into the batter.

2 Beat the egg whites with a pinch of salt to firm peaks. Fold the whites into the batter. Pour the mixture into a buttered Bundt pan. Place the pan in a baking dish and fill it half full with hot water. Bake for 45 minutes. Let the cake cool slightly and invert onto a serving dish.

Chocolate-Vanilla
Marbled Bundt Cake

Serves 4

Cake

12 Tbsps (6 oz or 175 g) butter, softened

2/3 cup (4 ½ oz or 130 g) sugar

1 tsp vanilla extract

3 eggs

1 ¾ cups (8 oz or 225 g) all-purpose flour

salt

1/2 tsp baking powder

2 oz (50 g) milk chocolate

Preparation time 20 minutes
Cooking time 30 minutes
Level easy

1 Preheat the oven to 375°F (190°C or Gas Mark 5). Cream the butter and sugar together. Add the vanilla and then the eggs. Sift in the flour, a pinch of salt and the baking powder.

2 Transfer half of the batter to another bowl. Melt the chocolate over a double boiler or the microwave. Let cool slightly, and when tepid add it to half of the batter. Stir until the color is uniform.

3 Butter a medium-sized Bundt pan. Fill the pan with spoonfuls of the batter, alternating chocolate and plain batter. Bake the cake for 30 minutes. Let cool and unmold before serving.

Rice Cake

Serves 4

Cake

3/4 cup plus 1 Tbsp (6 oz or 160 g) Originario rice (or short-grain risotto rice)

3 ⅔ cups (800 ml) milk

salt

1 cup plus 2 Tbsps (6 oz or 160 g) peeled almonds

3 eggs, separated

3/4 cup plus 1 ½ Tbsps (6 oz or 160 g) sugar

zest of 1/2 organic lemon

1 egg white

2 Tbsps (1 oz or 20 g) butter

Preparation time 20 minutes
Cooking time 45 minutes
Level easy

1 Preheat the oven to 300°F (150°C or Gas Mark 2). Cook the rice in the milk, adding a pinch of salt. When all of the milk has been absorbed, remove from heat and let cool completely.

2 Meanwhile, finely chop the almonds and add them to the cooked rice. Add the egg yolks, sugar and lemon zest and mix well.

3 Beat the egg whites to stiff peaks and carefully fold them into the batter.

4 Pour the batter into a buttered and floured baking dish and bake for 30 minutes. Unmold the cake and serve either warm or cold, sprinkled with confectioners' sugar and slivered almond if desired.

Almond Tart

Serves 6

Crust

4 cups (1 lb 2 oz or 500 g)
all-purpose flour

1 ¼ cups (9 oz or 250 g) sugar

11 Tbsps (5 ½ oz or 150 g)
butter

zest of 1 organic lemon

1/4 cup (60 ml) herb liqueur

1 egg plus 3 egg yolks

2 tsps baking powder

Filling

3 ½ cups (17 ½ oz or 500 g)
almonds

8 Tbsps (4 oz or 120 g) butter

1 ½ cups (10 ½ oz or 300 g)
sugar

5 eggs

Preparation time 50 minutes
Cooking time 45 minutes
Level medium

1 Mound the flour on a work surface and place the sugar, butter, lemon zest, liqueur, egg yolks and egg in the center. Working quickly, mix the dough together using the fingertips. Lastly, add the baking powder.

2 Preheat the oven to 350°F (180°C or Gas Mark 4). Form the dough into a ball, cover and let sit in a cool place for 30 minutes. Meanwhile, using a food processor, blend three-quarters of the almonds until they resemble fine meal. Add the butter, sugar and then the eggs, one at a time. Coarsely chop the remaining almonds and stir them into the filling.

3 Roll out the pastry into a 1/4-inch (1/2 cm) thick sheet and use it to line a buttered tart tin. Pour in the filling and bake for 45 minutes. Let the tart cool slightly before serving.

PASTRY CHEF'S TIP

For a distinctive almond flavor, blend 3-4 bitter almonds into the mixture for the filling or add a few drops of almond extract.

Chocolate Cream Pie

Serves 8

Crust

11 Tbsps (5 ½ oz or 160 g) butter

2 ⅔ cups (11 ½ oz or 330 g) all-purpose flour

3/4 cup plus 1 ½ Tbsps (5 ½ oz or 160 g) sugar

1 egg plus 2 egg yolks

1/3 cup (1 oz or 30 g) cocoa powder

1 Tbsp pine nuts

Pastry Cream

2 cups (500 ml) milk

2 tsps vanilla extract

4 egg yolks

2/3 cup (4 ½ oz or 125 g) sugar

7 Tbsps all-purpose flour

Preparation time 30 minutes
Cooking time 45 minutes
Level medium

1 Make the pastry cream: Bring the milk and vanilla extract to a boil. Beat the egg yolks with the sugar and sift in the flour. Whisk the hot milk into the eggs and return to the saucepan. Bring to a boil over low heat, stirring constantly, until the cream thickens. Remove from the heat and let cool.

2 Make the crust: Cut the butter into small pieces. Pour the flour into a mixing bowl and add the butter, sugar, egg, egg yolks and cocoa. Mix well to form a uniform dough. Cover the dough and refrigerate for 1 hour. Preheat the oven to 350°F (180°C or Gas Mark 4). Butter and flour a tart tin.

3 Roll out the dough into 2 thin sheets and line the tin with 1 sheet of dough. Pour in the pastry cream and then cover with the second sheet of dough. Press down the dough to seal, cutting off any extra dough if necessary. Top with pine nuts and bake for 35 minutes. Let cool completely before serving.

PASTRY CHEF'S TIP

To make the top and bottom of the pie crust stick together, brush the edges with beaten egg white.

Neapolitan Pastiera

Serves 6

Crust

2 cups (9 oz or 250 g)
all-purpose flour

13 Tbsps (6 ½ oz or 180 g)
butter

1/2 cup plus 1 Tbsp (2 ½ oz
or 70 g) confectioners' sugar

1 egg plus 1 egg yolk

1 tsp baking powder

salt

Filling

1 vanilla bean

1 cup (250 ml) milk

1 piece of organic lemon rind

7 oz (200 g) cooked wheat

7 oz (200 g) sheep's
milk ricotta

4 oz (120 g) candied
orange rind

2 eggs plus 3 egg yolks

1/3 cup (2 oz or 60 g) sugar

2 Tbsps orange-flower water

Preparation time 50 minutes
Cooking time 1 hour
Level medium

1 Prepare the crust following the instructions on p. 32. When the dough is ready, cover it with plastic wrap and let rest in a cool place for 1 hour. Preheat the oven to 325°F (170°C or Gas Mark 3).

2 Make the filling: Cut the vanilla bean in half lengthwise and place it in a saucepan with the milk. Bring to a boil and lower the heat, then add the lemon rind and the cooked wheat.

3 Cook over low heat until all of the liquid has been absorbed. Remove the lemon rind and vanilla bean and let the mixture cool.

4 Sieve the ricotta and add it to the cooled filling along with the candied orange. Beat the egg yolks with the sugar until thick and creamy and add them to the filling along with the whole eggs. Add the orange-flower water and mix well.

5 Butter and flour a tart tin. Roll out most of the pastry into a 1/5-inch (3 mm) thick sheet and use it to line the prepared tart tin. Pour the filling into the crust and roll out the remaining pastry. Cut the pastry into strips and form a diagonal lattice over the top. Bake the tart for 40 minutes.

Bolognese Fruit and Nut Cake

Serves 6

Cake

1/3 cup plus 2 Tbsps
(5 ½ oz or 150 g) honey

2/3 cup (4 ½ oz or 125 g) sugar

1 tsp aniseeds

1 tsp baking soda

2 cups (9 oz or 250 g)
all-purpose flour

3/4 cup plus 1 Tbsp
(3 ½ oz or 100 g) raisins

2/3 cup (3 ½ oz or 100 g)
almonds, chopped

3/4 cup (3 ½ oz or 100 g)
pine nuts, chopped

3 ½ oz (100 g) candied orange
or citron rind, chopped

3 ½ oz (100 g) chocolate
shavings or chips

butter

Preparation time 20 minutes
Cooking time 40 minutes
Level easy

1 Place the honey, sugar, aniseeds and baking soda in a saucepan along with 3/4 cup (200 ml) of hot water. Cook over low heat, stirring constantly, and then add the flour. Cook the mixture for 5 minutes and remove from heat.

2 Add the raisins, almonds, pine nuts, candied orange, chocolate chips and baking powder to the mixture and stir well.

3 Transfer the batter to a buttered, high-rimmed cake pan and bake for 30 minutes. Remove from the oven and cool completely before unmolding.

Cherry Clafoutis

Serves 4

Cake

3/4 cup plus 1 Tbsp (3 ½ oz or 100 g) all-purpose flour

2 eggs

6 ½ Tbsps sugar

2 tsps vanilla extract

salt

1 cup (250 ml) milk

1 pat of butter

1 lb (450 g) black cherries, pitted

Decoration

confectioners' sugar

Preparation time 10 minutes
Cooking time 20 minutes
Level easy

1 Preheat the oven to 425°F (220°C or Gas Mark 7). Mix the flour, eggs, sugar, vanilla and a pinch of salt in a mixing bowl. Slowly whisk in the milk, being careful not to let lumps form. The batter should be smooth and creamy.

2 Butter a deep, heavy baking dish and fill it two-thirds full with the batter. Add the cherries and then pour over the remaining batter.

3 Bake for at least 20 minutes. The cake should be deep golden-brown color. Sprinkle with confectioners' sugar and serve hot or at room temperature.

Chocolate Mille-feuille

by **Francesco Elmi**

Serves 4

Starter Dough

4 ½ cups (1 ¼ lb or 555 g)
all-purpose flour

1 cup (250 ml) water

3 tsps salt

Pastry

1 ⅓ cups plus 1 Tbsp (6 oz
or 175 g) all-purpose flour

1 ½ lb plus 4 Tbsps (750 g)
butter

2/3 cup (2 oz or 50 g)
cocoa powder

Cream

6 egg yolks (3 ½ oz
or 100 g in total)

2/3 cup (4 ½ oz or 130 g) sugar

1 ¼ cups (300 ml) milk

2 oz (50 g) dark chocolate,
chopped

3/4 cup (2 ½ oz or 70 g)
cocoa powder

Decoration

hazelnuts, coarsely chopped

cocoa powder

chocolate shavings (optional)

Preparation time 1 hour
Cooking time 30 minutes
Level difficult

1 Mix together the ingredients for the starter dough until smooth and let rest in the refrigerator. Mix together the ingredients for the pastry into a smooth dough and refrigerate for 30 minutes. Roll out the pastry dough on a lightly floured surface and place the starter in the center. Fold the pastry around the starter and close to form a package. Roll out the dough with a rolling pin, fold into thirds to form a rectangle and refrigerate for 15 minutes. Roll out the pastry again, fold into fourths and refrigerate for 15 minutes. Repeat 2 times.

2 Preheat the oven to 400°F (200°C or Gas Mark 6). Make the cream: Beat the egg yolks and sugar until thick. Bring the milk to a simmer in a saucepan. Add the egg mixture to the milk and stir to combine. Cook the mixture over low heat and add the chocolate and cocoa powder, stirring constantly. When the cream thickens, remove from heat. Let cool and then transfer to a pastry bag.

3 Roll out the pastry into a thin sheet and bake for 8 minutes. Let cool and then, using a round cookie cutter, cut out at least 12 rounds. Construct the mille-feuilles by alternating layers of pastry with the chocolate cream. Top each layer with chopped hazelnuts. Before serving, sprinkle each mille-feuille with cocoa powder, more hazelnuts and chocolate shavings if desired.

Lemon Meringue Tart

by **Francesco Elmi**

Serves 4

Crust

1 ½ cups (10 ½ oz or 300 g) butter, softened

1 ⅔ cups (7 oz or 200 g) confectioners' sugar

2 large eggs

1/3 cup plus 1 Tbsp (2 oz or 50 g) almond flour

4 cups (1 lb 2 oz or 500 g) all-purpose flour

1 tsp salt

1 tsp vanilla extract

Cream

4 egg yolks (2 ½ oz or 70 g in total)

2 small eggs

1/3 cup (2 ½ oz or 75 g) sugar

1/2 cup (125 ml) lemon juice

5 Tbsps (2 ½ oz or 75 g) butter

Meringue

7 Tbsps (100 ml) water

2 ½ cups (1 lb 2 oz or 500 g) sugar

4 egg whites

Preparation time 1 hour
Cooking time 35 minutes
Level medium

1 Make the crust: Mix together the butter, sugar, eggs, both types of flour, salt and vanilla extract to form a smooth dough. Form into a ball, cover with plastic wrap and let rest. Preheat the oven to 325°F (170°C or Gas Mark 3).

2 Make the cream: Beat the egg yolks and egg with the sugar until thick and foamy. Bring the lemon juice to a boil in a saucepan, remove from heat and whisk in the egg mixture. Return the saucepan to the heat and bring the mixture to 176°F (80°C). Add the butter, mix well and remove from heat.

3 Make the meringue: Heat the water and 2 cups (14 oz or 400 g) of sugar to 250°F (121°C). While the sugar syrup heats, begin to beat the egg whites with the remaining sugar in a standing mixer. When the syrup comes to the correct temperature, slowly drizzle it into the stiff egg whites. Continue beating until the meringue cools.

4 Roll out the pastry into a 1/5-inch (3 mm) thick sheet and use it to line a buttered and floured tart tin. Pour the lemon cream into the pastry shell, filling the shell three-quarters full. Bake the tart for 25 minutes. Let cool and spread the meringue over the top of the tart. Place the tart under a preheated broiler for a few minutes, until the meringue begins to color. Decorate the tart, if desired, with dehydrated lemon slices.

Apple Tart with Pastry Cream

by **Francesco Elmi**

Serves 8

Crust

1 ½ cups (10 ½ oz or 300 g) butter

1 ⅔ cups (7 oz or 200 g)
confectioners' sugar

2 extra-large eggs

4 cups (17 ½ oz or 500 g)
all-purpose flour

1/3 cup plus 1 Tbsp
(2 oz or 50 g) almond flour

1 tsp salt, 1 tsp vanilla extract

Sponge Cake

6 eggs plus 3 egg yolks

1 ½ cups (10 ½ oz or 300 g) sugar

2/3 cup (3 oz or 80 g) cornstarch

2 ⅓ cups plus 1 Tbsp (10 ½ oz
or 300 g) all-purpose flour

1 tsp baking powder

Pastry Cream

13 egg yolks (8 oz or 220 g in total)

3/4 cup (5 oz or 140 g) sugar

1/4 cup (1 oz or 30 g)
all-purpose flour

1 cup (250 ml) whipping cream

1 cup (250 ml) milk

1/2 vanilla bean,
sliced in half lengthwise

Decoration

4 Golden Delicious apples

Preparation time 1 hour 10 minutes
Cooking time 1 hour 10 minutes
Level medium

1 Make the pastry cream: Beat the egg yolks with the sugar until thick, sift in the flour and stir to combine. Beat the whipping cream to stiff peaks. Bring the milk and the vanilla bean to a boil. Remove the vanilla bean and slowly drizzle the boiling hot milk into the egg mixture, stirring constantly with a whisk.

2 Make the crust: Mix together the softened butter, confectioners' sugar, eggs, flour, almond flour, salt and vanilla extract to form a smooth dough. Cover with plastic wrap and let rest in a cool place for at least 30 minutes.

3 Make the sponge cake: Preheat the oven to 400°F (200°C or Gas Mark 6). Beat the eggs and egg yolks with the sugar and add the cornstarch. Sift in the flour and baking powder and mix well. Pour the batter into a cake pan lined with parchment paper and bake for 25 minutes. Lower the oven temperature to 325°F (170°C or Gas Mark 3). Peel the apples and slice them into very thin slices. Roll out the pastry into a 1/5-inch (3 mm) sheet and use it to line a buttered and floured tart tin the same size as the cake pan. Pierce the crust with a fork and pour over a layer of pastry cream. Place the sponge cake on top of the pastry cream and top with the remaining pastry cream. Decorate the top of the cake with the apple slices and bake for 30 minutes.

Mille-feuille with
Bergamot Cream and Strawberries

by **Roberto Rinaldini**

Serves 4

Crust

2 ⅔ cups plus 1 Tbsp (10 ½ oz or 300 g) all-purpose flour

2/3 cup (150 ml) water

1 ½ tsp salt

3/4 cup plus 3 ½ Tbsps (9 oz or 250 g) butter, cold

6 Tbsps confectioners' sugar

Chantilly Cream

6 egg yolks (3 ½ oz or 100 g)

6 Tbsps sugar

1/3 cup (1 ½ oz or 40 g) cornstarch

zest of 1 organic lemon

7 Tbsps (100 ml) bergamot liqueur

3/4 cup plus 1 Tbsp (200 ml) whipping cream

1/2 vanilla bean, split lengthwise

1 ¾ cups (400 ml) whipped cream

Filling

5 ½ oz (150 g) almond brittle, chopped

9 oz (250 g) strawberries, cleaned and sliced

Decoration

confectioners' sugar

Preparation time 1 hour 10 minutes
Cooking time 30 minutes
Level medium

1 Prepare the crust following the instructions on p. 34. Preheat the oven to 400°F (200°C or Gas Mark 6). Roll the finished dough out into five 1/2-inch (1 ½ cm) thick rounds. Place them on a baking sheet, pierce with a fork and sprinkle with confectioners' sugar. Bake for 10 minutes.

2 Make the Chantilly cream: Beat the egg yolks with the sugar and sift in the cornstarch. Add the lemon zest and bergamot liqueur. Bring the whipping cream and the vanilla bean to a simmer over low heat. Drizzle into the egg mixture, whisking constantly. Return the mixture to the saucepan and cook over low heat, stirring constantly, until the mixture thickens or reaches 180°F (82°C). Remove from heat, cool quickly and fold in the whipping cream.

3 Transfer the Chantilly cream to a pastry bag fitted with a ridged tip. Pipe the pastry cream onto a pastry round, top with almond brittle and strawberries, top with another pastry round and continue making layers, finishing with a layer of pastry. Sprinkle with confectioners' sugar and serve with sliced strawberries.

Hazelnut Tart
with Berries and Chocolate Cream

by **Roberto Rinaldini**

Serves 8

Crust

1 lb (425 g) butter

1 ⅓ cups plus 1 Tbsp (6 oz or 175 g) hazelnut flour

1 ¾ cups plus 2 Tbsps (8 oz or 225 g) confectioners' sugar

1/2 tsp salt, 4 large eggs

8 cups (2 ¼ lb or 1 kg) bread flour

zest of 1/2 organic lemon

Berry Puree

1 lb (500 g) fresh berries

2/3 cup (4 ½ oz or 120 g) sugar

2 ½ gelatin sheets

zest of 2 organic lemons

Chocolate Cream

1 ¼ cups (300 ml) milk

3 egg yolks (2 oz or 50 g in total)

1/3 cup (2 oz or 60 g) sugar

6 oz (170 g) dark chocolate

3/4 cup plus 1 Tbsp (200 ml) whipped cream

Glaze

3/4 cup plus 1 Tbsp (200 ml) whipping cream

3 ½ Tbsps (50 g) glucose syrup

7 oz (200 g) dark chocolate, chopped

Preparation time 1 hour
Cooking time 30 minutes
Level difficult

1 Make the crust: Beat the butter, sift in the hazelnut flour and confectioners' sugar, and add the salt. Add the eggs, the flour and the lemon zest and mix. Cover with plastic wrap and refrigerate for 2 hours. Roll out the dough into a 1/5-inch (3 mm) thick sheet, line a tart tin, and bake for 18 minutes.

2 Make the berry puree: Mix the sugar and the berries in a saucepan and warm over low heat. Soak the gelatin in cold water, then remove it and dissolve the sheets in the warm fruit mixture. Add the lemon zest to the puree and pour into the cooled pastry shell. Refrigerate for 30 minutes.

3 Make the chocolate cream: Mix together the milk, egg yolks and sugar in a saucepan and heat to 180°F (82° C). Then, melt the chocolate over a double boiler. Fold the melted chocolate into the egg and milk mixture, and refrigerate until the cream reaches room temperature. Fold in the whipped cream with a spatula and spread the chocolate cream over the chilled tart. Cover the tart with plastic wrap and return to the refrigerator.

4 Make the glaze: Heat the whipping cream and the glucose until the mixture reaches 175°F (80°C). Pour the hot mixture over the chopped chocolate and stir with a rigid spatula until the glaze is smooth. Let the glaze cool completely. Reheat the glaze to 95°F (35°C) and pour it over the top of the tart.

Peach Tart
with Spiced Almond Cream

by **Roberto Rinaldini**

Serves 8

Crust

1 cup (5 oz or 135 g) almond flour

3/4 cup (5 oz or 135 g) sugar

1 ¾ cups plus 1 Tbsp (8 oz or 225 g) confectioners' sugar

1 lb (425 g) butter, 1 tsp salt

4 large eggs

8 cups (2 ¼ lb or 1 kg) bread flour

zest of 1/2 organic lemon

Almond Cream

3/4 cup (7 oz or 200 g) butter

1 cup (7 oz or 200 g) sugar, 4 eggs

1 ⅔ cups (7 oz or 200 g) almond flour

1 ¼ cups (5 ½ oz or 160 g) all-purpose flour

zest of 1 organic lemon

1 tsp cinnamon, 1/4 Tonka bean

Peaches

1 lb 5 oz (600 g) yellow peaches

7 Tbsps (3 ½ oz or 100 g) butter, melted

1/3 cup (2 oz or 60 g) raw sugar

1/2 vanilla bean, halved and seeds scraped out

zest of 1 organic lemon

Preparation time 40 minutes

Cooking time 50 minutes

Level easy

1. Make the crust: Sift together the almond flour, sugar, confectioners' sugar and salt. Beat the butter until soft and add the almond mixture. Add the eggs and slowly stir in the flour a little at a time. Add the lemon zest, form into a ball, cover with plastic wrap and refrigerate. Preheat the oven to 350°F (180°C or Gas Mark 4).

2. Make the almond cream: Cream the butter and sugar together, then add the eggs, flour and lemon zest. Add the cinnamon and grate in the Tonka bean.

3. Make the peaches: Slice the peaches and toss them with the melted butter, raw sugar, vanilla seeds and lemon zest.

4. Roll out the pastry into a thin sheet and use it to line a buttered and floured tart tin. Spread the almond cream into the tart and top with the peaches. Bake for 50 minutes.

Millefeuille with Wild Berries

by **Paolo Staccoli**

Serves 6

Pastry

2 ¼ cups (9 ½ oz or 275 g) all-purpose flour

1 ½ cups (10 ½ oz or 300 g) butter

1/2 cup plus 2 Tbsps (140 ml) water

1 tsp salt

confectioners' sugar

Cream

1 cup (250 ml) milk

1/2 vanilla bean, split lengthwise

zest of 1 organic lemon

2 egg yolks

6 Tbsps sugar

2 Tbsps all-purpose flour

1 ¾ cups (400 ml) whipped cream

Filling

10 ½ oz (300 g) mixed edible berries

Preparation time 1 hour
Cooking time 20 minutes
Level medium

1. Prepare the crust following the instructions on p. 34. Roll out the finished dough into a 1/8-inch (2 mm) thick sheet. Place on a baking sheet lined with parchment paper, pierce with a fork, and let rest for 1 hour. Preheat the oven to 400-425°F (200-220°C or Gas Mark 6-7). Sprinkle the pastry with confectioners' sugar and bake for 8 minutes. Remove from the oven and let cool completely. Cut cooled pastry into 3 rectangles and set aside.

2. Make the cream: Bring the milk to a boil with the vanilla bean and the lemon zest. Strain the infusion. Beat the egg yolks with the sugar until thick, then sift in the flour and mix well. Drizzle in the hot milk, whisking constantly. Return the mixture to the saucepan and cook over low heat until the cream comes to a boil. Let cool and fold in the whipped cream.

3. Spread 2 of the pastry rectangles with part of the cream and transfer the remaining cream to a pastry bag fitted with a ridged tip. Pipe out little puffs of cream, alternating with berries, along the edge of one of the pastry sheets. Fill the center with berries. Place the second pastry sheet on top of the first and repeat. Top with the remaining pastry sheet and decorate with confectioners' sugar and mixed berries if desired.

Amarcord

by **Paolo Staccoli**

Serves 6

Sponge Cake

3 eggs

1/2 cup (3 ½ oz or 100 g) sugar

2/3 cup (3 oz or 85 g) all-purpose flour

1/4 cup (1/2 oz or 15 g) cocoa powder

Mousse

4 ½ oz (125 g) crème anglaise (see p. 98)

5 ½ oz (160 g) white chocolate couverture

1 cup (250 g) whipping cream

2 Tbsps Amarena cherries in syrup, drained and chopped

2 oz (50 g) dark chocolate

Syrup

1 ¼ cups (300 ml) water

1 cup (7 oz or 200 g) sugar

7 Tbsps (100 ml) Maraschino liqueur

Glaze

4 ½ Tbsps water, 1 sheet of gelatin

1/2 cup minus 1 Tbsp (3 oz or 90 g) sugar

1/4 cup (60 ml) whipping cream

1/3 cup plus 1 Tbsp (1 oz or 30 g) cocoa powder

Preparation time 1 hour 10 minutes

Cooking time 40 minutes

Level medium

1 Preheat 400°F (200° or Gas Mark 6). Make the sponge cake: In a small saucepan beat the eggs with the sugar. Add the flour, sift in the cocoa powder and fold in using bottom to top motions. Remove from the heat and pour the mixture into a buttered 8-inch (18 cm) round cake pan, filling it three-quarters full. Bake for 20 minutes.

2 Make the mousse: Heat the crème anglaise to 82°F (28°C). Melt the chocolate couverture over a double-boiler and whip the cream to soft peaks. Add the chocolate and whipped cream to the crème anglaise. Make the syrup: Bring the water and sugar to a boil and boil for 10 minutes, then stir in the Maraschino liqueur. Slice the sponge cake into 3 rounds. Brush 1 round with the syrup. Spread with the white chocolate mousse and top with the chopped Amarena cherries. Repeat to make 1 more layer, top with the third sponge cake round and spread over the remaining white chocolate mousse. Place in the freezer for 30 minutes.

3 Make the glaze: Bring the water, sugar and cream to a boil together and sift in the cocoa powder. Cook until the mixture reaches 217°F (103°C). Remove from heat and when the glaze reaches 140°F (60°C) stir in the previously soaked gelatin. Glaze the cooled cake and garnish with chocolate and berries if desired.

techniques&recipes

Small Pastries

Homemade beignets, miniature tarts and tiny cookies
are ideal desserts to serve with afternoon tea
or coffee—irresistible and delicious tiny temptations.

1 Bring the milk to boil over a low heat. Add the butter and salt. Sift in the flour and stir constantly with a wooden spoon.

2 Cook until the mixture is smooth and shiny and pulls away from the side of the pan.

3 Remove from heat, let cool slightly and start adding the eggs one at a time, stirring to incorporate completely before adding the next egg.

Serves 6
Pastry
1 cup (250 ml) milk
6 Tbsps (3 oz or 90 g) butter
salt
1 cup plus 3 Tbsps (5 ½ oz or 150 g) all-purpose flour
4 eggs

Icing
3/4 cup plus 1 Tbsp (3 ½ oz or 100 g) confectioners' sugar
1 egg white
lemon juice
food coloring

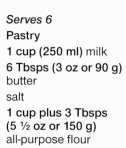

4 Continue mixing until the dough is soft. Transfer the dough to a pastry bag and pipe out walnut-sized balls onto a baking sheet lined with parchment paper. Leave 1/2-inch (1 ½ cm) spaces between the beignets.

5 Mix the sifted confectioners' sugar with the egg white and add a few drops of lemon juice. Stir to form a smooth and fluid frosting.

6 Add the food coloring and mix well to incorporate the color. Cover and let rest in the refrigerator for 10 minutes. Using a brush or a spoon, frost the tops of the beignets, let sit until the icing is dry and serve.

CHOUX PASTRY AND ROYAL ICING

Pastry Chef's Tip

Once the beignets have been formed, brush the top with a little water to avoid burning and help to bake uniformly. The confectioners' sugar for the icing must be sifted, otherwise the icing will be lumpy. The icing should be mixed vigorously for at least 10 minutes in order to combine properly.

Recipe on p. 150

1 Sift the flour onto a work surface and make a well at the center. Pass the egg yolks through a sieve and add them to the flour.

2 Add the softened butter, sugar, vanilla extract and lemon zest. Mix well to form a smooth dough; wrap in plastic wrap and let rest in the refrigerator at 42°F (6°C) for 30 minutes.

3 Roll out the dough on a lightly floured work surface into a 1/4-inch (1/2 cm) thick sheet. Using a 2-inch (5 cm) round cookie cutter cut out rounds that will form the base of the cookies.

Makes 20 cookies
2 cups (9 oz or 250 g) all-purpose flour
3 hard-boiled egg yolks
9 Tbsps (4 ½ oz or 125 g) butter, softened
1/2 cup (3 ½ oz or 100 g) sugar
1 tsp vanilla extract
zest of **1** organic lemon
milk
cherry jam

4 Using a slightly smaller round cookie cutter, cut a hole in the center of half of the cookie rounds to form tops.

5 Place the cookie bases on a baking sheet lined with parchment paper and top each base with a cookie top. Brush each cookie with a little milk.

6 Fill the hole in each cookie with 1 teaspoon of cherry jam and bake for 12 minutes at 325°F (170°C or Gas Mark 3).

JAM COOKIES

PASTRY CHEF'S TIP
This basic recipe may
be used to make many
variations of cookies;
they may be enriched
with chocolate chips,
topped with sugar or
filled with other types
of jam.

Recipe on p. 174

2 Remove the wafers from the oven and immediately place them over upside-down teacups to form a concave shape. Let cool, then unmold.

1 Beat the softened butter with the flour, confectioners' sugar and egg whites in a standing mixer with the whisk attachment.
Using the back of a spoon, spread the batter into rounds on a baking sheet lined with parchment paper. Bake for 8-10 minutes at 400°F (200°C or Gas Mark 6) or until the edges begin to brown.

Makes 30 wafers
7 Tbsps (3 ½ oz or 100 g)
butter, softened
3/4 cup plus 1 Tbsp (3 ½ oz or 100 g)
all-purpose flour
3/4 cup plus 1 Tbsp (3 ½ oz or 100 g)
vanilla-flavored confectioners' sugar
2-3 egg whites
at room temperature

WAFER CUPS

PASTRY CHEF'S TIP
To preserve the wafers, place them in an airtight plastic container with a little silicon salt, available from drugstores.

Recipe on p. 180

1 Place the egg whites in a bowl and add the sugar. By hand or using a standing mixer, whisk the egg white mixture.

2 Continue mixing until the mixture forms stiff peaks.

3 Transfer the mixture to a pastry bag and pipe out the meringues onto a baking sheet lined with parchment paper. Bake the meringues in a warm oven (200°F/100°C or Gas Mark 1) for 1-3 hours depending on the size. Meringues should always cook at a low temperature as this allows them to dry out completely. Meringues may be colored by adding food coloring to the batter before the eggs begin to form peaks.

Makes 30 meringues
2 egg whites
at room temperature
1 cup (7 oz or 200 g)
sugar

MERINGUES

1 Mound the flour on a work surface, add the butter and the salt and begin kneading into a dough. Add the warm water 1 teaspoon at a time to form a dough

2 Quickly work the dough until smooth, wrap with plastic wrap and refrigerate for 15 minutes at 37°F (3°C).

3 Roll out the dough on a lightly floured work surface into a 1/4-inch (1/2 cm) thick sheet. Cut out small rounds using a cookie cutter or a rolling cutter.

4 Place the rounds into buttered and floured miniature tart tins.

Makes 12 tartlet shells
2 cups (9 oz or 250 g) all-purpose flour
8 Tbsps (4 oz or 120 g) butter, softened
1 pinch of salt
3 Tbsps water
butter and flour for the tart tins

TART SHELLS

Pastry Chef's Tip
To make chocolate tart shells, add 1/2 cup (1 ½ oz or 40 g) of cocoa powder to the flour and proceed with the recipe.

Recipe on p. 181

Dessert 147

Chocolate Beignets

Serves 6

Beignets

1 ½ Tbsps water

3 ½ Tbsps milk

2 Tbsps (1 oz or 25 g) butter

6 ½ Tbsps all-purpose flour

2 eggs

Filling

9 oz (250 g) dark chocolate

1 cup (250 ml) whipping cream

Decoration

3 ½ oz (100 g) dark chocolate

Preparation time 50 minutes
Cooking time 20 minutes
Level medium

1 Preheat the oven to 425°F (220°C or Gas Mark 7). Melt the chocolate for the filling over a double boiler. Whip the whipping cream into stiff peaks and fold it into the chocolate.

2 Meanwhile, bring the water and milk to a boil with the butter. Remove from the heat and add the flour little by little, stirring constantly with a wooden spoon. Return to the heat and cook for 2 minutes, stirring continuously. Let cool and add the eggs one at a time.

3 Using a spoon to form 24 small balls of the mixture and place them on a buttered baking sheet. Bake for 6-7 minutes, until the beignets have risen, then turn the heat down to 375°F (190°C or Gas Mark 5) to finish cooking.

4 Remove from the oven, let cool and slice in half horizontally. Transfer the chocolate cream to a pastry bag and fill the beignets with the cream. Melt the remaining chocolate and drizzle it over the beignets before serving.

Pastry Chef's Tip

For a stronger-flavored filling, add 1/4 cup (60 ml) espresso coffee or 2 Tbsps rum or other liqueur to the melted chocolate.

Chantilly Cream Beignets

Serves 8

Beignets

1 cup (250 ml) milk

6 Tbsps (3 oz or 90 g) butter

1 cup plus 3 Tbsps (5 ½ oz or 150 g) all-purpose flour

4 eggs

salt

Cream

4 egg yolks

2/3 cup (4 oz or 120 g) sugar

1/2 cup (2 oz or 60 g) all-purpose flour

2 cups (500 ml) milk

1 tsp vanilla extract

1/3 cup (80 ml) whipping cream

Decoration

pink royal icing (see p. 138)

Preparation time 30 minutes
Cooking time 40 minutes
Level medium

Pastry Chef's Tip

Refrigerate the beignets for at least 1 hour before serving so that the Chantilly cream will harden slightly.

1 Preheat the oven to 400°F (200°C or Gas Mark 6). Bring the milk, butter and a pinch of salt to a boil over low heat. Pour in all of the flour and beat vigorously with a whisk. Continue cooking, stirring with a wooden spoon, until the dough begins to pull away from the sides of the pan. Transfer the dough to a mixing bowl.

2 When the dough is cool add the eggs one at a time, stirring to incorporate completely before adding the next egg. Transfer the mixture to a pastry bag fitted with a smooth tip and pipe out walnut-sized beignets onto a baking sheet lined with parchment paper. Leave a 1-2 inch (3-4 cm) space between each beignet. Bake for 20 minutes and let cool completely.

3 Meanwhile, make the pastry cream. Beat the egg yolks together with the sugar and sift in the flour. Bring the milk and vanilla extract to a boil and whisk it into the egg mixture. Return to the saucepan and bring to a simmer over low heat, stirring constantly with a whisk. When the cream has thickened, remove from heat and let cool. Whip the whipping cream and fold it into the pastry cream. Cut a small incision in the bottom of each beignet and, using a pastry bag, fill with the beignets with the chantilly cream. Frost the top of each beignet with the pink royal icing.

Lemon Cream Profiteroles

Serves 6

Beignets

2 organic lemons

2 cups (500 ml) milk

4 egg yolks

2/3 cup (4 ½ oz or 125 g) sugar

7 Tbsps all-purpose flour

20-25 ready-made beignets

Caramel

3/4 cup (5 oz or 150 g) sugar

2 Tbsps water

Preparation time 30 minutes
Cooking time 20 minutes
Level medium

1 Peel the lemons using a potato peeler. Heat the milk and lemon peel together. When the milk reaches a boil remove from heat and set aside for 10 minutes.

2 Meanwhile, beat the egg yolks with the sugar until thick. Sift in the flour and mix well. Strain and reheat the milk. Whisk the hot milk into the eggs and then return the saucepan. Cook over low heat, stirring constantly, until the cream thickens. Transfer to a bowl and let cool completely. Place the cream into a pastry bag. Make a small incision in the bottom of the beignets. Fill with the lemon cream and refrigerate.

3 Meanwhile, heat the sugar and water in a saucepan and cook over low heat until it begins to color. Remove from heat and let cool just until the caramel falls in thread-like ribbons from a spoon. Assemble the beignets into a pyramid shape and drizzle over the caramel. Let sit for 5 minutes before serving.

PASTRY CHEF'S TIP

To make the beignets at home, follow the choux pastry master recipe on p. 138.

Miniature Pear and Calvados
Tart Tatins with Acacia Honey

Serves 4

Tarts

2 Williams pears

4 Tbsps (2 oz or 50 g) butter

3 Tbsps acacia honey

3 Tbsps Calvados

10 ½ oz (300 g) puff pastry dough (see p. 34)

Decoration

ground cinnamon

crème anglaise (see p. 98)

Preparation time 25 minutes
Cooking time 20 minutes
Level easy

1 Preheat the oven to 400°F (200°C or Gas Mark 6). Peel and quarter the pears and then slice each quarter into thirds. Heat the butter in a non-stick frying pan and add the pears. Sauté for 1 minute and add the honey. Sauté for another 2 minutes, until the pears begin to brown. Sprinkle with Calvados and let the liquid evaporate. Let the pears cool. Roll out the puff pastry and cut out circles just slightly larger than the tart tins.

2 Place the caramelized pears in concentric circles in the bottom of four small round (not fluted) tart tins. Cover with pastry rounds and roll over the top with a rolling pin.

3 Bake for 15-18 minutes and remove from the oven. Let cool slightly. Invert the tarts onto individual serving plates and garnish with a little cinnamon or crème anglaise if desired.

PASTRY CHEF'S TIP

For an original variation, try using almond shortcrust instead of puff pastry.

Sabayon Cannoncini

Serves 8

Cannoncini

14 oz (400 g) puff pastry dough (see p. 34)

2 Tbsps sugar

Sabayon

5 egg yolks

2/3 cup (4 ½ oz or 130 g) sugar

7 Tbsps (100 ml) Marsala wine

1 Tbsp cornstarch

salt

Preparation time 30 minutes
Cooking time 40 minutes
Level medium

Pastry Chef's Tip

For added flavor, fold a few crumbled amaretto cookies into the cold sabayon and dip the ends of the cannoncini in melted dark chocolate and then in a mixture of chopped hazelnuts and almonds.

1 Preheat the oven to 400°F (200°C or Gas Mark 6). Cut the puff pastry into 1/2-inch (1 cm) wide strips and roll them around cannoli molds or stainless steel cylinders. The pastry should overlap slightly.

2 Place the wrapped cylinders on a baking sheet lined with wax paper and sprinkle with sugar. Bake for 18 minutes, until the cannoncini are puffed up and golden-brown. Remove from the oven and let cool completely.

3 Meanwhile, beat the egg yolks and the sugar over a double boiler. Add the Marsala, cornstarch and a pinch of salt and continue whisking until the mixture triples in volume. Remove from heat and pour into a mixing bowl. Refrigerate until cold. Transfer the mixture to a pastry bag and fill the cannoncini with the sabayon.

Babà

Serves 4

Babà

2 ⅔ tsps active dry yeast

3 Tbsps warm water

2 cups minus 1 Tbsp (8 ½ oz or 240 g) bread flour

4 eggs

9 Tbsps (4 ½ oz or 130 g) butter at room temperature

2 ½ Tbsps (1 ½ oz or 40 g) sugar

salt

Syrup

3/4 cup plus 1 ½ Tbsps (6 oz or 160 g) sugar

1 ¼ cups (300 ml) water

2/3 cup (150 ml) rum

Preparation time 30 minutes
Cooking time 15 minutes
Level easy

1. Dissolve the yeast in the warm water. Mix a dough using 2/3 cup (3 oz or 80 g) of flour and the yeast mixture. Let rest for 30 minutes on a floured work surface. Transfer to a bowl and add the eggs and softened butter. Add the remaining flour, sugar and a pinch of salt.

2. Work the dough by pushing down with the hands and fingertips to until the dough is soft and begins to form air bubbles. Let rise for 40 minutes. Preheat the oven to 350°F (180°C or Gas Mark 4). Butter ten 2 ½-inch (6 cm) diameter and 2-inch (5 cm) tall stainless steel molds.

3. Divide the dough between the molds, filling them only half full. Let rise again and then bake the babà for 15 minutes. Remove from the oven and let cool completely.

4. Meanwhile, make the syrup by boiling the sugar and the water until a thin syrup forms. Pour the hot syrup over the cooled babà. Just before serving, sprinkle the babà with rum.

Chocolate Beignets
with White-Chocolate Mousse

Serves 4

Beignets

3/4 cup (175 ml) water

5 Tbsps (2 ½ oz or 75 g) butter

3/4 cups plus 1 Tbsp (3 ½ oz or 100 g) all-purpose flour

1/2 cup plus 1 Tbsp (2 oz or 50 g) cocoa powder

1/4 cup (2 oz or 50 g) sugar

2 eggs

salt

Mousse

7 oz (200 g) white chocolate

2 gelatin sheets

1 egg plus 1 egg yolk

2/3 cup (4 oz or 120 g) sugar

2/3 cup (150 ml) whipping cream

Preparation time 30 minutes
Cooking time 20 minutes
Level medium

1 Preheat the oven to 400°F (200°C or Gas Mark 6). Bring the water and butter to a boil with a pinch of salt. Sift together the flour and cocoa powder and add the sugar. When the water boils, add the flour mixture and stir vigorously with a wooden spoon until the mixture begins to pull away from the sides of the pan. Remove from the heat and add the eggs one at a time, stirring constantly. Return to heat and cook for 1 minute. Transfer the dough to a pastry bag and make small puffs on a baking sheet lined with parchment paper. Bake for 20 minutes, remove from the oven and cool on a wire rack.

2 Melt the white chocolate for the mousse over a double boiler. Soak the gelatin sheets in cold water for a few minutes. Drain and squeeze out excess water. Beat the egg and egg yolk with the sugar and add the gelatin.

3 Beat the whipping cream to stiff peaks and fold it into the egg mixture. Refrigerate until firm. Slice the beignets in half and fill them with the white chocolate mousse.

Pastry Chef's Tip

These beignets may also be filled with the following cream: Puree 1 basket of raspberries with 2 Tbsps sugar. Whip 3/4 cup (200 ml) whipping cream until quite stiff, then fold in the raspberry puree.

Vol-au-vent
with Strawberries and Cream

Serves 4

Vol-au-vents

3/4 cup (7 oz or 200 g) plain low-fat yogurt

1 Tbsp vanilla-flavored confectioners' sugar

2 ½ Tbsps whipping cream

1 basket of strawberries

1 mint sprig

1 Tbsp sugar

12 ready-made puff pastry vol-au-vents (or, see Step 4)

Decoration

1 tsp sweetened cocoa powder

Preparation time 30 minutes

Level medium

1 Mix the yogurt with the confectioners' sugar. Whip the cream, fold it into the yogurt mixture and refrigerate.

2 Wash and dice the strawberries. Mince the mint leaves and add to the strawberries along with the sugar. Let sit for 30 minutes.

3 Fill the vol-au-vents with alternate layers of yogurt cream and strawberries. Sprinkle with cocoa powder and serve.

4 To make the vol-au-vents at home, cut 1 roll of puff pastry (see p. 34) into 24 rounds using a fluted cookie cutter. Using a smaller cookie cutter, remove the center from 12 of the rounds to form the tops. Place a top on each base and brush with egg wash. Place on a baking sheet lined with parchment paper and bake for 20 minutes at 400°F (200°C or Gas Mark 6).

Choux Mushrooms

Serves 8

Mushrooms

20 choux pastry mushrooms
(or, see below)

melted chocolate

Fillings

4 egg yolks

2/3 cup (4 oz or 120 g) sugar

1 tsp vanilla extract

6 ½ Tbsps all-purpose flour

2 cups (500 ml) milk

2 oz (60 g) dark chocolate,
chopped

salt

Decoration

cocoa powder

Preparation time 20 minutes
Cooking time 15 minutes
Level easy

PASTRY CHEF'S TIP

Prepare the "mushrooms" at home by following the recipe for choux pastry on p. 138.

1   Make the fillings: Beat the egg yolks and the sugar until thick. Add the vanilla, a pinch of salt and sift in the flour. Mix well to combine.

2   Bring the milk to a boil and whisk it into the egg mixture. Return the cream to the saucepan and cook over low heat, stirring constantly, until the cream thickens.

3   Pour half of the pastry cream over the chopped chocolate and stir until the chocolate has melted. Let the creams cool and then refrigerate until use.

4   Cut small incisions in the "legs" of the mushrooms and on the underside of the tops. Fill the legs with the chocolate cream and the tops with the vanilla cream. Stick the tops to the legs using a little melted chocolate and refrigerate until the chocolate has hardened. Sprinkle the mushrooms with cocoa powder and serve.

Sugar Cookies

Serves 4

Cookies

13 Tbsps (6 ½ oz or 180 g) butter

3/4 cup plus 1 ½ Tbsps (5 ½ oz or 160 g) sugar

1 egg yolk

2 hard-boiled egg yolks

zest of 1 organic orange

2 cups plus 2 ½ Tbsps (9 ½ oz or 270 g) all-purpose flour

salt

Decoration

raw sugar

Preparation time 20 minutes
Cooking time 15 minutes
Level easy

1. Preheat the oven to 325°F (170°C or Gas Mark 3). Cream the butter with the sugar and add the egg yolk. Pass the hard-boiled egg yolks through a sieve and add them to the dough.

2. Add a pinch of salt and the orange zest. Sift in the flour and mix well. Wrap the dough in plastic wrap and refrigerate until firm.

3. Roll out the dough on a lightly floured work surface. If the dough is very sticky roll it out between 2 pieces of parchment paper or plastic wrap. Cut out as many cookies as possible using cookie cutters.

4. Place the cookies on a waxed paper-lined baking sheet and sprinkle with raw sugar. Bake for 8-10 minutes and let cool before serving.

Brutti ma Buoni Cookies

Serves 4

Cookies

2/3 cup (3 ½ oz or 100 g) toasted almonds

3 Tbsps Passito di Pantelleria wine or another sweet dessert wine

2/3 cup (3 oz or 80 g) confectioners' sugar

1 egg white

salt

1 ½ Tbsps sugar

1 Tbsp cornstarch

Preparation time 15 minutes
Cooking time 40 minutes
Level easy

1 Preheat the oven to 265°F (130°C or Gas Mark 1). Coarsely chop two-thirds of the almonds and add the wine, confectioners' sugar, and whole almonds and stir to combine.

2 Beat the egg white with a pinch of salt until foamy. Add the sugar and the nut mixture and continue beating until white and shiny. Fold in the cornstarch.

3 Drop teaspoonfuls of batter onto a baking sheet lined with parchment paper, leaving a 3/4-inch (2 cm) space between each cookie.

4 Bake for 40 minutes and let cool completely before serving.

White Chocolate-Hazelnut Cookies

Makes 20 cookies

Cookies

9 Tbsps (4 ½ oz or 125 g) butter

2/3 cup (4 ½ oz or 125 g) sugar

2 egg yolks

1 ¼ cups (5 ½ oz or 155 g)
all-purpose flour

3/4 cup (4 oz or 110 g)
finely ground cornflour

1 tsp baking soda

1 ½ oz (40 g) white chocolate,
finely chopped

Decoration

20 hazelnuts

Preparation time 30 minutes
Cooking time 20 minutes
Level easy

1. Cream the butter and sugar together and add the egg yolks. Sift in the flour and cornstarch.

2. Add the baking soda and stir to combine, without over mixing. Flatten the dough into a disk and cover with plastic wrap. Refrigerate for at least 1 hour.

3. Preheat the oven to 325°F (170°C or Gas Mark 3). Add the white chocolate to the dough and return to the refrigerator for a few minutes. Roll out the dough on a lightly floured surface. Cut out 20 cookies using any kind of cutter and place a hazelnut in the center of each cookie.

4. Bake for 20 minutes on a baking sheet lined with parchment paper. Let cool completely before serving.

PASTRY CHEF'S TIP

Piedmontese hazelnuts are considered to be some of the best in the world and are known for their aromatic qualities. The highest quality variety is called "tonda gentile" and comes from the Langhe region.

Checkerboard Cookies

Serves 4

Cookies

3 cups (13 oz or 370 g) all-purpose flour

1 ¼ cups (9 oz or 250 g) sugar

3/4 cup (7 oz or 200 g) butter, softened

3 eggs

salt

1 tsp vanilla extract

1 oz (30 g) milk chocolate

Preparation time 20 minutes
Cooking time 10 minutes
Level easy

1 Sift the flour into a bowl. Add the sugar, softened butter, 2 eggs, a pinch of salt and the vanilla. Mix well to obtain a smooth dough. Melt the chocolate over a double boiler or in a microwave. Add the chocolate to half of the dough, kneading until the chocolate is incorporated. Wrap the two doughs separately in plastic wrap and refrigerate for 30 minutes. Preheat the oven to 350°F (180°C or Gas Mark 4).

2 Roll out each piece of dough with a rolling pin to a 1/2-inch (1 cm) thickness. Cut each kind of dough into 4 strips. Lay 4 strips of dough next to each other, alternating chocolate and plain. Lay the remaining four strips on top, making sure to alternate chocolate and plain. Press the strips together gently, then slice the layers into rectangular cookies, which should look like miniature checkerboards. Lay the cookies on a baking sheet lined with parchment paper. Bake for 10 minutes, then remove from the oven and cool on a wire rack.

Baci di dama

Serves 8

Cookies

1 ½ cups plus 1 ½ Tbsps (7 oz or 200 g) all-purpose flour

14 Tbsps (7 oz or 200 g) butter, softened

1 cup (7 oz or 200 g) sugar

2 ⅔ cups (7 oz or 200 g) ground hazelnuts

Filling

14 Tbsps (7 oz or 200 g) butter

1/4 cup (1 oz or 25 g) cocoa powder

1/2 cup (3 ½ oz or 100 g) raw sugar

1 Tbsp rum

Preparation time 30 minutes
Cooking time 20 minutes
Level easy

1. Preheat the oven to 375°F (190°C or Gas Mark 5). Mix the flour with the softened butter. Add the sugar and the hazelnuts. Mix well.

2. Line a baking sheet with parchment paper. Roll the dough into small balls and place them on the baking sheet. Bake for 20 minutes.

3. Meanwhile, mix the butter, cocoa, sugar and rum together to form a smooth cream.

4. Let the hazelnut cookies cool completely and then spread the bottom of 1 cookie with chocolate cream and stick it to another cookie to form a sandwich.

PASTRY CHEF'S TIP

For a richer filling, substitute the cocoa powder with melted dark chocolate or hazelnut cream.

Milk Chocolate Cookies

Serves 4

Cookies

9 Tbsps (4 ½ oz or 125 g) butter

2/3 cup (4 ½ oz or 125 g) sugar

2 egg yolks

1 vanilla bean,
halved lengthwise
and seeds scraped out

1 ¼ cups (5 ½ oz or 155 g)
all-purpose flour

3/4 cup (4 oz or 110 g)
finely ground cornflour

1 tsp baking soda

1/3 cup (2 oz or 60 g) milk
chocolate chips

Decoration

confectioners' sugar (optional)

Preparation time 30 minutes
Cooking time 15 minutes
Level easy

1 Cream the butter and sugar together, then add the egg yolks and the seeds from the vanilla bean. Sift in the flour, cornstarch and baking soda. Mix to combine, taking care not to overwork the dough.

2 Flatten the dough into a disk and wrap in plastic wrap. Refrigerate for at least 1 hour. Preheat the oven to 325°F (160°C or Gas Mark 3).

3 Divide the dough into 4 portions and mix the milk chocolate chips into each portion. Roll out the dough on a lightly floured surface and cut out cookies using the cutters of choice.

4 Place the cookies on a baking sheet lined with parchment paper and bake for about 15 minutes. Cool on wire racks and sprinkle, if desired, with confectioners' sugar.

PASTRY CHEF'S TIP

This is a good basic recipe that may be varied according to taste. Try adding 5 tablespoons of raisins or 4 tablespoons of shredded coconut to the dough before rolling out.

Two-Chocolate Cookies

Serves 4

Cookies

3 ½ oz (100 g) milk chocolate, chopped

7 Tbsps (3 ½ oz or 100 g) butter at room temperature

6 ½ Tbsps sugar

6 ½ Tbsps raw sugar

salt

1 egg

1 tsp vanilla extract

1 cup plus 3 Tbsps (5 ½ oz or 150 g) all-purpose flour

1/2 tsp baking powder

1/3 cup (2 oz or 50 g) pine nuts, chopped

5 oz (140 g) white chocolate, chopped

Preparation time 20 minutes
Cooking time 13 minutes
Level easy

1 Preheat the oven to 350°F (180°C or Gas Mark 4). Melt the milk chocolate over a double boiler or in the microwave.

2 Cream the butter with the sugar, raw sugar and a pinch of salt together. Add the egg and vanilla extract and continue beating. Drizzle in the cooled melted chocolate. When the mixture is smooth, sift in the flour and baking powder and stir with a wooden spoon. Add the chopped pine nuts and the white chocolate.

3 Roll the dough into walnut-sized balls and place them on a baking sheet lined with wax paper, leaving a 1-inch (3 cm) space between each cookie.

4 Flatten each ball into a cookie shape and bake for 13 minutes. Remove from the oven and let cool completely before serving. The cookies can be kept in a airtight container.

PASTRY CHEF'S TIP

Take care not to overheat the butter and egg while mixing them together as they can separate. To give the cookies a regular shape, they may be cooked in paper baking cups.

Amaretto Cookies

Serves 4

Amaretto Cookies

2 cups (10 ½ oz or 300 g)
blanched almonds

1 ¾ cups (12 oz or 350 g) sugar

3 egg whites

zest and juice
of 1 organic lemon

salt

1 Tbsp all-purpose flour

1 tsp cornstarch

almond extract

confectioners' sugar

Preparation time 20 minutes
Cooking time 30 minutes
Level easy

1 Blend the almonds in a food processor with a few tablespoons of sugar. Beat the egg whites, 1 teaspoon lemon juice and a pinch of salt to stiff peaks. Add the ground almonds and remaining sugar to the egg whites and sift in the flour and cornstarch. Mix carefully and then add the almond extract.

2 Butter and flour a baking sheet. Drop spoonfuls of the batter onto the baking sheet. Sprinkle with confectioners' sugar and let rest for 4-5 hours.

3 Preheat the oven to 210°F (100°C or Gas Mark 1/4). Bake the cookies for 30 minutes, turning the baking sheet from time to time to allow for even cooking. Remove from the oven and transfer the hot cookies to a wooden cutting board to cool. Once cool the cookies can be stored in an airtight tin.

PASTRY CHEF'S TIP

For chocolate amaretto cookies, sift 1/4 cup (1/2 oz or 15 g) of sweetened cocoa powder together with the flour.

Miniature Pistachio Tarts

Serves 4

Crust

10 Tbsps (5 oz or 140 g) butter, salt

1/2 cup (2 ½ oz or 70 g)
confectioners' sugar

3 egg yolks, 1/2 tsp baking soda

zest of 1 organic lemon

1 ⅔ cups (7 ½ oz or 210 g)
all-purpose flour

Pistachio Cream

4 egg yolks, 2 cups (500 ml) milk

1/2 cup (3 ½ oz or 100 g) sugar

6 ½ Tbsps all-purpose flour

1 Tbsp pistachio paste, salt

2 oz (60 g) dark chocolate

Preparation time 40 minutes
Cooking time 35 minutes
Level easy

Pastry Chef's Tip

To make pistachio paste, take 1 lb (500 g) of shelled pistachios and dry them out in the oven, then blanch them for a few seconds in boiling water and remove the skins. Chop them with a knife, then puree them in the food processor. Transfer to a large bowl and add 4 ½ oz (125 g) of almond flour and 10 drops of bitter-almond extract. Stir 2 ¼ cups (9 oz or 250 g) of sugar and 4 ½ Tbsps of water together in a saucepan, then bring to a boil without stirring further. When the mixture reaches 250°F (120°C) pour it over the pistachio mixture and stir. Transfer everything to the food processor and blend until smooth.

1 Cream the butter and the confectioners' sugar in a bowl with an electric mixer. Add the egg yolks one at a time and then add the lemon zest, baking soda and salt. Quickly mix in the flour, roll into a ball and wrap in plastic wrap. Refrigerate for 1 hour. Preheat the oven to 325°F (170°C or Gas Mark 3).

2 Meanwhile, make the cream. Beat the egg yolks with the sugar. Add a pinch of salt, sift in the flour and stir to combine. Bring the milk to a boil and slowly drizzle it into the egg mixture, whisking to incorporate completely. Return the mixture to the saucepan and cook over low heat until the cream thickens. Stir in the pistachio paste, remove from the heat and let cool completely. Roll out the pastry dough and cut out 4 rounds. Use them to line 4 buttered miniature tart tins and pierce the surfaces with a fork. Cover each tart with parchment paper and fill with dried beans or pie weights. Bake for 20 minutes. Remove the tarts from the oven, cool and unmold.

3 Fill each tart with the pistachio cream. Melt the dark chocolate and transfer it to a pastry bag made from folding a square of parchment paper into a cone. The cone should fit easily into the palm of the hand. Cut off the tip and decorate the tops of the tarts with the melted chocolate (see p. 378).

Cocoa-Rum Cookies

Serves 4

Cookies

1 ¼ cups (3 oz or 90 g) blanched hazelnuts

1/2 cup (3 ½ oz or 100 g) sugar

3/4 cup plus 1 Tbsp (3 ½ oz or 100 g) all-purpose flour

1/3 cup (1 oz or 30 g) cocoa powder

6 Tbsps (3 oz or 80 g) butter, cut into small pieces

salt

1 Tbsp dark rum

Preparation time 20 minutes
Cooking time 15 minutes
Level easy

1 Preheat the oven to 350°F (180°C or Gas Mark 4). Grind the hazelnuts with the sugar in a food processor.

2 Place the flour and cocoa powder in a mixing bowl. Add the hazelnut mixture and butter. Add a pinch of salt and pour over the rum.

3 Mix well to obtain a smooth dough. Wrap in plastic wrap and refrigerate for 20 minutes. Roll the dough into small walnut-sized balls, place on a baking sheet and press down lightly to flatten the bottom of the cookie. Bake for 15 minutes, remove from the oven and cool completely on a wire rack. Store in an airtight container.

Chocolate and Vanilla Wafers
with Almond Milk Gelée

Serves 6

Wafers

3 egg whites (3 ½ oz or 100 g in total)

3/4 cup plus 1 Tbsp (3 ½ oz or 100 g) confectioners' sugar

7 Tbsps (3 ½ oz or 100 g) butter, melted

3/4 cup plus 1 Tbsp (3 ½ oz or 100 g) all-purpose flour

1 Tbsp cocoa powder

Gelée

3/4 cup plus 1 Tbsp (200 ml) almond milk

2 Tbsps agar agar powder

3 ½ Tbsps sugar

Decoration

10 large strawberries

1 Tbsp raw sugar

slivered almonds

Preparation time 20 minutes
Cooking time 10 minutes
Level medium

PASTRY CHEF'S TIP

To make almond milk mince 1 ⅓ cups (7 oz or 200 g) of whole peeled almonds in a food processor and mix together with 1/2 cup (3 ½ oz or 100 g) of sugar. Place the mixture in a clean kitchen towel and tie closed at the top. Soak in 4 cups (1 l) of cold water for at least 6 hours, then squeeze out the almond mixture, strain the liquid and use it while fresh.

1 Preheat the oven to 400°F (200°C or Gas Mark 6). Beat the egg whites with the confectioners' sugar until soft peaks begin to form. Add the melted butter and sift in the flour. Divide the batter between 2 bowls and mix the cocoa powder into one. Refrigerate the batter for 30 minutes.

2 Line a baking sheet with parchment paper. Using a spoon to spread the batter, form 2-inch (5 cm) rounds, alternating chocolate and plain batter. Variegate the wafers by dropping a little of the opposite color onto each wafer and spreading it with the tines of a fork. Bake for 5 minutes. Remove from the oven and drape the hot wafers over upside-down tea cups or demitasse cups to cool.

3 Meanwhile, dissolve the agar-agar powder in half of the almond milk over low heat. Add the sugar and the remaining almond milk. Remove from heat and pour the mixture into hemispherical silicon molds. Refrigerate for 1 hour.

4 Dice the strawberries and sprinkle with the raw sugar. To serve, place an almond milk gelée in each wafer cup and top with the strawberries and slivered almonds.

Chocolate Wafers
with White Chocolate Cream

Serves 4

Wafers

2 egg whites (2 oz or 60 g in total)

1/2 cup (2 oz or 60 g) confectioners' sugar

4 Tbsps (2 oz or 60 g) butter, melted and cooled

6 ½ Tbsps all-purpose flour

2 Tbsps cocoa powder

Cream

2/3 cup (150 ml) milk

1 ½ oz (40 g) white chocolate, chopped

1 cup (250 ml) whipping cream

1 Tbsp confectioners' sugar

Decoration

1 oz (25 g) dark chocolate, shaved

Preparation time 30 minutes
Cooking time 8 minutes
Level easy

1. Beat the egg whites with the confectioners' sugar. Add the cooled melted butter and sift in the flour and cocoa powder. Refrigerate the batter until cooled and thickened.

2. Heat the milk in a saucepan and add the white chocolate. Melt over medium heat, stirring frequently. Let cool slightly, add the confectioners' sugar and pour into a whipped cream canister (siphon). Add the whipping cream to the canister, close and add the gas cartridge. Leave in a cool place. Preheat the oven to 400°F (200°C or Gas Mark 6).

3. Spread small spoonfuls of the wafer batter onto a baking sheet lined with parchment paper and spread into thin rounds with the back of a spoon. Bake for 4 minutes, then remove from the oven. Mold the hot wafers over the bottom of a demitasse cup or the neck of a bottle to form small cups.

4. When the wafer cups are cool, fill them with the chocolate cream. Garnish with dark chocolate shavings and serve immediately.

Rum-Chocolate Cups
with Mascarpone Cream

Serves 4

Chocolate Cups

1 egg white

2/3 cup (3 oz or 80 g) confectioners' sugar

1 tsp dark rum

1/3 cup (3 oz or 80 g) butter, melted

2/3 cup (3 oz or 80 g) all-purpose flour

4 Tbsps cocoa powder

Cream

4 oz (120 g) mascarpone

3 ½ oz (100 g) cream cheese

1 Tbsp confectioners' sugar

1 tsp vanilla extract

Decoration

1 basket of raspberries

mint leaves

Preparation time 30 minutes
Cooking time 5 minutes
Level easy

1 Preheat the oven to 400°F (200°C or Gas Mark 6). Beat the egg white and confectioners' sugar in a bowl and add the rum and melted butter. Sift in the flour and cocoa powder and mix to form a sticky, elastic dough. Refrigerate for 20 minutes.

2 Line a baking dish with parchment paper. Using the back of a spoon, spread the dough into circles 2 ½-inches (5 cm) in diameter.

3 Bake for 5 minutes. Remove from the oven and mold the chocolate rounds over upturned teacups or inside a muffin tin. Let sit for 1 minute, then remove the chocolate cups and let them cool.

4 Beat the mascarpone and cream cheese with the confectioners' sugar. Transfer to a pastry bag and fill each chocolate cup. Top with 1 raspberry and 1 mint leaf. Serve immediately.

Wafer Cups
with Sweet Robiola Cream and Strawberries

Serves 4

Wafer Cups

5 egg whites

1/4 cup (2 oz or 50 g) sugar

6 ½ Tbsps all-purpose flour

4 Tbsps (2 oz or 50 g) butter, softened

Filling

1 Tbsp raw sugar

zest of 1 organic lemon

6-7 strawberries, diced

5 ½ oz (150 g) robiola or other soft mild cheese

1 tsp confectioners' sugar

1 tsp vanilla extract

3 Tbsps whipping cream

Preparation time 40 minutes

Cooking time 3 minutes

Level easy

1 Sprinkle the raw sugar over the strawberries and add 1 teaspoon of lemon zest. Let sit for 30 minutes. Preheat the oven to 375°F (190°C or Gas Mark 5).

2 Beat the egg whites with the sugar and sift in the flour. Add the butter and quickly whisk the mixture until combined. Using the back of a spoon, spread the batter onto a baking sheet lined with parchment paper forming several small discs.

3 Bake for 3 minutes or until the discs begin to brown. Remove from the oven and mold the hot wafers over several upside-down teacups or demitasse cups to form little cups.

4 Whip the cheese and the confectioners' sugar together with the vanilla. Beat the whipping cream to soft peaks and fold into the cheese mixture. Fill the wafer cups with the cheese cream and top with the strawberries.

PASTRY CHEF'S TIP

For an unusual flavor, add a little freshly grated ginger to the strawberries.

Pear and Ricotta Tarts

Serves 8

Crust

2 cups (9 oz or 250 g)
all-purpose flour

3 Tbsps cocoa powder

1/2 cup (4 oz or 120 g) butter
at room temperature

3 Tbsps warm water

salt

Pears

2 pears, peeled

4 cups (1 l) Fragolino wine
or other light, sweet red wine

1 cup (7 oz or 200 g) raw sugar

Filling

7 oz (200 g) fresh ricotta

1 Tbsp confectioners' sugar

4 Tbsps cornflakes, crushed

Preparation time 40 minutes
Cooking time 20 minutes
Level medium

1. Mix together the flour, cocoa powder and salt and work in the butter using the fingertips. Little by little add the warm water. When the dough comes together, roll into a ball, wrap in plastic wrap and refrigerate for 30 minutes.

2. Meanwhile, immerse the whole pears in the wine. Add the raw sugar and transfer to a saucepan. Cook the pears in the wine until tender. Remove from the heat, transfer to a mixing bowl and let cool. Preheat the oven to 350°F (180°C or Gas Mark 4).

3. Butter and flour 8 small tart tins. Roll out the pastry into a thin sheet and cut out 8 rounds. Use the rounds to line the prepared tart tins. Pierce the crusts with a fork and bake for 15-20 minutes. Remove from the oven and let cool completely.

4. Beat together the ricotta and confectioners' sugar and add the crushed cornflakes. Slice the cooked pears, eliminating the core. Fill the tarts with the ricotta mixture and top with the pear slices.

Hazelnut Tartlets
with Chocolate Ganache

Serves 6
Crust
1/2 cup (2 ½ oz or 75 g) hazelnuts
1/2 cup (3 ½ oz or 100 g) sugar
7 Tbsps (3 ½ oz or 100 g) butter
2 egg yolks
1 cup plus 3 Tbsps (5 1/2 oz or 150 g) all-purpose flour
salt
Ganache
7 oz (200 g) dark chocolate (80% cocoa content)
1/3 cup (80 ml) whipping cream
Decoration
hazelnuts, toasted and chopped

Preparation time 25 minutes
Cooking time 15 minutes
Level easy

1 Grind the hazelnuts with the sugar in a food processor until they are the consistency of flour. Quickly mix together the butter, hazelnut mixture, egg yolks, flour and pinch of salt with the fingertips. Roll the dough into a ball and wrap in plastic wrap. Refrigerate for 1 hour. Preheat the oven to 350°F (180°C or Gas Mark 4).

2 Roll out the dough on a lightly floured work surface. Butter and flour 6 small tartlet tins and line them with the dough. Pierce the dough with a fork and cover each tart with parchment paper. Fill the tarts with dried beans or pie weights and bake for 15 minutes. Cool on a wire rack.

3 Meanwhile, melt the chocolate over a double boiler or in the microwave. Whisk in the cream. Place a spoonful of ganache in the center of each tartlet shell. Let cool and sprinkle with the chopped hazelnuts.

PASTRY CHEF'S TIP
Nuts should always be ground with sugar, as the sugar absorbs the oils that may create a bitter aftertaste.

Mini Layered Cream Tarts

Serves 4

Crust

2 cups (9 oz or 250 g)
all-purpose flour

2 cups (2 oz or 50 g)
multigrain cereal flakes

2/3 cup (4 oz or 120 g) sugar

1 egg

1/2 cup (4 oz or 120 g) butter

1 tsp vanilla extract

Filling

1 cup (250 ml) milk

1/2 vanilla bean,
sliced lengthwise

2 egg yolks

1/3 cup (2 oz or 60 g) sugar

1/4 cup (1 oz or 30 g)
all-purpose flour

3 ½ oz (100 g) dark chocolate,
chopped

Preparation time 40 minutes
Cooking time 30 minutes
Level easy

1 Place all of the ingredients for the crust in a large bowl and mix together using the fingertips. When the dough comes together, transfer it to a clean work surface and knead briefly with the palm of the hand. Roll into a ball, wrap in plastic wrap and refrigerate. Bring the milk and vanilla bean to a boil, then discard the vanilla bean.

2 Beat the egg yolks with the sugar until they are thick and pale yellow in color. Sift in the flour and mix. Slowly drizzle the hot milk into the egg mixture, whisking constantly. Return to the stove and cook over medium heat until the cream coats the back of a spoon. Divide the cream between two bowls and add the chocolate to one, stirring until melted. Preheat the oven to 350°F (180°C or Gas Mark 4).

3 Roll out the crust dough and cut it into 4 rounds. Use the dough to line 4 small tart tins. Pierce with a fork and bake for 12 minutes. Remove from the oven and cool. Unmold the tarts and fill them half with the pastry cream, then finish with the chocolate cream.

PASTRY CHEF'S TIP
To save time, use purchased shortcrust tart shells for this recipe.

Apple Tartlets

Serves 6

Pastry

7 Tbsps (3 ½ oz or 100 g) butter
at room temperature

6 Tbsps sugar

1 tsp vanilla extract

1 ⅔ cups (7 oz or 200 g)
all-purpose flour

Filling

2 Golden Delicious apples,
peeled and chopped

1 Tbsp raw sugar

1 Tbsp pine nuts, chopped

Cream

3/4 cup plus 1 Tbsp
(200 ml) milk

2 egg yolks

1/3 cup (2 oz or 60 g)
raw sugar

1 Tbsp cornstarch

1/2 tsp cinnamon

Preparation time 30 minutes

Cooking time 40 minutes

Level easy

1. Preheat the oven to 350°F (180°C or Gas Mark 4). Cream the butter and the sugar and add the vanilla. Slowly add the flour.

2. Mix to form a smooth and compact dough. Let rest for 10 minutes. Roll the dough into a thin sheet and cut into rounds that will fit into miniature tartlet tins. Butter and flour the tins and line them with the dough.

3. Sauté the apples in a large non-stick pan with the sugar and the pine nuts for 5 minutes.

4. Meanwhile, prepare the cream. Using an immersion blender or electric whisk, blend the milk and egg yolks with the raw sugar.

5. Add the cornstarch and cinnamon and blend quickly to incorporate. Place a few cooked apples in the bottom of each tart and top with the cream. Bake for 18 minutes.

PASTRY CHEF'S TIP

For a simple variation, try substituting the apples with the same quantity of pears. Omit the cinnamon and sprinkle the tarts with a few chocolate chips before baking.

Miniature Tarts
with Fresh Fruit

Serves 4

Crust

1 ⅔ cups (7 oz or 200 g)
all-purpose flour

8 Tbsps (4 oz or 110 g)
butter, diced

1/2 cup (3 ½ oz or 100 g) sugar

1 egg plus 1 egg yolk

zest of 1 organic lemon

salt

Cream

2 egg yolks

1/3 cup (2 oz or 60 g) sugar

1 tsp vanilla extract

2 ½ Tbsps all-purpose flour

1 cup (250 ml) milk

Decoration

2 kiwis, peeled and sliced

raspberries

Preparation time 30 minutes
Cooking time 35 minutes
Level medium

1 Mound the flour on a work surface and make a well at the center. Place the butter, sugar, egg and egg yolk in the center. Add the lemon zest and salt and mix quickly using the fingertips until the dough comes together. Knead the dough using the palm of the hand until smooth. Wrap in plastic wrap and refrigerate for 2 hours.

2 Beat the egg yolks with the sugar and vanilla until thick. Sift in the flour and stir to combine. Bring the milk to a boil and slowly whisk it into the egg mixture. Return to the saucepan and cook over low heat, stirring constantly, until the cream thickens. Transfer to a bowl and let cool completely. Preheat the oven to 325°F (170°C or Gas Mark 3).

3 Roll out the pastry into a thin sheet. Butter and flour miniature tart tins and line the dough into the tins. Pierce the surface of the tarts with a fork and bake for 14 minutes. Remove from the oven, let cool and fill with the pastry cream. Top each tart with a slice of kiwi and 1 raspberry.

Miniature Spicy Chocolate Tarts

Serves 4

Crust

10 Tbsps (5 ½ oz or 150 g) butter, softened

1/2 cup (3 ½ oz 100 g) sugar

2 egg yolks

2 ⅓ cups plus 1 Tbsp (10 ½ oz or 300 g) all-purpose flour

salt

Filling

1 egg

2/3 cup (4 oz or 120 g) sugar

7 oz (200 g) chili-flavored dark chocolate, chopped (see p. 93)

2 gelatin sheets

7 Tbsps whipping cream

Preparation time 30 minutes
Cooking time 15 minutes
Level medium

1 Preheat the oven to 350°F (180°C or Gas Mark 4). Cream the softened butter with the sugar. Add the egg yolks, flour and a pinch of salt. Mix together quickly and form into a ball. Cover with plastic wrap and refrigerate for 10 minutes.

2 Roll out the dough until 3/4-inch (2 cm) thick. Using a round cookie cutter, cut out twelve 2 ½-inch (5 cm) rounds. Use the dough rounds to line 12 miniature tart tins and pierce the base with a fork. Bake for 10 minutes, remove from the oven, unmold and let cool. Meanwhile, make the filling: Beat the egg and the sugar with an electric beater until thick and creamy.

3 Melt the chocolate over a double boiler. Soak the gelatin in cold water for a few minutes. Drain and squeeze out the excess water. Add the gelatin to the hot chocolate and stir with a wooden spoon. Whisk the chocolate into the egg mixture until smooth.

4 Whip the whipping cream to stiff peaks and fold it into chocolate mixture. Transfer the mousse to a pastry bag and pipe into the tart shells.

Raspberry Cheese Pastries

Serves 4

Dough

1 ¼ cups plus 3 Tbsps (6 ½ oz
or 180 g) all-purpose flour

6 Tbsps sugar

4 Tbsps warm milk

1 egg yolk

Filling

3 ½ oz (100 g) ricotta

3 ½ oz (100 g) cream cheese

1 Tbsp confectioners' sugar

1 tsp vanilla extract

zest of 1 organic lemon

1 basket of raspberries

melted butter

Decoration

confectioners' sugar

Preparation time 25 minutes
Cooking time 25 minutes
Level medium

1 Preheat the oven to 350°F (180°C or Gas Mark 4). Mix the flour and sugar together and whisk in the warm milk and egg yolk. Place the dough on a work surface and knead to form an elastic dough. Cover with plastic wrap and let rest for 30 minutes in a cool place.

2 Beat the ricotta and cream cheese with 1 tablespoon of confectioners' sugar, the vanilla extract and lemon zest. Set aside. Butter and flour 4 individual tart tins. Roll out the dough into a thin sheet and cut out 4 squares, larger than the tart tins.

3 Line the tins with the dough. Fill with the ricotta mixture and top with raspberries. Fold the corners of the dough over the top of the filling and pinch together to seal. Brush with melted butter and bake for 25 minutes. Sprinkle the pastries with confectioners' sugar and serve.

Ricotta Pastries

Serves 4

Pastry

1 lb 5 oz (600 g) shortcrust dough (see p. 32)

1 egg yolk, beaten

Filling

3/4 cup (5 ½ oz or 150 g) semolina flour

5 ½ oz (150 g) fresh ricotta

1/2 cup (3 ½ oz or 100 g) vanilla sugar

1 egg

1 tsp orange-flower water

3 ½ oz (100 g) candied citron, diced

1 tsp ground cinnamon

salt

Decoration

confectioners' sugar

Preparation time 40 minutes
Cooking time 30 minutes
Level medium

1 Preheat the oven to 350°F (180°C or Gas Mark 4). Mix together all the filling ingredients, adding enough milk to form a smooth batter of medium consistency.

2 Roll out the shortcrust dough out into a 1/5-inch (1/2 cm) thick sheet, trimming the sheet to make a rectangle. Place teaspoonfuls of the filling along one side of the dough, leaving a 1-inch (2 ½ cm) space between them. Fold the dough over and press down between the mounds of filling. Cut between each one to form small raviolis.

3 Transfer the pastries to a parchment paper-lined baking sheet and brush with the lightly beaten egg yolk. Bake until golden-brown, remove from the oven and let cool. Sprinkle with confectioners' sugar before serving.

Almond Pastries

Serves 4

Pastry

2 ⅓ cups plus 1 Tbsp (300 g) all-purpose flour

1 egg plus 1 egg white

2 Tbsps (1 oz or 30 g) butter, melted

zest of 1 organic lemon

3 Tbsps confectioners' sugar

Filling

2 cups (10 ½ oz or 300 g) blanched almonds

1 cup minus 1 Tbsp (6 ½ oz or 180 g) sugar

7 Tbsps (3 ½ oz or 100 g) butter, diced

3 tsps orange-flower water

Preparation time 15 minutes
Cooking time 20 minutes
Level easy

1 Prepare the filling by blending the almonds with the sugar, butter and orange-flower water in a food processor.

2 Mound the flour on a work surface and make a well at the center. Add the egg and melted butter to the well along with the lemon zest. Mix with the fingertips and when the dough comes together use the palm of the hand to knead it until smooth. Form into a ball, cover with plastic wrap and refrigerate for 30 minutes. Preheat the oven to 325°F (170°C or Gas Mark 3).

3 Roll out the dough into a thin sheet. Cut out ovals using a rolling cutter or a sharp knife. Place a spoonful of the almond filling at the center of each oval and fold the pastry over itself. Transfer the pastries to a baking sheet. Lightly beat the egg white, brush each pastry with the egg white and sprinkle with confectioners' sugar. Bake for 20 minutes.

Pineapple and Orange Tarts

Serves 4

Tarts

juice of 2 oranges

2 Tbsps raw sugar

2 cinnamon sticks

1/2 pineapple, peeled, cored and diced

10 ½ oz (300 g) shortcrust pastry dough (see p. 32)

9 oz (250 g) puff pastry dough (see p. 34)

2 Tbsps (1 oz or 20 g) butter, melted

Decoration

confectioners' sugar

candied orange slices, julienned (optional)

Preparation time 30 minutes
Cooking time 35 minutes
Level medium

1 Strain the orange juice in a chinois sieve and add the raw sugar. Transfer to a saucepan and bring to a boil with the cinnamon sticks. Remove from heat, let cool and add the pineapple. Let sit for 1 hour. Preheat the oven to 375°F (190°C or Gas Mark 5).

2 Roll out the shortcrust dough on a lightly floured work surface. Cut out 4 rounds and use them to line 4 aluminum tart tins. Pierce the surfaces with a fork. Drain the pineapple and top the tarts with the fruit.

3 Roll out the puff pastry and cut out 4 rounds, just larger than the tarts. Top the tarts with the puff pastry rounds, pinching around the edges so the two doughs stick to each other. Brush with melted butter and cut a few incisions on the top of each tart.

4 Bake for 25 minutes. Remove from the oven, let cool and sprinkle with confectioners' sugar. Top with julienned candied orange slices, if desired.

Wheat Tarts
with Ricotta and Lemon

Serves 4

Crust

2 Tbsps (1 oz or 30 g) butter

1 egg

2 Tbsps sugar

1 cup plus 3 Tbsps (5 1/2 oz or 150 g) all-purpose flour

Filling

4 oz (120 g) cooked wheat

4 ½ Tbsps milk

2 Tbsps honey

peel of 1/2 organic lemon

3 ½ oz (100 g) ricotta

1 handful of pine nuts

confectioners' sugar

Preparation time 40 minutes
Cooking time 30 minutes
Level easy

1 Preheat the oven to 350°F (180°C or Gas Mark 4). Melt the butter in a double boiler. Let cool. Beat the egg and sugar together. Add the butter and flour and mix until the dough is smooth and elastic. Refrigerate for 30 minutes.

2 Heat the cooked wheat, milk, honey and lemon peel. Simmer the mixture until the milk has been absorbed by the wheat. Remove from the heat and let cool. Remove the lemon peel and stir in the ricotta with a wooden spoon.

3 Roll out the dough into a thin sheet and cut out 4 rounds. Place the rounds on the bottom of 4 individual tart tins. Use the remaining dough to cut out 4 strips. Place the strips around the edges of the tins and press down to seal the bottom and sides.

4 Pour the cooked wheat filling into the tarts and top with the pine nuts. Bake for 25 minutes. Sprinkle with confectioners' sugar.

Mini Chocolate-Almond Tarts

Serves 6

Crust

1/2 tsp active dry yeast

1 Tbsp warm milk

4 ¾ cups plus 1 Tbsp (1 lb 5 oz or 600 g) all-purpose flour

7 Tbsps (3 ½ oz or 100 g) butter

2/3 cup (4 oz or 120 g) sugar

2 eggs plus 4 egg yolks

grated zest of 1 organic lemon

Filling

1 cup (5 ½ oz or 150 g) toasted almonds

10 ½ oz (300 g) dark chocolate, chopped

5 Tbsps grape jam

1 Tbsp bitter herb liqueur, like Centerbe

1 pinch of ground cinnamon

Preparation time 30 minutes
Cooking time 20 minutes
Level easy

1 Preheat the oven to 400°F (200°C or Gas Mark 6). Dissolve the yeast in the warm milk. Sift the flour onto a work surface and make a well at the center. Add the butter, sugar, yeast mixture, eggs, egg yolks and lemon zest.

2 Mix together to form a smooth and compact dough. Roll out the dough into a thin sheet and cut out rounds with a cookie cutter. Place half of the rounds in miniature tart tins. Reserve the other half for the top of the tarts.

3 Make the filling: Grind the almonds in a food processor and transfer to a mixing bowl. Add the chopped chocolate, jam, liqueur and a pinch of cinnamon. Mix well to form a very thick mixture.

4 Place 1 teaspoon of filling in each tart and cover the tarts with the reserved dough rounds. Pinch the edges to seal and bake for 15 minutes. Sprinkle with confectioners' sugar, if desired, and serve.

Pastry Chef's Tip

Centerbe liquor may be substituted with an anise liqueur like Pastis.

Mini Plum Pies

Serves 4

Crust

7 Tbsps (3 ½ oz or 100 g) butter

3/4 cup (3 ½ oz or 90 g) confectioners' sugar

1 egg

2 ⅓ cups plus 1 Tbsp (10 ½ oz or 300 g) all-purpose flour

zest of 1 organic lemon

zest of 1 organic orange

1 Tbsp sugar

Filling

4 Tbsps plum preserves

Preparation time 20 minutes

Cooking time 15 minutes

Level medium

1 Cream the butter and sugar together and mix in the egg. Sift in the flour and mix with a wooden spoon. Add the citrus zest and stir to form a smooth dough. Roll into a ball, cover with plastic wrap and refrigerate until firm. Preheat the oven to 325°F (160°C or Gas Mark 3).

2 Roll out the dough on a lightly floured work surface and cut out four 3-inch (7 cm) rounds using a fluted cookie cutter. Place a tablespoonful of plum preserves on one side of each round and fold in half. Pinch the edges down to seal.

3 Place the parcels on a baking sheet lined with parchment paper and sprinkle with sugar. Bake for 15 minutes, remove from the oven and cool completely before serving

Mini Citrus-Yogurt Cups

Serves 4

Mini cups

10 ½ oz (300 g) shortcrust dough (see p. 32)

1 cup (9 oz or 250 g) plain low-fat yogurt

1 Tbsp confectioners' sugar

1/2 tsp vanilla extract

grated zest of 1 organic orange

grated zest of 1 organic lemon

3 ½ oz (100 g) dark chocolate

2 ripe apricots, pitted and diced

Preparation time 45 minutes
Cooking time 10 minutes
Level easy

1 Preheat the oven to 325°F (170°C or Gas Mark 3). Roll out the shortcrust dough into a thin sheet and cut out rounds with a cookie cutter. Place the rounds in miniature tart tins or hemispherical molds.

2 Pierce the dough with a fork and bake for 10 minutes. Remove from the oven, unmold and cool completely. Mix together the yogurt, sugar, vanilla and orange and lemon zest.

3 Melt the chocolate over a double boiler. Dip the outside of the pastry cups into the chocolate and set on a wire rack to harden.

4 Once cooled, fill the cups with the yogurt mixture and place one piece of apricot in each cup. Serve cold.

PASTRY CHEF'S TIP

To prevent the formation of air pockets while baking the pastry cups, cover the unbaked dough with wax paper and fill with dried beans, uncooked rice or pie weights.

Chocolate Cake Squares
with Strawberries

Serves 4

Chocolate Cake

3 ½ oz (100 g) milk chocolate

2 oz (50 g) dark chocolate

5 Tbsps (2 ½ oz or 75 g) butter, softened

1/3 cup (2 ½ oz or 75 g) sugar

1 Tbsp brandy

2 eggs, lightly beaten

3 ½ oz (100 g) mascarpone

1/3 cup (1 ½ oz or 40 g) all-purpose flour

1 Tbsp cornstarch

3/4 cup (2 ½ oz or 75 g) almonds, toasted and ground

Decoration

2 oz (50 g) white chocolate

1 basket of strawberries, hulled and halved

Preparation time 30 minutes

Cooking time 25 minutes

Level easy

1 Preheat the oven to 350°F (180°C or Gas Mark 4). Melt the milk chocolate and dark chocolate together over a double boiler or in a microwave.

2 Using an electric mixer, cream the butter and sugar. Beat in the melted chocolate, brandy, eggs and finally the mascarpone.

3 Sift in the flour and cornstarch and add the ground almonds. Mix to combine and pour the batter into small rectangular tins or silicon molds.

4 Bake for 20 minutes and let cool completely. Melt the white chocolate and let cool.

5 Unmold the chocolate cakes and place a dollop of melted white chocolate on top of each cake. Top with a strawberry half. Let cool completely before serving.

Pastry Chef's Tip

This dessert may also be decorated with seasonal edible berries such as raspberries or blackberries.

Mini Cherry Clafoutis

Serves 6

Clafoutis

3 eggs plus 1 egg yolk

3/4 cup (4 ½ oz or 135 g) raw sugar

1 tsp vanilla extract

1 cup (250 ml) whipping cream

1 cup (250 ml) milk

2 Tbsps (1 oz or 20 g) butter, melted

30 ripe cherries, pitted but with stalks attached

Decoration

confectioners' sugar

Preparation time 25 minutes
Cooking time 20 minutes
Level easy

1 Preheat the oven to 375°F (190°C or Gas Mark 5). Beat the eggs, egg yolk and sugar together until thick. Add the vanilla extract, cream, milk and melted butter. Let the batter rest for 15 minutes.

2 Pour the batter into miniature muffin tins, filling each tin two-thirds full. Drop one cherry in each tin. Place the muffin tins on a baking sheet and bake for 20 minutes.

3 Remove from the oven, unmold and sprinkle with confectioners' sugar before serving.

PASTRY CHEF'S TIP

The same recipe may be used to make one large clafoutis. Bake a single cake for 2 more minutes.

Strawberry Mousse
in Chocolate Cups

Serves 8

Mini cups

7 oz (200 g) dark chocolate couverture

Mousse

5 ½ oz (150 g) strawberries, hulled

1/3 cup (2 oz or 60 g) sugar

1 Tbsp white rum

1 gelatin sheet

1 cup plus 3 Tbsps (280 ml) whipping cream

chocolate sauce

Preparation time 30 minutes
Cooking time 10 minutes
Level medium

1. Place half of the strawberries and all of the sugar in a frying pan and sauté for a few minutes. Add the rum and cook for a few more minutes. Remove from the heat. Soak the gelatin in cold water. Drain and squeeze out the excess water. Add the gelatin to the cooked strawberries. Add the remaining raw strawberries and puree in a blender or food processor.

2. Whip the whipping cream to stiff peaks and fold into the strawberry mixture. Refrigerate. Melt the chocolate over a double boiler or in a microwave.

3. Coat the inside of 20 waxed paper cups with melted chocolate. Refrigerate the cups until the chocolate hardens, then remove from the paper. Fill the chocolate cups with strawberry mousse and drizzle with chocolate sauce. Chill before serving.

PASTRY CHEF'S TIP

Frozen strawberries or raspberries may be used for the puree. If desired, decorate the mousse cups with fresh strawberries.

Rum-Meringue Truffles

Serves 4

Truffles

1/4 cup (60 ml) whipping cream

1 tsp white rum

7 oz (200 g) milk chocolate, finely chopped

2 oz (60 g) meringues (see p. 144)

3 Tbsps cocoa powder

Preparation time 25 minutes
Cooking time 10 minutes
Level easy

1 Heat the cream and rum in a small saucepan. Add the chocolate and whisk until it has melted and the mixture is smooth. Let cool in the refrigerator for 5 minutes, stirring at least 3 times, until the mixture begins to thicken.

2 Crush the meringues and add them to the chocolate mixture. Using the hands, form walnut-sized balls.

3 Place the truffles on a baking sheet and refrigerate for at least 15 minutes. Once chilled, roll them in the cocoa powder. Keep the truffles in a cool place and serve at the end of a meal with dessert wines or liqueurs.

Baked Hazelnut Truffles

Makes 20 truffles

Truffles

1 oz (30 g) milk chocolate

4 Tbsps (2 oz or 60 g) butter, softened

1 cup minus 1 Tbsp (6 ½ oz or 185 g) sugar

1/2 tsp vanilla extract

1 egg yolk, lightly beaten

1 ⅔ cups (7 oz or 200 g) all-purpose flour

1/2 tsp baking powder

1/3 cup (1 ½ oz or 40 g) ground hazelnuts

confectioners' sugar

Preparation time 30 minutes
Cooking time 30 minutes
Level easy

PASTRY CHEF'S TIP

These truffles can be made using other types of nuts in place of the hazelnuts. If desired, omit the nuts completely and add 1 tablespoon of rum for more flavor.

1 Melt the chocolate over a double boiler. Cream the softened butter, sugar and vanilla in a mixer or with an electric beater. Add the egg yolk and melted chocolate. Sift in the flour and baking powder and continue mixing.

2 Finally add the hazelnuts. Refrigerate the dough for 3 hours. Preheat the oven to 350°F (180°C or Gas Mark 4).

3 Break off small pieces of the truffle dough and, using the hands, roll it into balls. Roll the truffles in the confectioners' sugar and place them on a buttered baking sheet.

4 Bake for 25 minutes. Remove from the oven and cool completely. Sprinkle with more confectioners' sugar, if desired.

Milk Chocolate
and Coconut Truffles

Serves 4

Truffles

7 oz (200 g) milk chocolate, chopped

1 ⅔ cups (5 ½ oz or 150 g) shredded coconut

5 Tbsps whipping cream

3/4 cup (2 oz or 60 g) ground hazelnuts

1 tsp cocoa powder

Preparation time 15 minutes
Cooking time 5 minutes
Level easy

1 Place the chocolate and the cream in a double boiler and melt, stirring constantly. Once the mixture is smooth, remove from heat.

2 Add the hazelnuts and cocoa powder and mix to combine. Let the mixture cool until is thickens and is easy to work with.

3 Form walnut-sized balls by rolling a teaspoonful of the mixture between the palms of the hands. Roll each ball in the shredded coconut and refrigerate for at least 2 hours before serving.

PASTRY CHEF'S TIP
Take care not to let any water from the double boiler fall into the melted chocolate as it could cause the chocolate and cream to crystallize immediately. The chocolate and cream may be melted in the microwave on a medium setting. Stir the mixture frequently even when using the microwave.

Mini Walnut Brownies

Serves 6

Brownies

4 ½ oz (125 g) milk chocolate

6 Tbsps (3 oz or 90 g) butter

2 cups (9 oz or 250 g)
confectioners' sugar

1 tsp vanilla extract

2 eggs

2/3 cup (3 oz or 80 g)
all-purpose flour

1/3 cup (1 oz or 30 g)
cocoa powder

1/2 tsp baking powder

1 cup (4 oz or 120 g)
walnuts, chopped

Preparation time 30 minutes
Cooking time 40 minutes
Level medium

1 Preheat the oven to 350°F (180°C or Gas Mark 4). Melt the chocolate over a double boiler or in a microwave.

2 Beat the butter, sugar and vanilla together using an electric mixer. Add the eggs and beat well. Stir in the melted chocolate. Sift in the flour, cocoa powder and baking powder. Mix gently with a spatula. Add the walnuts and stir to combine.

3 Pour the batter into a rectangular baking dish lined with parchment paper and smooth the top with a spatula. Bake for 35 minutes. Let cool and cut into small rectangles. Serve the brownies in miniature paper baking cups.

PASTRY CHEF'S TIP

Brownies are an American classic. Try serving them hot with a scoop of vanilla ice cream for brownies à la mode.

Sponge Cake Sandwiches
with Chocolate Cream

Serves 6

Cake

1 sponge cake round (see p. 38)

1 cup (250 ml) Alchermes liquor

sugar

Pastry Cream

4 egg yolks

2/3 cup (4 ½ oz or 125 g) sugar

6 ½ Tbsps all-purpose flour

2 cups (500 ml) milk

1 vanilla bean, halved lengthwise

Chocolate Cream

2 oz (50 g) dark chocolate

3/4 cup (200 ml) whipping cream

4 egg yolks

2/3 cup (4 ½ oz or 125 g) sugar

Preparation time 30 minutes

Cooking time 1 hour

Level medium

1 Cut the sponge cake into small rounds and set aside. Make the pastry cream: Beat the egg yolks with the sugar until thick and pale yellow in color, sift in the flour and stir to incorporate. Heat the milk and vanilla bean in a saucepan. Strain the milk and whisk it into the egg mixture. Return to the saucepan and cook over medium heat until the cream coats the back of a spoon. Remove from the heat and set aside.

2 Make the chocolate cream: Melt the chocolate and cream over a double boiler. Beat the egg yolks with the sugar and add the melted chocolate. Beat until smooth.
Spread half of the sponge cake rounds with chocolate cream and the other half with pastry cream. Make sandwiches out of the sponge cake rounds. Brush the exterior of the sandwiches with Alchermes liquor and roll in sugar. Let sit until firm, then serve.

PASTRY CHEF'S TIP

Sponge cake may be used in many types of desserts, thanks to its soft texture. In this recipe, the sponge cake can be cut into any shape desired.

Chocolate-Vanilla Caramels

Serves 6

Caramels

5 ½ oz (150 g) vanilla-flavored
dark chocolate, chopped

1 cup (250 ml)
whipping cream

1 ¼ cups (9 oz or 250 g) sugar

2 tsps honey

1 Tbsp (15 g) butter

Preparation time 20 minutes
Cooking time 40 minutes
Level difficult

PASTRY CHEF'S TIP

If vanilla-flavored chocolate is unavailable, infuse the cream with 1 vanilla bean for 5 minutes before adding it to the caramel. To make a caramel lollipop, let a large drop of the hot caramel mixture fall into a bowl filled with cornstarch, immediately place a plastic or wooden stick into the caramel and let cool completely.

1 Melt the chocolate over a double boiler. Heat the whipping cream in a small saucepan. Caramelize 3 tablespoons sugar a small heavy-bottomed copper saucepan over low heat.

2 Once the sugar has dissolved, add another tablespoon of sugar, and repeat until the sugar is gone. Slowly add the hot cream to the caramel and then the honey. Remove from the heat and pour in half of the chocolate. Return to the heat and cook until it reaches 235°F (113°C). To measure doneness without a candy thermometer, after 6-7 minutes of cooking drop a small spoonful of caramel onto a plate and when it cools, test to see that it is the correct consistency.

3 Remove from heat and stir in the butter and remaining chocolate. Mix well and pour the caramel into a baking dish, smoothing it out into an even layer. When cool, cut the caramel into small cubes and wrap them in greaseproof or wax paper. Store in a sealed container.

Florentine Cookies
with Gianduia Mousse

by **Stefano De Pietri**

Serves 6

Florentine Cookies

8 Tbsps (4 oz or 120 g) butter

3 Tbsps glucose syrup or honey

2/3 cup (4 oz or 120 g) sugar

3 Tbsps whipping cream

2 cups (200 g) sliced almonds

9 oz (250 g) candied orange paste or orange-flavored marzipan

Mousse

9 oz (250 g) gianduia chocolate (see p. 64)

2/3 cup (150 ml) whipping cream

1 ½ oz (40 g) hazelnut cream (like Nutella)

Preparation time 40 minutes
Cooking time 30 minutes
Level medium

1. Preheat the oven to 325°F (160°C or Gas Mark 3). Heat the butter, glucose syrup or honey, sugar and the whipping cream in a double boiler or in the microwave until melted. Remove from heat and add the almonds and the candied orange paste.

2. Spread the mixture onto a silicone baking mat and cut out 1-inch (3 cm) diameter circles. Transfer the rounds to a cookie sheet and bake for 18-20 minutes or until the cookies are a caramel color.

3. Melt the gianduia chocolate in a double boiler. Whip the cream into soft peaks and fold it into the melted chocolate. Add the hazelnut cream and gently stir to combine.

4. Let the mixture cool until it has thickened and transfer to a pastry bag. Pipe out a little of the gianduia cream onto half of the florentine cookies. Top the frosted rounds with the remaining rounds and serve the cookies.

Pastry Chef's Tip

To make the candied orange paste finely chop 9 oz (250 g) of candied orange until it forms a dough-like consistency. Hazelnut cream is available in specialty food stores or can be prepared at home by grinding the same quantity of hazelnuts into a paste.

Tartlets with Port Cream
and Nut Brittle

by **Stefano De Pietri**

Serves 6

Tartlets

1 lb (500 g) shortcrust pastry
(see p. 32)

Port Cream

5 eggs

1 lb 2 oz (500 g) butter

2 ½ cups (1 lb 2 oz or 500 g)
sugar

4 Tbsps lemon juice

3/4 cup plus 1 Tbsp (200 ml)
white Port wine

Nut Brittle

2 ½ cups (1 lb 2 oz or 500 g)
sugar

juice of 1 organic lemon

1 cup (3 ½ oz or 100 g)
pecan halves

1 ¼ cups (5 ½ oz or 150)
pistachios, shelled and peeled

1 cup (5 ½ oz or 150 g)
hazelnuts

Preparation time 40 minutes
Cooking time 20 minutes
Level easy

1 Preheat the oven to 350°F (180°C or Gas Mark 4). Roll out the shortcrust dough into a thin sheet about 1/8-inch (2 mm) thick. Cut out rounds and use them to line buttered and floured miniature tart tins. Pierce the dough with a fork and bake for 6-8 minutes.

2 Mix together the ingredients for the port cream in a small saucepan and cook over low heat, whisking constantly until the cream reaches 185°F (85°C). Remove from the heat and let cool completely. Fill the tartlet shells with the port cream and refrigerate until the cream has set.

3 Meanwhile, make the nut brittle. Heat the sugar in a pan with the lemon juice until the sugar becomes a golden-brown color. Add the nuts and stir to combine. Using 2 lightly oiled spoons, drop small spoonfuls of the nut mixture onto a baking sheet lined with parchment paper.

4 Press down on each mound of the nut mixture to form an oblong shape that will fit on the top of the tartlets. Decorate the tartlets with the nut brittle and serve.

techniques&recipes

Mousses and Creams

Bavarian creams, puddings, charlottes,
fruit or chocolate mousses, spiced soufflés
and original tiramisus are among these delicious desserts.

1 Soak the gelatin sheets in a little cold water for a few minutes.

2 Beat the egg yolks with the sugar until thick and smooth.

3 Heat the milk with the vanilla and then slowly whisk it into the egg mixture. Return the mixture to the saucepan and cook over low heat, stirring constantly with a wooden spoon. When the cream begins to simmer, remove from heat and stir in the gelatin sheets one at a time. Let the cream cool completely.

4 Once cool, whip the whipping cream to stiff peaks and fold it into the cream.

5 Pour the Bavarian cream into a mold or several individual molds and refrigerate for 3-4 hours before serving.

Serves 4
4 gelatin sheets
4 egg yolks
1/3 cup (2 oz or 60 g) sugar
1 cup (250 ml) milk
1 tsp vanilla extract
1 cup (250 ml) whipping cream

BAVARIAN CREAM

Pastry Chef's Tip

Remember to let the cream cool completely before folding in the whipped cream, otherwise the whipped cream could lose its volume. To unmold the Bavarian cream, immerse the bottom of the mold in a hot water bath for a few seconds.

Recipe on p. 224

1 Beat the egg yolks with the sugar and add the cocoa powder and rum.

2 Soak the gelatin sheets in cold water. Bring the milk and cream to a boil and add the chocolate shavings. Remove from heat and add the drained gelatin sheets.

3 Slowly whisk the milk mixture into the eggs and sugar, stirring constantly until completely incorporated.

4 Pour the mixture into a damp pudding mold. Refrigerate for 1 hour and unmold.

Serves 4

3 egg yolks

6 ½ Tbsps sugar

1/3 cup (1 oz or 20 g) cocoa powder

1 Tbsp rum

2 gelatin sheets

1 ¼ cups (300 ml) milk

3/4 cup plus 1 Tbsp (200 ml) whipping cream

7 oz (200 g) white chocolate shavings

PUDDING

PASTRY CHEF'S TIP

For an original variation, pour the pudding into decorative individual molds.

Recipe on p. 235

1 Heat the wild berries in a frying pan with the lemon zest, sugar and agar agar.

2 Melt the chocolate and whip the cream. Fold the chocolate into the cream.

3 Add the berry mixture to the chocolate cream.

4 Fold the berries into the cream using bottom to top motions. Transfer to a serving bowl and refrigerate for 1 hour.

Serves 6
7 oz (200 g) wild berries
zest of **1** organic lemon
6 ½ Tbsps raw sugar
1/2 tsp agar agar
3 ½ oz (100 g)
white chocolate, chopped
7 Tbsps (100 ml)
whipping cream

MOUSSE

Pastry Chef's Tip

Take care when folding together the cream and the chocolate and when incorporating the berries into the mousse as the whipped cream is very delicate and may lose its airiness, leaving the mousse thick and heavy.

Recipe on p. 245

Bavarian Cream
with Raspberries

Serves 4

Bavarian

3/4 cup plus 1 Tbsp (200 ml) milk

1 vanilla bean, halved lengthwise

6 oz (170 g) white chocolate

2 gelatin sheets

2 egg yolks

3/4 cup (5 ½ or 150 g) sugar

1 cup (250 ml) whipping cream

1 basket of raspberries

Preparation time 20 minutes
Cooking time 15 minutes
Level easy

1 Heat the milk and vanilla bean. Let cool slightly, then scrape the vanilla seeds out of the bean and add them to the milk. Discard the bean. Chop the chocolate and melt it in the warm milk.

2 Soak the gelatin in cold water. Drain, squeeze out the excess water and add to the milk and chocolate. Stir to dissolve the gelatin. Beat the egg yolks with the sugar until thick and creamy. Whisk the warm milk mixture into the eggs and let cool.

3 Whip the whipping cream to stiff peaks and fold into the chocolate cream. Fold in the raspberries. Line a loaf pan with plastic wrap and pour the cream into the pan. Refrigerate for at least 3 hours. Slice and serve.

Pastry Chef's Tip

Try freezing the raspberries for about 40 minutes before adding them to the cream mixture. A frozen film will form around the berries that will help them to maintain their shape and color within the dessert.

Coffee Bavarian Cream
with Two Chocolate Sauces

Serves 6

Bavarian Cream

6 gelatin sheets

2 cups (500 ml) milk

10 coffee beans

4 egg yolks

3/4 cup (5 ½ oz or 150 g) sugar

1/2 cup (120 ml) prepared espresso coffee

7 Tbsps (100 ml) whipping cream

1/4 cup (60 ml) brandy

Sauces

3 ½ oz (100 g) white chocolate, chopped

3 ½ oz (100 g) dark chocolate, chopped

7 Tbsps whipping cream

1 Tbsp instant coffee granules

Preparation time 20 minutes
Cooking time 15 minutes
Level easy

1 Soak the gelatin sheets in cold water for a few minutes. Meanwhile, bring the milk and coffee beans to a boil. Strain the milk and set aside.

2 Beat the egg yolks with the sugar until thick. Whisk in the hot milk and the espresso coffee. Transfer the mixture to a saucepan and heat over low heat, stirring constantly. Continue cooking the mixture until it coats the back of a wooden spoon and begins to thicken. Drain the gelatin, squeeze out the excess water and stir into the coffee mixture.

3 Whip the whipping cream and fold it into the mixture. Coat the inside of a Bundt pan or individual ramekins with the brandy and pour in the coffee cream. Refrigerate for 4-5 hours.

4 Make the sauces: Melt the two types of chocolate separately, adding half of the cream to each. Stir until the chocolate is melted and the cream has been incorporated. Sprinkle the unmolded Bavarian cream with instant coffee and serve with the two chocolate sauces.

PASTRY CHEF'S TIP

For a shiny look and a sauce that will not harden too quickly, try adding a little warm water to the chocolate sauce.

Chocolate-Orange Bavarian Creams

Serves 4

Bavarian Creams

1 cup (250 ml) milk

julienned zest
of 1 organic orange

4 gelatin sheets

3 oz (80 g) dark chocolate,
chopped

2 egg yolks

1/2 cup (3 1/2 oz or 100 g)
sugar

1 cup (250 ml)
whipping cream

1/2 cup (125 ml)
Grand Marnier

Decoration

julienned zest
of 1 organic orange

dark chocolate shavings

Preparation time 25 minutes
Cooking time 5 minutes
Level easy

1 Bring the milk to a boil with the orange zest. Soak the gelatin sheets in cold water for a few minutes. Drain and squeeze out the excess water. Transfer half the hot milk to a bowl and dissolve the chocolate in the milk.

2 Beat the egg yolks and the sugar together and add the chocolate and the milk. Return to the saucepan and cook over low heat. Add the gelatin and mix until the cream begins to thicken. Remove from heat, sieve the mixture and let cool. Whip the whipping cream and fold into the cooled chocolate mixture.

3 Coat 4 individual molds with Grand Marnier. Pour the chocolate cream into the molds and refrigerate for 3 hours. Unmold the Bavarian creams and decorate with julienned orange zest and shaved chocolate. The dessert may be accompanied by a Gran Marnier-flavored crème anglaise if desired.

PASTRY CHEF'S TIP

For a lighter version of this dessert, substitute the cream with 3 egg whites, beaten to stiff peaks.

Jasmine-Infused
White Chocolate Cream

Serves 4

Cream

3 gelatin sheets

1 cup (250 ml) milk

2 oz (60 g) edible
jasmine flowers

salt

1 vanilla bean,
halved lengthwise

3 egg yolks

1/4 cup (2 oz or 50 g) sugar

3 ½ oz (100 g) white
chocolate, shaved

1 ¼ cups (300 ml)
whipping cream

Sauce

7 Tbsps (100 ml) milk

1/4 cup (2 oz or 50 g) sugar

7 Tbsps (100 ml) mint syrup

Decoration

fresh edible jasmine flowers

Preparation time 25 minutes
Cooking time 10 minutes
Level easy

1 Soak the gelatin sheets in cold water for a few minutes. Bring the milk to a boil with the jasmine flowers, a pinch of salt and the vanilla bean. Remove from the heat and set aside to infuse. Meanwhile, beat the egg yolks with the sugar until thick and pale yellow.

2 Whisk the hot milk infusion into the egg yolks and stir until the mixture coats the back of a spoon. Strain the mixture and add the white chocolate shavings. Drain the gelatin, squeeze out the excess water and add to the white chocolate cream. Stir until the chocolate is melted and the gelatin incorporated, then set aside to cool.

3 Whip the whipping cream to stiff peaks and fold it into the cooled white chocolate cream. Pour into a mold and refrigerate until cool. Meanwhile make the sauce: Bring the milk and sugar to a boil. Remove from the heat and stir in the mint syrup. Let cool. Serve the white chocolate cream with the mint sauce and decorate with fresh jasmine flowers.

PASTRY CHEF'S TIP

If the sauce is too thin, whisk in 1/2 tablespoon of cornstarch dissolved in a little cold milk.

Lemon Bavarian Cream
with Pineapple

Serves 4

Bavarian Cream

1 ⅓ cups (320 ml) milk

3/4 cup (5 oz or 140 g) sugar

zest of 1 organic lemon

4 egg yolks

3 gelatin sheets

1 ¾ cups (400 ml) whipping cream

Pineapple

3 ⅓ cups (1 ½ lb or 670 g) sugar

2 cups (500 ml) water

1/2 pineapple, peeled

Decoration

1 organic lemon, thinly sliced

Preparation time 20 minutes
Cooking time 5 hours
Level difficult

Pastry Chef's Tip

The pineapple pieces may be cooked for a shorter time in the microwave on the highest setting. The exact amount of time required will depend on the thickness of the pineapple pieces.

1. Begin preparing the pineapple at least 1 day in advance. Heat the sugar and the water until it reaches 86°F (30°C); the liquid should be thicker but not colored. Cut the pineapple into very thick slices using a mandoline or an electric slicer. Cut the slices into smaller pieces and place the pieces in a baking dish. Pour the syrup over the pineapple and marinate the pineapple for at least 12 hours.

2. Preheat the oven to 200°F (100°C or Gas Mark 1). Drain off the marinade and place the pineapple pieces on a baking sheet lined with parchment paper. Bake for 4-5 hours.

3. Make the creams: Soak the gelatin sheets in water, then drain. Bring the milk and 2 tablespoons of sugar to a boil with the lemon zest. Beat the egg yolks with the remaining sugar in a stainless steel bowl. Whisk the boiling milk into the egg mixture. Place the bowl on top of a pot of simmering water and cook the cream until it reaches 180°F (82°C).

4. Remove from the heat and add the previously soaked gelatin sheets. Stir to combine. Whip the whipping cream to stiff peaks and fold it into the cooled cream mixture. Transfer the cream to individual silicon molds and refrigerate for at least 2 hours. Unmold the Bavarian creams and serve them with the pineapple pieces and lemon slices.

Chocolate Bônet

Serves 8

Bônet

4 cups (1 l) milk

3 ½ oz (100 g) ladyfingers

4 oz (120 g) small amaretto cookies

1/4 cup (60 ml) strong coffee

1 Tbsp instant coffee granules

2 Tbsps rum

2 Tbsps Marsala wine

5 eggs

1 cup (7 oz or 200 g) sugar

1/2 cup (2 oz or 50 g) cocoa powder

Preparation time 15 minutes
Cooking time 50 minutes
Level medium

PASTRY CHEF'S TIP

Bônet, also known as bunet, is a typical dessert from the Langhe region of Piedmont. The name means "beret" or "cap" in the local dialect. This may be because of the round molds sometimes used to make bônet. If desired, replace the amaretto cookies with crumbled torrone (nougat) or almond cookies.

1 Preheat the oven to 400°F (200°C or Gas Mark 6). Bring the milk to a boil in a saucepan and let it cool.

2 Meanwhile, finely chop the ladyfingers with the amaretto cookies in a food processor or with a knife. Add them to the milk. Stir in the coffee, instant coffee, rum and Marsala wine. Beat the eggs with the sugar and cocoa powder to obtain a smooth, thick cream. Whisk the milk mixture into the egg mixture.

3 Sprinkle a pudding mold with sugar and heat on the stove for a few minutes, until the sugar begins to caramelize. Remove from the heat and roll the mold around to evenly distribute the caramel. Set aside and let the caramel harden.

4 Pour the batter into the mold and bake in a hot water bath in the oven for 40 minutes. Remove from the heat and cool. Serve cold or at room temperature.

White Chocolate Pudding

Serves 8

Pudding

7 Tbsps all-purpose flour

6 cups (1 ½ l) milk

8 egg yolks

3 oz (80 g) white chocolate, chopped

1/2 cup plus 1 Tbsp (4 oz or 115 g) vanilla sugar

Decoration

mint leaves (optional)

Preparation time 30 minutes

Cooking time 30 minutes

Level easy

1 Heat the flour and 1/2 cup (120 ml) milk in a saucepan over low heat. Whisk in the egg yolks one by one until fully incorporated.

2 Melt the chocolate over a double boiler. Add the sugar and melted chocolate to the egg mixture and stir in the remaining milk.

3 Return to the heat and cook, stirring constantly, until the mixture just comes to a boil.

4 Pour into a pudding mold and let cool completely before serving. Decorate with mint leaves if desired.

Pastry Chef's Tip

This elegant pudding could served on a plate decorated with chocolate sauce. For a more color, garnish with mixed edible berries or strawberries.

Lavender Pudding

Serves 4

Pudding

1 ¼ cups (300 ml) milk

1/4 cup (1 ½ oz or 45 g) sugar

2 tsps vanilla extract

1 Tbsp agar agar powder

5 drops of lavender oil

1/2 tsp raw sugar

Decoration

1 Tbsp raw sugar

lavender flowers

Preparation time 5 minutes

Cooking time 10 minutes

Level easy

1 Heat the milk, sugar and vanilla extract. Add the agar agar and dissolve in the milk.

2 Cook over low heat stirring constantly for 5 minutes. Let cool slightly and then add the lavender oil and raw sugar. Pour the pudding into individual molds and let cool.

3 When cool refrigerate for another 2 hours. Sprinkle with raw sugar and garnish with lavender flowers.

PASTRY CHEF'S TIP

Essential oils are often used in perfumes but they can also be used in the kitchen. When cooking with essential oils it is important to use small doses and to dissolve the oils in milk, yogurt or cream.

Almond and Pistachio Pudding

Serves 4

Pudding

1/3 cup plus 1 Tbsp
(2 oz or 50 g) rice flour

1/3 cup plus 1 Tbsp
(2 oz or 50 g) cornstarch

4 ¾ cups (1200 ml) milk

6 ½ Tbsps sugar

2 Tbsps rose water

1/3 cup (2 oz or 50 g)
blanched almonds, chopped

Decoration

1/3 cup (1 oz or 30 g)
shelled pistachios, chopped

ground cinnamon

2 Tbsps honey

Preparation time 30 minutes
Cooking time 30 minutes
Level medium

1 Pour the rice flour and cornstarch into a mixing bowl. Add enough milk to form a smooth, thick batter.

2 Bring the remaining milk to a boil and add the sugar. Let simmer over low heat for about 15 minutes. Gradually add the rice flour batter, stirring constantly with a wooden spoon. Reduce the heat and continue cooking for another 15 minutes, stirring frequently and taking care not to burn the bottom of the pan.

3 Add the rose water and half of the almonds and simmer for another 5 minutes. Let cool slightly and then pour it into individual ramekins. Before serving, sprinkle with the remaining almonds, pistachios and ground cinnamon and drizzle with honey.

Yogurt Pudding
with Blueberry Sauce

Serves 4

Pudding

7 oz (200 g) plain low-fat yogurt at room temperature

2 Tbsps sugar

1 gelatin sheet

3/4 cup (180 ml) whipping cream

Sauce

1 basket of blueberries

1 Tbsp sugar

1 pinch of ground cinnamon

1/2 cup (120 ml) red wine

Preparation time 25 minutes
Cooking time 20 minutes
Level easy

1 Mix the yogurt with the sugar. Soak the gelatin sheet in a little cold water. Drain and squeeze out the excess liquid. Place the gelatin and a little cream in a small pan and cook over low heat just until the gelatin dissolves. Pour the mixture into the yogurt and mix well.

2 Whip the remaining whipping cream to stiff peaks and carefully fold it into the yogurt mixture. Transfer to 4 hemispherical molds and refrigerate until firm, then place the puddings in the freezer for 20 minutes.

3 Meanwhile, pour the blueberries into a small saucepan, reserving a few for decoration. Add the sugar, cinnamon and wine to the berries. Cook over low heat until the berries begin to pop open, making a saucy liquid.

4 Unmold the pudding and top with the sauce. Decorate the plates with the reserved blueberries cut in half.

Coconut Pudding

Serves 4

Pudding

1 coconut

7 Tbsps (100 ml) milk

1 tsp agar agar powder

4 thin slices of white
sandwich bread

1 Tbsp vanilla-flavored
confectioners' sugar

Decoration

shredded coconut

cocoa powder

Preparation time 10 minutes
Cooking time 15 minutes
Level easy

1 Extract the milk from the coconut (about 7 Tbsps or 100 ml) and shred the meat, leaving 1 piece whole for decoration, and set aside.

2 Heat the regular milk over low heat and sprinkle in the agar agar powder. Add the coconut milk and shredded coconut meat and mix well. Line a rectangular baking dish with plastic wrap and pour the coconut mixture into the prepared pan. Refrigerate for 1 hour. Preheat the oven to 350°F (180°C or Gas Mark 4).

3 Place the bread slices on a baking sheet. Sprinkle with the confectioners' sugar and toast in the oven, turning until golden-brown on both sides.

4 Unmold the pudding onto a clean cutting board and cut into 4 squares. Place the pudding on the toasted bread and serve sprinkled with the shredded coconut and cocoa powder.

Milk Chocolate-Rum Pudding

Serves 6

Pudding

1 ¼ cups (300 ml) milk

3/4 cup plus 1 Tbsp (200 ml) whipping cream

7 oz (200 g) milk chocolate, chopped

3 egg yolks

6 ½ Tbsps sugar

1 Tbsp aged rum

1/3 cup (1 oz or 25 g) cocoa powder

3 gelatin sheets

Preparation time 30 minutes
Cooking time 15 minutes
Level easy

1. Bring the milk and cream to a boil in a small saucepan, remove from heat and stir in the chocolate until melted.

2. Beat the egg yolks with the sugar until thick and pale yellow. Stir in the rum and cocoa powder and set aside.

3. Soak the gelatin in cold water for a few minutes. Drain and squeeze out the excess liquid. Add the gelatin to the chocolate mixture. When cool, whisk the egg yolks into the chocolate mixture.

4. Line a rectangular loaf pan with plastic wrap and pour in the chocolate cream. Refrigerate for at least 1 hour. Unmold and serve.

PASTRY CHEF'S TIP

This pudding may be served with whipped cream, a sweet sauce such as crème anglaise or sabayon, or a fruit compote spiked with a liqueur of choice.

Mini Milk Chocolate Charlottes

Serves 4

Charlotte

4 Tbsps orange-flower liqueur
or Grand Marnier

20 ladyfingers, cut in half

8 oz (230 g) milk chocolate

2/3 cup (150 ml)
whipping cream

4 eggs, separated

salt

3/4 cup (5 ½ oz or 150 g) sugar

Preparation time 30 minutes
Cooking time 5 minutes
Level easy

1 Line 4 mini spring-form pans with parchment paper. Dilute the orange-flower liqueur or Grand Marnier with a few spoonfuls of water and use the mixture to brush the ladyfingers. Line the spring-form pans with the ladyfingers.

2 Melt the chocolate over a double boiler or in a microwave and then stir in the whipping cream. Beat the egg whites with a pinch of salt, slowly add the sugar and continue beating to stiff peaks.

3 Whisk the egg yolks into the chocolate mixture one at a time. Fold the egg whites into the chocolate mixture and stir carefully to incorporate. Pour the mixture into the spring-form pans and refrigerate overnight. Unmold before serving.

PASTRY CHEF'S TIP
The ladyfingers may be soaked in any liqueur, or in coffee.

White Chocolate-Raspberry
Cheesecakes

Serves 4

Cheesecakes

2 ½ oz (70 g) white chocolate, chopped

8 ½ oz (240 g) soft, fresh goat's milk cheese

6 Tbsps whipping cream

1 cup plus 1 Tbsp (4 ½ oz or 130 g) confectioners' sugar

1 egg, lightly beaten

4 chocolate wafer cookies

Decoration

raspberries

mint leaves

Preparation time 20 minutes
Cooking time 30 minutes
Level easy

1 Preheat the oven to 325°F (170°C or Gas Mark 3). Melt the chocolate in the microwave or over a double boiler, stirring frequently. Beat the goat's cheese together with the cream and confectioners' sugar in a standing mixer until light and fluffy.

2 Slowly add the melted chocolate and the beaten egg to the cheese mixture, stirring with a wooden spoon or a spatula.

3 Line 4 ceramic ramekins with parchment paper. Place a chocolate cookie in the bottom of each ramekin and fill two-thirds full with the cheese mixture.

4 Bake for 20 minutes, remove from the oven, cool completely and refrigerate for 1 hour. Serve the cheesecakes topped with a few raspberries and mint leaves.

PASTRY CHEF'S TIP

The chocolate wafer cookies may be replaced with slices of chocolate cake or another kind of cookie.

Brachetto Mousse

Serves 4

Mousse

1 ¼ cups (300 ml)
Brachetto wine
(or sweet Marsala)

2 Tbsps sugar

1 ½ gelatin sheets

2/3 cup (150 ml)
whipping cream

10 ½ oz (300 g)
puff pastry dough

2 Tbsps (1 oz or 30 g)
butter, melted

1 Tbsp confectioners' sugar

Preparation time 30 minutes
Cooking time 15 minutes
Level easy

1 Boil the wine and sugar and reduce to a third of the original volume. Soak the gelatin in cold water for a few minutes. Drain and squeeze out the excess water. Set 2 tablespoons of the wine reduction aside and dissolve the gelatin in the remaining reduction. Let cool.

2 Whip the whipping cream and then carefully fold the wine reduction into the whipped cream. Pour the wine cream into 4 ramekins and refrigerate for 1 hour. Preheat the oven to 375°F (190°C or Gas Mark 5).

3 Roll out the puff pastry and make diagonal incisions along the surface. Brush the pastry with melted butter and sprinkle with sugar. Cut the pastry into 2-inch (5 cm) by 1/2-inch (1 cm) rectangles. Bake until golden brown, remove from the oven and let cool. Unmold the ramekins onto serving plates and decorate with puff pastry cookies. Drizzle the reserved wine reduction over the top of the mousse.

White Chocolate Mousse
with Lemon Jelly

Serves 4

Mousse

9 oz (250 g) white chocolate, chopped

2 egg whites

salt

2/3 cup (150 ml) whipping cream

2 gelatin sheets

grated zest of 1 organic lemon

5 Tbsps lemon juice

Lemon Jelly

juice of 2 lemons

3 Tbsps water

1 Tbsp sugar

1 tsp agar agar or 1 gelatin sheet

Preparation time 25 minutes
Cooking time 10 minutes
Level medium

1 Melt the white chocolate over a double boiler or in the microwave. Beat the egg whites and a pinch of salt to stiff peaks. Then beat the whipping cream to stiff peaks and set aside. Soak the gelatin in cold water for a few minutes, drain and squeeze out the excess water.

2 Meanwhile, mix together the lemon zest and lemon juice. Heat the mixture slightly and then add the gelatin sheets and stir until dissolved. Pour the white chocolate over the whipped cream and fold together. Let cool and then add the lemon juice mixture. Carefully fold in the egg whites, making gentle movements from the top to the bottom of the mixture. Transfer the mixture to a large bowl, cover with plastic wrap and refrigerate until firm.

3 Meanwhile, make the jelly: Mix together the lemon juice, water and sugar in a small saucepan. Briefly heat the mixture and add the agar agar or the soaked gelatin sheet. Stir until dissolved. Strain the mixture and pour into silicon jelly molds. Refrigerate until firm. Unmold the jellies and roughly chop them. Serve the white chocolate mousse with a spoonful of lemon jelly.

PASTRY CHEF'S TIP

For a herbed variation, try infusing the lemon juice with a few sprigs of lemon thyme for 15 minutes before adding the gelatin sheets.

White Chocolate-Coconut Mousse

Serves 4

Mousse

9 oz (250 g) white chocolate, chopped

2 gelatin sheets

3 ½ Tbsps coconut milk

5 Tbsps coconut liqueur

7 Tbsps (100 ml) whipping cream

2 egg whites

salt

grated zest of 1 organic lime

Preparation time 20 minutes
Cooking time 10 minutes
Level easy

1 Melt the white chocolate over a double boiler or in the microwave, remove from the heat and cool until tepid. Soak the gelatin in cold water for a few minutes. Drain and squeeze out the excess water. Dissolve the gelatin in the coconut milk and coconut liqueur and set aside.

2 Meanwhile, whip the whipping cream into stiff peaks. Fold the melted chocolate into the whipped cream. Add the coconut mixture to the whipped cream mixture and fold carefully to incorporate.

3 Beat the egg whites and a pinch of salt to stiff peaks and fold into the coconut mixture. Fold in the lime zest and transfer the mixture to a bowl. Refrigerate until firm.

PASTRY CHEF'S TIP

This mousse may also be made in a "dark" version. Substitute the white chocolate with top-quality dark chocolate, the coconut liqueur with dark rum and omit the lime zest.

Tropical Fruit Mousse

Serves 4

Mousse

2 papayas

1 mango

3 gelatin sheets

1 ¼ cups (300 ml) whipping cream

1/2 cup (120 ml) water

1 cup (7 oz or 200 g) sugar

Decoration

2 kiwis

Preparation time 15 minutes
Cooking time 10 minutes
Level easy

1 Peel and deseed the papayas and mango. Chop into pieces and puree separately; refrigerate. Soak the gelatin in cold water for a few minutes, drain and squeeze out the excess liquid. Dissolve the gelatin in a small pan over low heat. Stir half of the dissolved gelatin into each of the fruit purees.

2 Meanwhile, beat the whipping cream to stiff peaks. Prepare a simple syrup by simmering the sugar with the water for 10 minutes. Add half of the sugar syrup to each fruit puree and then fold half of the whipped cream into each fruit mixture. Pour the mousses into individual molds and refrigerate or freeze for about 2 hours.

3 Puree the kiwis. Unmold the mousses onto serving plates and decorate with the kiwi puree.

Berry Mousse

Serves 4

Mousse

7 oz (200 g) mixed edible berries

zest of 1 organic lemon

6 ½ Tbsps raw sugar

1/2 tsp agar agar powder

3 ½ oz (100 g) white chocolate, chopped

7 Tbsps (100 ml) whipping cream

Decoration

wafer cookies

Preparation time 10 minutes
Cooking time 10 minutes
Level easy

1. Heat the berries with the lemon zest, sugar and agar agar.

2. Melt the chocolate over a double boiler. Remove from the heat and stir until cool.

3. Whip the whipping cream to stiff peaks and fold it into the chocolate. Fold in the berry mixture.

4. Refrigerate for 1 hour. Serve the mousse with wafer cookies.

PASTRY CHEF'S TIP

Serve the mousse with a sauce made by boiling 4 tablespoons of mixed berries with 2 tablespoons of sugar and a little water. Let cool and pour over the mousse.

Dark Chocolate Mousse
with Strawberries

Serves 4

Mousse

9 oz (250 g) dark chocolate, chopped

2/3 cup (150 ml) whipping cream

2 gelatin sheets

5 Tbsps white rum

2 egg whites

2 Tbsps sugar, salt

Decoration

2 small baskets of strawberries, hulled and sliced

Preparation time 15 minutes

Cooking time 5 minutes

Level easy

1. Melt the chocolate over a double boiler. Remove from the heat and let cool. Whip the cream and fold it into the chocolate.

2. Soak the gelatin in cold water. Drain and squeeze out the excess water. Add the gelatin and the rum to the chocolate mixture.

3. Beat the egg whites with a pinch of salt until foamy. Add the sugar and beat to stiff peaks. Fold the egg whites into the mousse. Refrigerate for 4 hours and decorate with sliced strawberries.

PASTRY CHEF'S TIP

Mousse is one of the many cooking terms borrowed from the French. It usually describes a soft light cream made with eggs, either sweet or savory.

Mini Yogurt Mousses
with Orange

Serves 4

Mousse

2/3 cup (150 ml) rice milk

2 tsps agar agar

2/3 cup (4 oz or 120 g) sugar

1 ½ cups (12 ½ oz or 350 g) low-fat yogurt

2 Tbsps orange marmalade

Preparation time 10 minutes
Cooking time 5 minutes
Level easy

1 Heat the rice milk over low heat, add the agar agar and stir until dissolved. Add the sugar and let cool. Stir in the yogurt.

2 Pour the mixture into a rectangular container and freeze.

3 Puree the orange marmalade and pour it over the frozen yogurt mixture. Refrigerate for 3 hours. Cut into cubes or ovals and serve.

PASTRY CHEF'S TIP

Agar agar is a thickening agent made from algae derivatives and is frequently used in Asian cuisine. It can be used as a substitute for animal-based gelatin and is available in powder, flakes or tablets.

Milk Chocolate Mousse

Serves 6

Mousse

5 ½ oz (150 g) milk chocolate

3 Tbsps sugar

8 Tbsps water

2 egg whites

1 ½ gelatin sheets

2 Tbsps instant coffee granules

1 ¾ cups (400 ml) whipping cream

Preparation time 20 minutes

Cooking time 5 minutes

Level easy

Pastry Chef's Tip

The secret to a perfect mousse is its lightness. It is important to add the ingredients to the egg whites gradually and in small quantities. Make sure to use a gentle folding technique when incorporating ingredients into the egg whites, being careful not to lose the airy consistency.

1 Shave a few spoonfuls of chocolate and set aside. Roughly chop the remaining chocolate. Heat the sugar in a small saucepan with 6 tablespoons of water and cook over low heat until the liquid becomes thick and syrupy. When the syrup comes to a boil, remove from the heat and set aside.

2 Beat the egg whites until they begin to form peaks. Slowly pour the sugar syrup into the egg whites, beating continuously, until all of the syrup has been incorporated. Continue to beat the egg whites until the mixture has cooled and the whites form stiff peaks. Soak the gelatin sheets in cold water.

3 Meanwhile, melt the chocolate over a double boiler or in the microwave. Heat the remaining 2 tablespoons of water and add the instant coffee. Stir to dissolve. Drain the gelatin sheets and squeeze out the excess water. Add to the coffee and stir to dissolve. Add the coffee mixture to the egg whites and then fold in the melted chocolate. Whip the cream and fold it into the chocolate mixture. Spoon the mousse into 6 coffee or tea cups. Cover with plastic wrap and refrigerate for 1 hour. Top the mousse with the reserved chocolate shavings and serve.

Chocolate Tiramisù

Serves 4

Tiramisù

8 ladyfingers

7 Tbsps (100 ml) egg liqueur (such as Vov)

3 oz (80 g) milk chocolate, chopped

4 Tbsps whipping cream

4 egg yolks

2 Tbsps sugar

1 Tbsp sweet Marsala wine

2 oz (60 g) mascarpone

Garnish

1 Tbsp instant coffee granules

wafer cookies (optional)

Preparation time 40 minutes
Cooking time 20 minutes
Level easy

1 Slice the ladyfingers in half and soak them in the egg liqueur. Line 4 glass bowls or cups with the ladyfingers.

2 Meanwhile, melt the chocolate and cream over a double boiler or in the microwave. Let cool, and when tepid, pour the chocolate sauce over the ladyfingers.

3 Beat the egg yolks and the sugar in a round-bottomed bowl over a double boiler over medium heat. When the mixture is thick and foamy, pour over the Marsala and continue beating until the mixture has tripled in volume. Remove from the heat and immerse the pan in a cold water bath to stop the cooking. Fold in the mascarpone and spoon the sauce over the chocolate. Let sit for 5 minutes and then sprinkle with the instant coffee. Decorate with wafer cookies if desired.

Pastry Chef's Tip

Mascarpone pairs well with chocolate thanks to its thick consistency and high fat content.

Vanilla Tiramisù

Serves 4

Cake

3/4 cup (200 ml) water

3 Tbsps sugar

5 Tbsps Alchermes

1 round of sponge cake
(see p. 38)

Cream

1 cup (250 ml) milk

1 vanilla bean,
sliced in half lengthwise

2 egg yolks

1/3 cup (2 oz or 60 g) sugar

3 Tbsps all-purpose flour

2 oz (50 g) robiola cheese

2 oz (50 g) ricotta

5 Tbsps whipping cream

Decoration

amaretto cookies

Preparation time 25 minutes

Cooking time 5 minutes

Level easy

1. Heat the milk with the vanilla bean. Beat the egg yolks with the sugar and sift in the flour. Whisk in the hot milk and return to the saucepan. Cook over low heat until the cream thickens. Remove the vanilla bean, pour into a bowl and let cool. Add the robiola and ricotta and mix until creamy. Whip the whipping cream to stiff peaks and fold into the pastry cream.

2. Bring the water and sugar to a boil and add the Alchermes. Remove from the heat and cool. Soak the sponge cake in the cooled syrup. Cut the sponge cake into rounds that fit into the serving dishes.

3. Layer the sponge cake and pastry cream in the serving dishes. Top with crumbled amaretto cookies and refrigerate for at least 30 minutes before serving.

Chocolate Zuccotto

Serves 6

Zuccotto

2 sponge cake rounds
(see p. 38)

3/4 cup plus 1 Tbsp (200 ml)
sweet liqueur or Vin Santo

4 oz (120 g) dark chocolate

2 cups (500 ml)
whipping cream

1 cup (7 oz or 200 g) sugar

1/3 cup (1 oz or 30 g)
cocoa powder

Decoration

chocolate shavings (optional)

Preparation time 40 minutes
Level medium

1 Cut 1 sponge cake into strips and use them to line a bombe mold. Pour half of the sweet liqueur or Vin Santo over the sponge cake to moisten.

2 Shave the chocolate with a sharp knife. Beat the whipping cream with the sugar and divide it between 2 bowls. Add the chocolate shavings to one of the bowls and stir to combine. Add the cocoa powder to the second bowl.

3 Fill the zuccotto with alternating layers of the two creams. Moisten the second round of sponge cake with the remaining liqueur or Vin Santo and place it on top of the zuccotto. Cover with plastic wrap and freeze for 3-4 hours. Unmold and decorate, if desired, with chocolate shavings.

4 The name of this typical Italian dessert comes from the word zucca, meaning pumpkin, and refers to its rounded shape.

Bread Pudding
with Marsala and Raisins

Serves 6

Cream

1 ¾ cups (400 ml) milk

3/4 cup plus 1 Tbsp (200 ml) whipping cream

2 tsps vanilla extract

4 egg yolks

2/3 cups (4 oz or 120 g) sugar

1 tsp cornstarch

2 Tbsps raisins

2 Tbsps Marsala wine

12 ½ oz (350 g) brioche bread

butter

Preparation time 15 minutes
Cooking time 20 minutes
Level easy

1 Preheat the oven to 350°F (180°C or Gas Mark 4). Heat the milk, cream and vanilla extract in a saucepan.

2 Beat the egg yolks with the sugar and add the cornstarch. Whisk in the milk mixture and return to the saucepan. Cook over low heat until the cream coats the back of a spoon.

3 Remove from heat and let cool. Soak the raisins in the Marsala wine and a little water.

4 Dice the brioche bread and use it to line the bottom of 6 buttered ramekins. Divide the raisins and their soaking liquid between the ramekins. Top with any remaining brioche bread. Pour the pastry cream into the ramekins. Bake for 12 minutes and serve.

Neapolitan-Style Trifle

Serves 6

Trifle

1 ⅓ lb (600 g) sponge cake
(see p. 38)

3/4 cup (60 ml) rum

10 ½ oz (300 g) ricotta

3/4 cup (5 ½ oz or 150 g) sugar

2 oz (60 g) extra-dark
chocolate, finely chopped

1 tsp vanilla extract

Decoration

3 egg whites

2 ½ Tbsps confectioners' sugar

colored sprinkles

Preparation time 40 minutes
Level easy

1. Cut the sponge cake horizontally into layers. Brush each layer with the rum. The cake should be moist and very soft. Stir the ricotta, sugar, chocolate and vanilla together. Mix well to combine.

2. Place a little sponge cake at the bottom of 6 small glass bowls. Top with a layer of the ricotta cream. Continue making alternating layers until all of the ingredients have been used up.

3. Beat the egg whites until they form stiff peaks. Carefully fold in the confectioners' sugar. Spread a layer of the meringue over the trifles, top with the colored sprinkles and refrigerate overnight.

PASTRY CHEF'S TIP

Ladyfingers may be used in place of the sponge cake. The trifle may be sprinkled with freshly ground cinnamon for added flavor.

Italian Chocolate Trifle

Serves 4

Trifle

1/3 cup (2 oz or 60 g) sugar

3/4 cup plus 1 Tbsp (200 ml) hot water

4 Tbsps Alchermes liqueur

10 ½ oz (300 g) sponge cake (see p. 38)

2 ½ oz (70 g) dark chocolate, chopped

Cream

2 egg yolks

1/3 cup plus 1 Tbsp (2 oz or 80 g) sugar

1 tsp vanilla

1/4 cup (1 oz or 30 g) all-purpose flour

1 cup (250 ml) milk

Preparation time 35 minutes

Cooking time 10 minutes

Level easy

1 Beat the egg yolks and sugar together until thick and creamy. Add the vanilla and flour.

2 Heat the milk in a saucepan. Whisk the hot milk into the egg mixture. Return to the saucepan and cook over low heat for at least 5 minutes.

3 Dissolve the sugar for the trifle in the hot water, add the Alchermes and let cool. Brush the sponge cake rounds with the Alchermes syrup.

4 Melt the chocolate over a double boiler. Make layers of the sponge cake, pastry cream and chocolate in a trifle bowl. Refrigerate for 2 hours before serving.

Mocha Panna Cottas

Serves 6

Panna cottas

3/4 cup plus 1 Tbsp (200 ml) milk

3/4 cup plus 1 Tbsp (200 ml) whipping cream

3 Tbsps sugar

2 gelatin sheets

1/4 cup (60 ml) sweetened espresso coffee

7 oz (200 g) dark chocolate, finely chopped

Preparation time 20 minutes
Cooking time 10 minutes
Level easy

1 Bring the milk, cream and sugar to a boil in a saucepan. Soak the gelatin in cold water for a few minutes, then drain and squeeze out excess water.

2 Add the gelatin and espresso to the milk mixture. Mix well and let cool slightly. Whisk the chocolate into the milk mixture.

3 Stir until the chocolate melts. Pour the mixture into 8 ramekins lined with plastic wrap. Refrigerate for 3 hours. Unmold the panna cottas and serve.

PASTRY CHEF'S TIP

For a softer panna cotta, do not heat the cream with the milk. Instead, whip the cream, and after the chocolate has been added, let the mixture cool in the refrigerator, then fold in the whipped cream. Then pour the mixture into the ramekins.

Lemon Panna Cottas
with Raspberry Coulis

Serves 6

Panna cotta

3 gelatin sheets

2 cups (500 ml) whipping cream

6 ½ Tbsps sugar

1 vanilla bean, halved lengthwise

zest of 1 organic lemon

Raspberry Coulis

7 oz (200 g) raspberries

1/2 cup (3 ½ oz or 100 g) sugar

Decoration

a few mint leaves

1 organic lemon

Preparation time 15 minutes

Cooking time 15 minutes

Level easy

1 Soak the gelatin in a little cold water until soft. Meanwhile, heat the cream with the sugar, vanilla bean and lemon zest for 5 minutes. Remove from the heat and strain the cream.

2 Drain the gelatin, squeeze out the excess water and dissolve it in the hot cream. Pour the mixture into individual ramekins and refrigerate for 2-3 hours.

3 Puree the raspberries together with the sugar. Strain the puree to eliminate the seeds.

4 Unmold the panna cottas onto individual serving plates and decorate with the raspberry coulis. Garnish with the mint leaves and julienned lemon zest.

Pastry Chef's Tip

To keep the cream a pure white color, add the sugar after removing the cream from the heat.

Pastry Cream
with Almond Brittle

Serves 4

Pastry Cream

2 cups (500 ml) milk

4 egg yolks

1/2 cup (3 ½ oz or 100 g) sugar

1/2 cup (2 oz or 60 g)
all-purpose flour

Almond Brittle

1 ½ cups (5 ½ oz or 150 g)
slivered almonds

1/4 cup (2 oz or 50 g) sugar

3 Tbsps water

salt

Preparation time 15 minutes
Cooking time 15 minutes
Level easy

1 Toast the slivered almonds in the oven or in a non-stick frying pan for 5 minutes. Line a baking sheet with parchment paper.

2 Let the sugar and water caramelize over medium heat. Add the almonds and pour the mixture onto the baking sheet. Smooth the brittle into a thin layer using a buttered spatula. Let cool.

3 Bring the milk to a simmer in a saucepan. Beat the egg yolks with the sugar. Sift in the flour. Whisk in the hot milk and then return to the saucepan. Cook over low heat, stirring constantly, until the cream thickens. Let cool.

4 Pour the pastry cream into small serving bowls and refrigerate. Chop the brittle into small pieces and use it to garnish the cooled pastry cream.

Pastry Chef's Tip

To prevent the caramel from crystallizing, add a few drops of lemon juice to the sugar syrup when the syrup reaches 275°F (140°C).

Champagne Cream with Raspberries

Serves 4

Champagne Cream

1 cup (250 ml) Champagne

1 egg plus 2 egg yolks

1/3 cup (2 oz or 60 g) sugar

3/4 cup plus 1 Tbsp (200 ml) whipping cream

Raspberry Sauce

1 basket of raspberries

2 Tbsps raw sugar

Garnish

1 basket of raspberries

Preparation time 20 minutes
Cooking time 5 minutes
Level easy

1. Reduce the Champagne in a small pan over low heat for 3-4 minutes.

2. Meanwhile, beat the egg yolks with the egg and add the sugar. Whisk in the Champagne reduction and transfer to a double boiler. Cook over low heat, whisking constantly until the sauce is thick and foamy. Let cool.

3. Whip the whipping cream to stiff peaks and fold into the Champagne mixture. Puree the raspberries for the sauce with the raw sugar and strain to remove the seeds.

4. Layer the cream and raspberry puree (reserving some for garnish) in 4 glass bowls or martini glasses and refrigerate until firm. Decorate with a drizzle of raspberry puree and the remaining raspberries.

PASTRY CHEF'S TIP

Try substituting the raspberries with the same quantity of strawberries for a slight variation. For a layered effect, cook the raspberry puree for 5 minutes and then whisk in 2 Tbsps (1 ½ oz or 40 g) of butter. Layer the raspberry sauce with the Champagne cream, freezing the dessert briefly before adding each next layer.

Red Wine
and Cherry Parfait

Serves 4

Parfaits

1 ½ lb (700 g) cherries
1/2 cup (3 ½ oz or 100 g) sugar
1/2 cup (120 ml) red wine
1 clove
zest of 1/2 organic lemon
7 Tbsps (100 ml) whipped cream

Preparation time 10 minutes
Cooking time 10 minutes
Level easy

1 Pit the cherries and place in a saucepan with the sugar, red wine, clove and lemon zest. Bring the mixture to a boil and cook over medium heat for about 10 minutes. Remove from the heat and let cool completely.

2 Divide the cooked cherries between 4 glasses or small glass serving bowls. Top the cherries with 1 tablespoon of the cooking liquid and a dollop of whipped cream. Decorate, if desired, with cherries.

PASTRY CHEF'S TIP
Try substituting the whipped cream with vanilla ice cream.

Strawberry Parfait
with Yogurt Cream

Serves 4

Parfaits

6 ½ oz (180 g) strawberries, hulled

1 Tbsp sugar

10 ladyfingers

1 ⅔ cups (14 oz or 400 g) plain low-fat yogurt

2 Tbsps vanilla-flavored confectioners' sugar

1/2 cup (120 ml) whipping cream

Decoration

4 strawberries

dark chocolate shavings

hazelnuts, finely chopped (optional)

Preparation time 25 minutes

Level easy

1. Puree the strawberries with the sugar and set aside. Cut the ladyfingers into pieces. Whip the yogurt together with the confectioners' sugar; beat the whipping cream to stiff peaks and fold it into the yogurt mixture using a silicon spatula.

2. Soak the ladyfinger pieces in the strawberry puree. Layer them and the yogurt cream into 4 glass bowls. Decorate the parfaits with sliced strawberries, dark chocolate shavings and finely chopped hazelnuts if desired. Refrigerate until firm and serve cold.

White Chocolate Sabayon
with Mixed Berries

Serves 4

Sabayon

4 egg yolks

2 Tbsps sugar

2 ½ oz (70 g) white chocolate, chopped

7 oz (200 g) mixed berries (raspberries, strawberries, blackberries, currants, blueberries)

Preparation time 20 minutes
Cooking time 15 minutes
Level easy

1. Beat the egg yolks and sugar over a double boiler.

2. Cook the mixture, stirring vigorously with a whisk.

3. Meanwhile melt the white chocolate. Slowly pour the melted chocolate into the egg mixture and continue beating until doubled in volume.

4. Place the berries in 4 martini glasses and top with the white chocolate sabayon sauce. Serve immediately.

PASTRY CHEF'S TIP

For an elegant variation, replace the white chocolate with the same quantity of dark chocolate.

Chantilly Cream Cups
with Chocolate Cookies

Serves 4

Cups

4 egg yolks

2/3 cup (4 ½ oz or 125 g) sugar

1 tsp vanilla extract

6 ½ Tbsps all-purpose flour

2 cups (500 ml) milk

3 Tbsps whipping cream

5 ½ oz (150 g) semi-sweet chocolate

15-20 langues-de-chat cookies (or other thin cookies)

1 Tbsp pine nuts, toasted

Preparation time 25 minutes
Cooking time 15 minutes
Level medium

1 Beat the egg yolks with a whisk until foamy and then add the sugar and vanilla and mix well. Add the flour and mix well.

2 Bring milk to a boil in a saucepan. Whisk the boiling hot milk into the egg mixture. Return the mixture to the saucepan and cook over low heat for 5 minutes to thicken. Remove from the heat, pour into a bowl and refrigerate. Whip the cream and refrigerate.

3 Melt the chocolate over a double boiler and dip the langues-de-chat in the chocolate. Let them cool on a tray lined with parchment paper. Reserve some melted chocolate for decorating.

4 When the pastry cream is cool, fold in the whipped cream with a wooden spoon. Layer the chantilly cream and the remaining melted chocolate in dessert cups or small bowls. Top with toasted pine nuts and serve with the chocolate-coated cookies.

PASTRY CHEF'S TIP

In cooking and baking, the term thicken means to increase the density of a sauce, soup or other liquid by cooking off liquid or by adding a thickener such as cornstarch, butter, cream or egg yolks.

Basil Chantilly Cream
with Raspberries

Serves 6

Cream

2 cups (500 ml) milk

zest of 1 organic lemon

12 basil leaves

2 egg yolks

1/2 cup plus 1 Tbsp (4 oz or 110 g) sugar

1/3 cup (1 ½ oz or 40 g) all-purpose flour

1 basket of raspberries

1 cup (250 ml) water

9 ladyfingers

3 Tbsps whipping cream

Preparation time 30 minutes
Cooking time 25 minutes
Level easy

1 Heat the milk with the lemon zest. Add the basil and let sit for 2 hours. Strain the milk and bring to a boil. Beat the egg yolks with 1/2 cup (3 ½ oz or 100 g) of sugar and then sift in the flour. Whisk in the boiling milk and transfer the mixture back to the saucepan. Cook over low heat for 10 minutes. Remove from the heat and let cool.

2 Place the raspberries, water and 1 tablespoon of sugar in a small saucepan and cook over low heat. When the sugar begins to caramelize remove from the heat and puree the mixture. Whip the whipping cream to stiff peaks and fold it into the cooled pastry cream.

3 Dip the ladyfingers in the raspberry sauce. Pour the remaining raspberry sauce into a trifle bowl, line the bowl with the ladyfingers and top with the Chantilly cream.

Layered Mascarpone
and Chocolate Creams

Serves 6

Cream

2 eggs, separated

1 egg yolk

1 cup (7 oz or 200 g) sugar

7 oz (200 g) mascarpone

1 Tbsp brandy

2 oz (60 g) dark chocolate

1 gelatin sheet

Preparation time 20 minutes

Cooking time 5 minutes

Level easy

1. Beat the egg yolks together with the sugar until thick and foamy. Add the mascarpone and mix until smooth. Add the brandy. Beat the egg whites to stiff peaks and fold into the mascarpone mixture.

2. Divide the cream between 2 bowls. Melt the chocolate over a double boiler. Soak the gelatin sheet in a little cold water for a few minutes, drain and squeeze out any excess liquid. Add the gelatin to the melted chocolate and let cool slightly. Fold the chocolate mixture into one of the bowls of mascarpone cream.

3. Chill 6 small bowls or cups and fill half full with the chocolate cream. Top with the mascarpone cream and chill before serving, if desired with ladyfingers or other small cookies.

Brown Rice Pudding
with Apples and Chocolate

Serves 4

Cream

2 Golden Delicious apples

2 Tbsps raw sugar

1/2 cup (3 ½ oz or 100 g) brown rice

2 cups (500 ml) milk

2 Tbsps sugar

1 Tbsp honey

2 Tbsps whipping cream

2 ½ oz (70 g) dark chocolate, chopped

1 banana, sliced

Preparation time 30 minutes
Cooking time 45 minutes
Level easy

1 Preheat the oven to 350°F (180°C or Gas Mark 4). Peel, core and thinly slice the apples. Line a baking tray with parchment paper.

2 Place the apple slices on the tray and sprinkle them with the raw sugar. Bake for 20 minutes. Blend the uncooked rice in a food processor until it resembles a coarse meal.

3 In a small saucepan bring the ground rice, milk and sugar to a simmer and cook for about 20 minutes, adding water if necessary. Puree the cooked rice with the honey and let cool.

4 Heat the cream and add the chocolate, stirring until the mixture is smooth. Cut the cooked apple into pieces. Layer the apple, banana, rice pudding and chocolate sauce in individual serving bowls. Refrigerate for 30 minutes and serve.

White Chocolate Crème brûlée

Serves 6

Crème brûlée

1 ¾ cups (400 ml)
whipping cream

1 vanilla bean,
halved lengthwise

4 ½ oz (130 g) white
chocolate, chopped

6 egg yolks

6 ½ Tbsps raw cane sugar

Preparation time 25 minutes
Cooking time 15 minutes
Level medium

1 Heat the cream and the vanilla bean in a small saucepan. Once the cream begins to simmer, remove from the heat, and using a small knife, scrape the seeds out of the vanilla bean and into the cream. Discard the bean.

2 Melt the chocolate over a double boiler or in a microwave, stirring frequently. Remove from the heat and stir in the egg yolks one at a time.

3 Whisk in the hot cream, transfer the mixture to a saucepan and return to the stove. Cook the mixture until it begins to thicken and coats the back of a spoon.

4 Strain the mixture and pour it into 6 ramekins. Refrigerate overnight. Before serving, sprinkle the crème brûlées with raw cane sugar and caramelize the sugar using a kitchen blow-torch or by placing the ramekins under a preheated broiler for a few minutes. Serve immediately.

Chocolate Crème brûlée

Serves 6

Crème brûlée

3/4 cup plus 1 Tbsp (200 ml) whipping cream

7 Tbsps (100 ml) milk

2 egg yolks

3 Tbsps sugar

1 tsp cornstarch

2 drops of hazelnut extract

3 oz (80 g) extra-dark chocolate, chopped

1 Tbsp raw cane sugar

Preparation time 25 minutes
Cooking time 15 minutes
Level easy

PASTRY CHEF'S TIP

If using the broiler to finish the crème brûlées, it is best to place the ramekins in a baking dish filled with cold water and broil until the sugar has caramelized. This way the heat from the grill will not overcook the crème brûlées.

1 Heat the cream and milk in a saucepan without boiling. Beat the egg yolks and the sugar in a mixing bowl. Add the cornstarch and hazelnut extract. Slowly whisk in the warm milk mixture. Transfer to a double boiler and make sure that the water never comes to a boil.

2 Cook the cream until it coats the back of a spoon. Add the chopped chocolate and stir to combine. Remove from the heat and pour into 4 ceramic ramekins. Refrigerate until ready to serve. Preheat the broiler.

3 Sprinkle the crème brûlées with the raw cane sugar and broil until the sugar caramelizes. Serve immediately.

Crema Catalana

Serves 4

Cream

2 cups (500 ml) milk
zest of 1/2 organic lemon
1 cinnamon stick
4 eggs, separated
1/2 cup (3 ½ oz or 100 g) sugar
2 Tbsps cornstarch
4 Tbsps raw sugar
grated nutmeg

Preparation time 20 minutes
Cooking time 15 minutes
Level medium

1 Bring the milk to a boil with the lemon zest and cinnamon stick and simmer for 10 minutes. Strain the milk.

2 Beat the egg yolks with the sugar and sift in the cornstarch. Add 2 tablespoons of the hot milk and whisk to combine. Whisk in the remaining milk and return to the saucepan. Cook over low heat, stirring constantly, for 5 minutes or until the cream thickens. Take care not to let the cream boil. Pour the mixture into 4 ramekins and refrigerate for 12 hours.

3 Remove the ramekins from the refrigerator just before serving and sprinkle with 1 tablespoon each of raw sugar and a grating of nutmeg. Place under a preheated broiler for a few minutes to caramelize the sugar. Let cool for a few minutes before serving.

PASTRY CHEF'S TIP

For a rich variation, add a few tablespoons of dark chocolate shavings and minced hazelnuts to the hot cream.

Frozen Yogurt Parfait
with Peaches and Red Currants

Serves 4

Parfaits

4 ripe peaches, peeled and diced

2 tsps freshly squeezed lemon juice

2 Tbsps raw sugar

10 ½ oz (300 g) plain frozen yogurt

3/4 cup plus 1 Tbsp (200 ml) milk

3-4 ice cubes

Decoration

1 basket of red currants

Preparation time 20 minutes

Level easy

1 Place the peaches in a non-metallic mixing bowl. Sprinkle over the lemon juice and raw sugar. Cover and let sit for 20 minutes. Puree the frozen yogurt with the milk and ice cubes in a blender for about 1 minute.

2 Place the peaches, with a little of their liquid, in the bottom of 4 glasses. Pour over the yogurt mixture and top with the red currants, if desired. Serve immediately.

Milk Chocolate Pots de Crème

Serves 6

Pots de Crème

1/2 vanilla bean, halved lengthwise

1 ½ cups plus 2 Tbsps (375 ml) milk

2 ½ oz (70 g) milk chocolate, chopped

2/3 cups (150 ml) whipping cream

3 egg yolks

1/2 cup (3 ½ oz or 100 g) sugar

Decoration

4 Tbsps cocoa powder

whipped cream

1 oz (30 g) dark chocolate, shaved

Preparation time 30 minutes
Cooking time 30 minutes
Level easy

PASTRY CHEF'S TIP

For an even prettier presentation, use heat-resistant glass cups instead of ramekins.

1. Preheat the oven to 325°F (170°C or Gas Mark 3). Place the vanilla bean in a saucepan with the milk. Bring to a simmer and remove from heat. Let the milk infuse for 10 minutes and then remove the vanilla bean. Add the chocolate and then the cream. Stir until the chocolate is melted and set aside.

2. Beat the egg yolks with the sugar until thick and pale yellow. Slowly whisk the chocolate mixture into the eggs.

3. Pour the chocolate cream into 6 ramekins and place them in a baking dish. Fill the baking dish half full of hot water and bake for 30 minutes, or until the cream has just set. Let the pots de crème cool and then decorate with cocoa powder, whipped cream and chocolate shavings.

Mini Chocolate Cakes
with Strawberry Centers

Serves 4

Cake

2 oz (50 g) extra-dark chocolate
(70% cocoa content)

1 Tbsp whipping cream

3 ½ Tbsps (2 ½ oz or 70 g)
strawberry jam

3 ½ oz (100 g) dark chocolate
(50 % cocoa content)

3 Tbsps (3 oz or 80 g) butter

2 eggs

6 Tbsps sugar

2 Tbsps all-purpose flour

Preparation time 15 minutes
Cooking time 15 minutes
Level medium

1 Preheat the oven to 400°F (200°C or Gas Mark 6). Melt the extra-dark chocolate with the cream over a double boiler. Add the strawberry jam and mix well. Transfer to the freezer and let harden slightly.

2 Melt the remaining chocolate with the butter and let cool slightly. Beat the eggs and sugar until thick and creamy. Fold in the chocolate and butter mixture.

3 Butter and flour 6 ramekins. Fill the ramekins two-thirds full with the chocolate batter. Remove the chocolate-strawberry mixture from the freezer. Scoop out 6 balls using a melon baller and drop one ball into the center of each ramekin. Top with the remaining batter. Bake for 12 minutes. Cool slightly and invert onto serving plates.

Pastry Chef's Tip

For a delicious winter dessert, substitute the strawberry jam with a chestnut or hazelnut cream or fill the center with white chocolate for a beautiful contrast.

Caramelized Pumpkin Soufflés

Serves 4

Soufflés

9 oz (250 g) pumpkin,
peeled and diced

3/4 cup (5 ½ oz or 150 g) sugar

butter

1 cup (250 ml) whipped cream

1 vanilla bean,
halved lengthwise

2 Tbsps rum

salt

2 eggs

Decoration

fresh mint leaves

Preparation time 20 minutes
Cooking time 1 hour 15 minutes
Level medium

1. Preheat the oven to 375°F (190°C or Gas Mark 5). Bake the pumpkin for about 30 minutes. Transfer to a blender and puree until smooth. Place 1/2 cup (3 ½ oz or 100 g) of sugar and 1 tablespoon of water in a saucepan and cook over low heat until the mixture turns an amber-brown color. Pour the caramel into 4 buttered ramekins and turn the ramekins so that the caramel coats the bottom and sides. Heat the cream with the vanilla bean.

2. Remove from the heat, remove the vanilla bean and add the remaining sugar, rum and the pumpkin puree. Stir in a pinch of salt. Beat the eggs until foamy, add 3 tablespoons of the pumpkin mixture and stir to combine. Pour the egg mixture into the pumpkin mixture and stir.

3. Divide the batter between the ramekins. Bake in a water bath in at 350°F (180°C or Gas Mark 4) for about 45 minutes. Let cool and refrigerate until ready to serve. Unmold the soufflés onto individual serving plates and decorate with the mint leaves.

PASTRY CHEF'S TIP

For a more flavorful variation, substitute the vanilla bean with a few pinches of freshly ground nutmeg. To make sure that the pumpkin stays moist while baking, wrap it in a piece of aluminum foil.

Almond Rice Pudding

Serves 4

Soufflés

1 ¼ cups (9 oz or 250 g)
Originario rice
(or short-grain risotto rice)

3 cups (750 ml) milk

1/2 cup (125 ml)
whipping cream

4 Tbsps (2 oz or 50 g)
butter, melted

1/2 cup (3 ½ oz or 100 g) sugar

2 Tbsps grappa

1/2 cup (2 ½ oz or 75 g)
almonds, chopped,
plus extra for garnish

Preparation time 30 minutes
Cooking time 45 minutes
Level easy

1. Cook the rice in the milk for 40 minutes. Remove from the heat and let sit for at least 10 minutes. Drain off any excess milk and stir in the cream, melted butter and sugar.

2. Add the grappa and puree the mixture in a food processor. Stir in the chopped almonds.

3. Pour the mixture into 4 ramekins and refrigerate for at least 2 hours. Serve the rice pudding cold topped with chopped almonds.

PASTRY CHEF'S TIP

Add a few drops of essential oil (cinnamon, mandarin, orange or eucalyptus) to the pudding mixture before chilling for added flavor.

Dark Chocolate Soufflés
with Basil Sabayon

Serves 4

Soufflés

9 oz (250 g) dark chocolate

6 eggs, separated

1 egg white

1/2 cup (3 ½ oz or 100 g) raw cane sugar

1 tsp vanilla extract

1/4 cup (1 oz or 25 g) cocoa powder

2 ½ Tbsps cornstarch, salt

1 pat of butter, all-purpose flour

Sabayon

3 egg yolks, 6 basil leaves

1/3 cup (2 oz or 60 g) sugar

2/3 cup (150 ml) whipping cream

Decoration

seeds of 1 ripe pomegranate

1/2 papaya, peeled and diced

Preparation time 20 minutes
Cooking time 30 minutes
Level medium

1 Preheat the oven to 350°F (180°C or Gas Mark 4). Make the soufflé: Melt the chopped chocolate over a double boiler. Beat the egg yolks with the sugar and the vanilla. Sift in the cocoa powder and cornstarch. Add the melted chocolate and mix well.

2 Beat the 7 egg whites and a pinch of salt to stiff peaks and carefully fold them into the egg mixture. Butter and flour 6 aluminum ramekins. Fill the ramekins three-quarters full with the soufflé batter and bake for 30 minutes. Cool the soufflés for at least 15 minutes.

3 Meanwhile, make the sabayon: Beat the egg yolks with the sugar. Whisk in the whipping cream and chopped basil leaves. Serve the soufflés with the sabayon on plates decorated with pomegranate seeds and diced papaya.

Chocolate-Pumpkin Soufflés

Serves 4

Soufflés

1/2 cup (2 oz or 60 g) diced pumpkin or other winter squash

4 large eggs, separated

1/2 cup (3 ½ oz or 100 g) raw cane sugar

1 Tbsp all-purpose flour

1/2 tsp vanilla extract

salt

5 Tbsps cocoa powder

7 Tbsps (3 ½ oz or 100 g) melted butter

Sauce

2 oz (60 g) extra-dark chocolate

2 Tbsps whipping cream

Preparation time 10 minutes
Cooking time 25 minutes
Level easy

1 Preheat the oven to 350°F (180°C or Gas Mark 4). Bake the pumpkin for 25 minutes. Meanwhile, beat the egg yolks until they are thick and pale yellow in color. Add the sugar, flour, vanilla and a pinch of salt. Mix well and add the cocoa powder and melted butter.

2 Mash or puree the cooked pumpkin and stir into the batter. Preheat the oven to 400°F (200°C or Gas Mark 6). Beat the egg whites and a pinch of salt to stiff peaks. Fold them into the soufflé batter.

3 Butter 4 ramekins and sprinkle them with sugar. Pour the batter into the ramekins and bake for 20-25 minutes. Meanwhile, melt the chocolate and whipping cream over a double boiler. Serve the soufflés with the chocolate sauce as soon as they come out of the oven.

Chocolate Roll

Serves 6

Cake

3 eggs

2/3 cup (5 oz or 135 g) sugar

4 Tbsps all-purpose flour, sifted

1/4 cup (1 oz or 25 g)
cocoa powder, sifted

Cream

1 ¼ cups (300 ml)
whipping cream

3 ½ oz (100 g) white chocolate

Preparation time 20 minutes
Cooking time 15 minutes
Level medium

1 Preheat the oven to 400°F (200°C or Gas Mark 6). Using an electric whisk, beat the eggs with 1/2 cup (3 ½ oz or 95 g) sugar. When the mixture lightens in color and begins to form ribbons, carefully fold in the sifted flour and cocoa powder. Pour the batter into a rectangular baking sheet lined with parchment paper.

2 Spread the batter with a spatula to form a uniform layer. Bake for 15 minutes. Meanwhile, place a clean kitchen towel on a work surface and top with paper towels. Sprinkle the remaining sugar over the paper towels. Invert the hot sponge cake onto the paper towels and roll up the sponge cake like a jelly roll.

3 Meanwhile melt the white chocolate over a double boiler or in a microwave. Whip the whipping cream to stiff peaks and fold in the melted white chocolate. Unroll the sponge cake, spread the chocolate cream over the cake and re-roll the cake. Cover the cake and refrigerate until firm. Slice the chocolate roll and serve.

Pastry Chef's Tip

The white chocolate for the filling may be substituted with 2/3 cup (150 ml) of sweetened condensed milk.

Mont Blanc

Serves 6

Mont Blanc

3 ¼ lb (1 ½ kg) chestnuts

1 cup (250 ml) milk

2 cups (14 oz or 400 g) sugar

1/2 cup plus 1 Tbsp (2 oz or 50 g) cocoa powder

2 Tbsps rum

Decoration

2 cups (500 ml) whipping cream

semi-sweet chocolate, shaved

Preparation time 25 minutes

Cooking time 45 minutes

Level easy

1 Boil the chestnuts for about 45 minutes. Drain and peel. Using a food mill, puree the chestnuts and set aside.

2 Heat the milk in a saucepan and stir in the sugar, cocoa powder and rum. Pour the mixture over the chestnuts and stir to combine.

3 Push the mixture through a potato ricer, letting the vermicelli-like strings fall directly onto a serving plate to form a mountain. Whip the cream and use it to cover the chestnut strings. Alternatively transfer the whipped cream to a pastry bag and form small puffs around the outside of the chestnut puree. Sprinkle with shaved chocolate and serve chilled.

Pastry Chef's Tip

Marrons glacé, whole or in small pieces, may be used to decorate the Mont Blanc along with candied violets and cherries. The dessert should be served chilled, but not too cold.

Concord Grape Jelly

Serves 4

Jelly

1 ½ cups (7 oz or 200 g)
Concord grapes

2 Tbsps sugar

2 tsps water

7 Tbsps (100 ml)
sweet Moscato wine
(or another sweet dessert wine)

1 tsp powdered agar agar

Decoration

whole Concord grapes

mint leaves

Preparation time 15 minutes
Cooking time 10 minutes
Level easy

1 Blend the grapes, sugar and water in a food processor.

2 Strain the mixture, pushing any larger pieces through the strainer with the back of a spoon.

3 Bring the wine to a simmer in a small saucepan. Remove from heat and dissolve the agar agar in the wine. Add the strained grape juice. Mix well.

4 Pour into 4 triangular, silicon molds or aluminum molds lined with plastic wrap.

5 Refrigerate for 2 hours. Invert the jellies onto individual serving plates and garnish with the Concord grapes and mint leaves.

Sauternes Jelly

Serves 4

Jelly

1 ¼ cups (300 ml)
Sauternes wine

1 tsp lemon juice

1 Tbsp sugar

1 tsp agar agar

Decoration

4 mint sprigs

4 blackberries

Preparation time 15 minutes
Cooking time 2 minutes
Level easy

1 Heat the wine in a saucepan over low heat. Add the lemon juice, sugar and agar agar powder. Dissolve, stirring frequently, and cook for 2 minutes until the liquid is smooth. Cut a sheet of wax paper into 4 triangles. Roll the triangle around a rolling pin to form a cylinder and tape it closed.

2 Place the wax paper cylinders in narrow glasses and pour the wine mixture into the wax-paper molds. Refrigerate until firm.

3 Remove the glasses from the refrigerator and unwrap the jelly. Place the jellies on a plate and decorate with mint sprigs and blackberries.

Pastry Chef's Tip

For a more flavorful version of this dessert, top the jellies with a few crumbled amaretto cookies. This jelly can also accompany creamy cheeses.

Strawberry Aspic

Serves 4

Aspic

5 gelatin sheets

1 ⅓ cups (320 ml)
Moscato Passito wine
(or another sweet dessert wine)

15 black peppercorns

9 basil leaves,
plus extra for garnish

10 ½ oz (300 g) strawberries

Preparation time 20 minutes
Cooking time 10 minutes
Level easy

1 Soak the gelatin in a little cold water. Pour the wine into a small saucepan and bring to a boil along with the peppercorns and 5 basil leaves. Remove from the heat and strain the liquid. Drain the gelatin and squeeze out any excess liquid. Add the gelatin to the wine and stir until dissolved.

2 Slice the strawberries and add half of them to the wine mixture. Place 1 basil leaf in the bottom of 4 individual ramekins. Pour a little of the wine mixture into the ramekins, refrigerate until firm and then divide the remaining wine mixture between the ramekins. Refrigerate for at least 2 hours.

3 Unmold the aspics onto serving plates and top with the remaining strawberries and basil leaves.

PASTRY CHEF'S TIP

When making gelatins or aspics do not freeze the gelatin as it may crystallize as it chills and then melt when it comes back to room temperature.

Mint Mousse Filled
with Coconut Cream
by **Stefano De Pietri**

Serves 6
Chocolate Wafers

6-7 egg yolks (4 oz
or 115 g in total)

1 cup plus 2 Tbsps (7 oz
or 225 g) sugar

5-6 egg whites (6 ½ oz
or 190 g in total)

7 Tbsps raw sugar

2/3 cup (2 ½ oz or 75 g)
all-purpose flour

1 cup (2 ½ oz or 75 g)
cocoa powder

Mint Mousse

1 ¾ lb (800 g) white
chocolate couverture

1 ¾ cups (400 ml) milk

1 handful of mint leaves

6 gelatin sheets, 2 Tbsps
mint liqueur

3 cups plus 2 Tbsps (800 ml)
whipping cream

Coconut Cream

1 gelatin sheet, 2 eggs

1 ⅔ cups (5 ½ oz or 150 g)
shredded coconut

5 egg yolks (3 oz or 85 g in total)

1/2 cup minus 1 Tbsp (3 oz
or 90 g) sugar

7 Tbsps (3 ½ oz or 100 g) butter

1 package of
granulated gelatin

Preparation time 50 minutes
Cooking time 30 minutes
Level difficult

1 Preheat the oven to 350°F (180°C or Gas Mark 4). Make the wafers: Beat the egg yolks with the sugar. Separately, beat the egg whites and raw sugar to stiff peaks. Fold the egg whites into the yolks and sift in the flour and cocoa powder. Line a rimmed baking sheet with parchment paper and pour in the batter. Bake for 15-18 minutes and then cool completely. Cut into 2-inch (4 cm) rounds and set aside.

2 Make the mousse: Soak the gelatin sheets in cold water. Melt the couverture over a double boiler. Bring the milk, mint leaves and mint liqueur to a boil. Remove from heat and add the drained gelatin. Whisk the milk into the couverture and add the cream. Set aside.

3 Make the coconut cream: Soak the gelatin in cold water for a few minutes and drain. Mix together the coconut, egg yolks, eggs, sugar and gelatin and cook over low heat until the mixture reaches 150°F (65°C). Remove from heat and cool to 95°F (35°C). Add the butter and mix well.

4 Pour the coconut cream into six 1 ½-inch (3 cm) diameter hemispherical silicon molds and freeze. Pour a third of the mint mousse into six 3-inch (8 cm) diameter hemispherical silicon molds and place an unmolded frozen coconut cream in the center of each mold. Fill with the remaining mousse and top with a cookie. Freeze for 4 hours. Unmold the mousses and glaze with the gelatin dissolved in a little water. Freeze for 12 hours.

Surprise Tiramisù

by **Francesco Elmi**

Serves 4

Base

4 ladyfingers

1 demitasse cup of prepared espresso coffee

Cream

3 Tbsps water

1 cup minus 1 Tbsp (6 ½ oz or 180 g) sugar

9 egg yolks (5 ½ oz or 150 g in total)

4 gelatin sheets

1 lb (500 g) mascarpone

1 cup (250 ml) whipping cream

1 ⅔ cups (380 ml) semi-whipped cream

Filling

4 Tbsps (60 ml) whipping cream

2/3 cup plus 1 Tbsp (160 ml) glucose syrup (or 2/3 cup or 4 ½ oz or 130 g sugar)

1/3 cup plus 1 Tbsp (1 oz or 30 g) cocoa powder

2 demitasse cups of prepared espresso coffee

1/2 cup plus 1 Tbsp (140 ml) water

Preparation time 50 minutes

Cooking time 20 minutes

Level medium

1. Make the cream: Bring the water and sugar to a boil until it thickens, forming a syrup. Beat the egg yolks in a standing mixer and slowly add the sugar syrup, beating continuously.

2. Soak the gelatin sheets in cold water, drain and squeeze out the excess liquid. Beat together the mascarpone and whipping cream until thick and soft. Pour a little cream over the gelatin to dissolve and add it to the semi-whipped cream. Fold the semi-whipped cream into the mascarpone mixture. Refrigerate until use.

3. Make the filling: Bring the cream and the glucose syrup or sugar to a boil. Add the cocoa powder and return to a boil. Add 2 demitasse cups of espresso and remove from heat. Transfer the mixture to a bowl and freeze.

4. Soak the ladyfingers in the espresso, then divide between 4 martini glasses or glass bowls. Top with a layer of the mascarpone cream and chill for 10 minutes. Spread a spoonful of the frozen espresso mixture over the cream and chill for another 10 minutes. Finish with a layer of mascarpone cream and sprinkle with cocoa powder. Top with dried fruit or coffee-flavored sugar if desired.

Vanilla Soufflés
with Saffron Peaches
by **Francesco Elmi**

Serves 4

Soufflés

4 Tbsps (2 oz or 65 g) butter

1/2 cup (2 oz or 65 g) all-purpose flour

1 cup (250 ml) milk

2 vanilla beans, halved lengthwise

1/3 cup (2 oz or 65 g) sugar

4 eggs, separated

Peaches

1 ¼ cups (9 oz or 250 g) sugar

2 cups (500 ml) water

1 lb (500 g) yellow peaches, peeled and sliced

1/2 cinnamon stick

1 pinch of saffron

4 Tbsps (2 oz or 60 g) butter

3/4 cup (5 ½ oz or 150 g) raw sugar

1/4 cup (60 ml) peach liqueur

Preparation time 40 minutes
Cooking time 25 minutes
Level medium

1 Prepare the peaches: Bring the sugar and water to a boil. Add the peaches, cinnamon stick and saffron and cook for 3-4 minutes. Remove from the heat and let infuse for 12 hours. Preheat the oven to 350°F (180°C or Gas Mark 4).

2 Drain the peaches and sauté them together with the butter and raw sugar. Pour over the peach liqueur and flambé the fruit. Remove from the heat and divide the peaches between 4 individual ramekins or soufflé cups.

3 Make the soufflés: Prepare a roux by melting the butter over medium heat and whisking in the flour. Cook the roux for a minute but do not let it color. Bring the milk to a boil with the vanilla beans. Remove from the heat, strain and whisk the milk into the roux. Continue to stir for a few minutes and then incorporate the egg yolks.

4 Beat the egg whites to stiff peaks and fold them into the soufflé base. Spoon the soufflé into the ramekins with the peaches, filling them three-quarters full. Bake for 10-12 minutes and serve immediately.

Nut Charlotte
with Pistachio, Chocolate and Coffee Creams
by **Roberto Rinaldini**

Serves 6
Cake
9 egg whites (10 ½ oz
or 300 g in total)
1 cup plus 1 ½ Tbsps (8 oz
or 220 g) sugar
1 ⅓ cup plus 1 Tbsp (6 oz
or 175 g) bread flour
1 cup (4 ½ oz or 125 g) cornstarch
11-12 egg yolks (7 oz
or 200 g in total)
3 ½ oz (100 g) mixed pine nuts,
pistachios and currants

Pistachio Cream
4-5 egg yolks (2 ½ oz
or 75 g in total)
1/3 cup (2 oz or 60 g) sugar
1 cup (250 ml) whipping cream
2 gelatin sheets
2 oz (60 g) pistachio paste

Chocolate Cream
4-5 egg yolks (2 ½ oz
or 75 g in total)
1/3 cup (2 oz or 60 g) sugar
1 cup (250 ml) whipping cream
5 oz (135 g) dark chocolate
couverture (72% cocoa content),
chopped and softened

Coffee Cream
2/3 cup (150 ml) Marsala wine
3/4 cup (5 ½ oz or 150 g) sugar
4 Tbsps espresso coffee
2/3 cup (150 ml) whipping cream
4 gelatin sheets
8 egg yolks (5 oz or 140 g in total)
1 ¾ cups (400 ml) whipped cream

Preparation time 40 minutes
Cooking time 25 minutes
Level difficult

1 Preheat the oven to 350°F (180°C or Gas Mark 4). Make the cake: Beat the egg whites until foamy and slowly add the sugar. Beat to stiff peaks. Sift the flour and cornstarch together. Fold the yolks into the whites and fold in the flour mixture. Pour the batter into baking sheet lined with parchment paper. Sprinkle with nuts and currants and bake for 7 minutes.

2 Make the pistachio cream: Mix the yolks, sugar and cream in a small saucepan and cook gently to 180°F (82°C). Transfer to a bowl and freeze to 95°F (35°C). Soak the gelatin in warm water and drain. Add the gelatin and pistachio paste (see p. 170) to the cooled cream and whisk until smooth. Make the chocolate cream: Follow the directions for the pistachio cream, adding softened chocolate instead of gelatin and pistachio paste. Make the coffee cream: Whisk together the Marsala wine, sugar, coffee and cream over a double boiler and cook to 180°F (82°C). Remove from the heat, transfer to a bowl and freeze to 95°F (35°C). Soak the gelatin in warm water, drain and mix into the cooled cream. Fold in the yolks and whipped cream.

3 Assemble the charlotte: Line a 5-inch-high stainless-steel, spring-form pan with strips of cake. Cut out a round of cake and fit it into the pan. Spread over the pistachio cream and freeze for 20 minutes. Make a layer of chocolate cream and freeze for 20 minutes. Finish with a layer of coffee cream and freeze for 20 minutes. Decorate with red currants, raspberries, pistachios and vanilla beans if desired.

Pavlova with Chantilly Cream
and Vanilla-Infused Berries
by **Roberto Rinaldini**

Serves 6

Meringue

5 egg whites

1 cup (7 oz or 200 g) sugar

1 Tbsp lemon juice

1 ⅔ cups (7 oz or 200 g) confectioners' sugar

Chantilly Cream

6 egg yolks (3 ½ oz or 100 g in total)

1/4 cup (2 oz or 50 g) sugar

2 Tbsps cornstarch

1 ¼ cup (300 ml) whipping cream

1/2 vanilla bean halved lengthwise

zest of 1 organic lemon

3/4 cup plus 1 Tbsp (200 ml) whipped cream

Fruit

7 Tbsps (100 ml) water

1/2 cup (3 ½ oz or 100 g) sugar

2 vanilla beans, halved lengthwise

7 oz (200 g) fresh raspberries

10 ½ oz (300 g) fresh strawberries, hulled and quartered

5 ½ oz (150 g) wild strawberries

Preparation time 40 minutes

Cooking time 8 hours

Level difficult

1 Preheat the oven to 175°F (80°C or Gas Mark 1/4). Make the meringue: Beat the egg whites in a standing mixer until foamy and slowly add the sugar and lemon juice. Continue beating until the egg whites form stiff peaks. Sift the confectioners' sugar and fold it into the egg whites using a spatula.

2 Transfer the meringue to a pastry bag and pipe out four 1-inch high rounds onto a baking sheet lined with parchment paper. Bake for 8 hours. Make the Chantilly cream: Beat the egg yolks and sugar until thick and sift in the cornstarch. Heat the whipping cream with the vanilla and lemon zest. Strain the cream and whisk it into the yolk mixture.

3 Return to the saucepan and cook until the mixture reaches 180°F (82°C). Cool the cream quickly and fold in the whipped cream. Make the fruit: Bring the water, sugar and vanilla beans to a boil. Let cook until syrupy and then cool.

4 Mix together the berries and pour over the cooled syrup. Let sit for 50 minutes. Strain the juice from the berries and pour it into shot glasses to serve as a pre-dessert drink. Reserve the berries. Compose the dessert by layering the meringues with the Chantilly cream and top with the berries.

techniques&recipes

Frozen Desserts

Semifreddos, sorbets and granitas made from fruit,
cream or chocolate are a cool, refreshing and delicious option.

1 Beat the egg yolks together with the sugar over a double boiler; mix until thick and foamy. Soak the gelatin in cold water, drain and dissolve in the mixture.

2 Beat the whipping cream into stiff peaks and carefully fold it into the yolk mixture.

3 Beat the egg whites to stiff peaks and fold into the mixture, folding from the bottom to the top to keep the airy consistency.

Serves 6
1 cup (7 oz or 200 g) sugar
4 eggs, separated
1 ¾ cups (400 ml) whipping cream
1 ½ gelatin sheets

SEMIFREDDO

Pastry Chef's Tip

This basic recipe may be modified as desired by adding various ingredients (the recipe photographed here uses this base with the addition of torrone). Transfer the batter to individual ramekins or molds lined with plastic wrap and freeze until firm.

Recipe on p. 310

1 Heat 2 cups (14 oz or 400 g) of sugar and the water in a saucepan and cook until it reaches 230°F (110°C) and the syrup is thick. In a standing mixture beat the egg whites together with the remaining 1/2 cup (3 ½ oz or 100 g) of sugar.

2 With the mixer running at medium speed, drizzle the syrup into the whites and continue mixing until the meringue is cool to the touch.

Serves 6
2 ½ cups
(1 lb 2 oz or 500 g) sugar
7 Tbsps (100 ml) water
12 egg whites
(14 oz or 400 g in total)

ITALIAN MERINGUES

Pastry Chef's Tip

Remember to watch the meringue topping carefully when broiling it, which should take no more than 2-3 minutes. A meringue-topped dessert should be lightly browned in parts. Dark brown or black meringue is an indication of overcooking.

Recipe on p. 313

Meringue with Fig
and White Chocolate Parfaits

Serves 4

Parfaits

2 oz (60 g) white chocolate, chopped

1/4 cup (60 ml) whipping cream

2 Tbsps milk

1 egg white

4 meringues (see p. 144)

6 ripe green figs

Preparation time 20 minutes
Cooking time 10 minutes
Level medium

1 Melt the white chocolate over a double boiler with the cream and milk, stirring until smooth. Let cool slightly. Beat the egg white and add it to the mixture.

2 Pour into a whipped cream canister (soda siphon), close, insert the gas cartridge and shake lightly. Place the canister in a pan of hot water (175°F or 80°C) to keep warm.

3 Crumble the meringues into the bottom of 4 small glasses.

4 Peel the figs and slice them into quarters using a paring knife. Place the fig quarters on top of the crushed meringues.

5 Top the parfaits with warm white-chocolate foam and serve immediately.

PASTRY CHEF'S TIP

A whipped cream canister, or siphon, similar to a seltzer bottle, is an insulated canister with an hermetic seal, usually made from stainless steel. It is double-walled and may be used to keep whipped cream, creams, sauces or cold foams at a constant temperature for up to 8 hours.

Meringue with Fig
and White Chocolate Parfaits

Serves 4

Parfaits

2 oz (60 g) white chocolate, chopped

1/4 cup (60 ml) whipping cream

2 Tbsps milk

1 egg white

4 meringues (see p. 144)

6 ripe green figs

Preparation time 20 minutes
Cooking time 10 minutes
Level medium

1 Melt the white chocolate over a double boiler with the cream and milk, stirring until smooth. Let cool slightly. Beat the egg white and add it to the mixture.

2 Pour into a whipped cream canister (soda siphon), close, insert the gas cartridge and shake lightly. Place the canister in a pan of hot water (175°F or 80°C) to keep warm.

3 Crumble the meringues into the bottom of 4 small glasses.

4 Peel the figs and slice them into quarters using a paring knife. Place the fig quarters on top of the crushed meringues.

5 Top the parfaits with warm white-chocolate foam and serve immediately.

PASTRY CHEF'S TIP

A whipped cream canister, or siphon, similar to a seltzer bottle, is an insulated canister with an hermetic seal, usually made from stainless steel. It is double-walled and may be used to keep whipped cream, creams, sauces or cold foams at a constant temperature for up to 8 hours.

Pastry Chef's Tip
For a lighter sorbet, substitute the whipping cream with 1 egg white beaten to stiff peaks and folded into the cooled syrup. For a smoother sorbet, add 2/3 cup (150 ml) of sparkling water to the cooled syrup.

Recipe on p. 324

1 Zest the lemons and juice them.

2 Dissolve the sugar in the water in a small saucepan over medium heat.

3 Cook until the liquid has a syrupy consistency. Add the lemon juice and cook for another 15 minutes. Let cool.

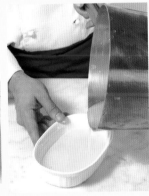

4 Whip the cream and add the cooled syrup. Mix to combine and then freeze for a few hours. Remove from the freezer and blend before serving.

5 Alternatively, omit the whipping cream and freeze the syrup, removing it from the freezer and stirring every 30 minutes, so that the mixture does not freeze solid.

Serves 4
2 organic lemons
3/4 cup plus 2 Tbsps
(6 oz or 170 g) sugar
3 ½ cups (850 ml) water
3/4 cup (200 ml)
whipping cream

SORBET

PASTRY CHEF'S TIP
Remember to watch the meringue topping carefully when broiling it, which should take no more than 2-3 minutes. A meringue-topped dessert should be lightly browned in parts. Dark brown or black meringue is an indication of overcooking.

Recipe on p. 313

Torrone Semifreddo
with Gianduia Sauce

Serves 4

Semifreddo

4 eggs, separated

1/2 cup (3 ½ oz or 100 g) sugar

1 ¾ cups (400 ml) whipping cream

salt

5 ½ oz (150 g) hazelnut torrone (nougat), finely chopped

1/2 tsp instant coffee granules

Sauce

2 Tbsps whipping cream

2 oz (50 g) gianduia chocolate (see p. 64)

Preparation time 20 minutes
Cooking time 5 minutes
Level easy

1. Beat the egg yolks and sugar in a mixing bowl. In another bowl, whip the whipping cream and then fold into the egg yolk mixture.

2. Beat the egg whites and a pinch of salt into stiff peaks and then fold into the eggs and cream. Carefully fold in three-quarters of the torrone and all the instant coffee.

3. Line 4 ramekins with foil and pour in the semifreddo. Freeze for at least 3 hours. Just before serving, heat the whipping cream and gianduia for the sauce until melted.

4. Unmold the semifreddos, drizzle with gianduia sauce and top with the remaining torrone.

Pastry Chef's Tip

For best results with semifreddos, beat the egg yolks and sugar over a double boiler until the mixture reaches 167°F (75°C). For a softer dessert, add 1 gelatin sheet, soaked and drained, to the whipped cream before folding it into the egg yolk base.

Pistachio Semifreddo

Serves 4

Semifreddo

1 ½ oz (40 g) extra-dark chocolate

4 Tbsps chocolate-flavored puffed rice

7 oz (200 g) pistachio ice cream

1/2 cup (120 ml) whipping cream

Decoration

4 blackcurrant or redcurrant sprigs

dark chocolate, shaved

Preparation time 25 minutes
Cooking time 3 minutes
Level medium

1 Line a baking sheet with plastic wrap. Place 4 individual spring-form molds (without the bottom) on the baking sheet.

2 Melt the chocolate over a double boiler. Pour the melted chocolate over the puffed rice and mix well. Place 1 tablespoon of the rice mixture in each spring-from mold. Use a spatula to make an even layer.

3 Place the ice cream in a bowl and mix it with a spatula until creamy. Whip the whipping cream and incorporate it into the ice cream. Fill the spring-from molds with the ice cream mixture and refrigerate for 30 minutes.

4 Remove from the refrigerator and unmold the semifreddos. Place each semifreddo on a serving plate and decorate with chocolate shavings and redcurrant sprigs, if desired.

PASTRY CHEF'S TIP

For extra flavor, mix 1 tablespoon Maraschino liqueur into the pistachio ice cream.

Pistachio Semifreddo
with Vanilla Sauce

Serves 6

Semifreddo

2 gelatin sheets

5 egg yolks (3 oz or 80 g in total)

3/4 cup plus 2 Tbsps (6 oz or 170 g) sugar

1 ¼ cups (5 ½ oz or 150 g) shelled pistachios

1/3 cup (2 oz or 50 g) pine nuts

1/3 cup (80 ml) water

1 ¾ cups (400 ml) whipping cream

3-4 egg whites (4 ozor 120 g in total)

Vanilla Sauce

1 ¾ cups (400 ml) whipping cream

4 egg yolks

1/4 cup (2 oz or 50 g) sugar

1/3 vanilla bean, halved lengthwise and seeds scraped out

Decoration

2 ½ cups (1 lb 2 oz or 500 g) sugar

1 ¼ cups (300 ml) glucose syrup

3/4 cup plus 1 Tbsp (200 ml) water

2 tsps rum

Preparation time 55 minutes
Cooking time 20 minutes
Level difficult

1. Make the semifreddo: Soak the gelatin in water, drain and squeeze out. Dissolve in a little warm water. Beat the yolks over a double boiler with 2/3 cup (4 oz or 120 g) of sugar until they reach 165°F (75°C) and are thick and foamy. Add the gelatin. Refrigerate at 40°F (6°C).

2. Toast the pistachios and pine nuts in a frying pan, add the remaining sugar and 1/3 cup (80 ml) of water and cook until golden-brown. Pour onto a sheet of wax paper. When cool, coarsely chop and fold into the cooled semifreddo. Whip the cream to stiff peaks and fold into the semifreddo. Beat the egg whites to stiff peaks and fold them in. Pour the mixture into 6 ramekins lined with plastic wrap and freeze.

3. Make the vanilla sauce: Heat the cream to 165°F (75°C). Beat the yolks with the sugar and the vanilla seeds. Add to the cream and cook over low heat, stirring constantly, until it reaches 180°F (82°C). Remove from the heat, cover with plastic wrap and freeze until cool.

4. Make the decoration: Heat the decoration ingredients in a saucepan until they reach 360°F (182°C). Drizzle thin threads of the mixture over the top of a small round stainless-steel bowl (see p. 380) and repeat 6 times to make 6 domes. Unmold the semifreddos and top with the sauce. Decorate with the domes.

Meringue-Topped Apple Sorbet

Serves 4

Sorbet

2 red apples

2/3 cup (4 ½ oz or 130 g) sugar

2 gelatin sheets

1 egg, separated

1 egg yolk

1 Tbsp Calvados or other apple brandy

Meringue

1 egg white

3 Tbsps sugar

6 ½ Tbsps confectioners' sugar

Preparation time 25 minutes
Cooking time 20 minutes
Level medium

PASTRY CHEF'S TIP

A kitchen torch may also be used to brown the meringue topping. For a caramel flavor, sprinkle the top of the meringue with a little raw sugar before browning.

1 Preheat the oven to 350°F (180°C or Gas Mark 4). Slice the apples in half and core them. Place on a baking sheet and sprinkle with 1 tablespoon of sugar. Bake until tender. Puree the apple pulp and pass it through a sieve.

2 Soak the gelatin sheets in a little cold water, drain and squeeze out the excess water. Beat together the 2 egg yolks with the remaining sugar and the Calvados over a double boiler. When the mixture is thick and foamy remove from the heat and add the apple puree and the gelatin. Let cool.

3 Meanwhile, beat the egg white to stiff peaks and fold into the apple mixture. Fill 4 glass cups with the mixture and freeze for 2 hours. Preheat the broiler.

4 Beat the egg white for the meringue in a standing mixer or with an electric whisk. When the white is foamy add both kinds of sugar. Beat until thick and shiny. Transfer the meringue to a pastry bag and top each glass with a layer of meringue. Broil for a few minutes or until the meringue is golden-brown.

Coconut Granita
with Milk Chocolate Sauce

Serves 4

Granita

1 ¾ cups (400 ml) sweetened coconut milk

Sauce

3 oz (80 g) milk chocolate

3 Tbsps whipping cream

Decoration

2 ⅔ cups (9 oz or 250 g) shaved fresh coconut meat

Preparation time 15 minutes

Cooking time 5 minutes

Level easy

1. Pour the coconut milk into a large stainless-steel bowl and freeze for at least 2 hours, beating it with an electric mixer every 30 minutes.

2. Meanwhile, melt the chocolate with the cream over a double boiler or in the microwave. Stir the mixture until cooled.

3. Pour the chocolate sauce in the bottom of 4 glasses, sprinkle over the shaved coconut and top with the granita.

PASTRY CHEF'S TIP

Instead of beating the granita with a mixer every 30 minutes it can be left in the freezer for the full 2 hours and then blended just before serving.

Strawberry Sorbet

Serves 4

Sorbet

8 oz (230 g) strawberries, washed and hulled

1/2 cup plus 1 Tbsp (140 ml) sugar syrup

juice of 1 lemon

1 egg white

Decoration

chocolate sauce

Preparation time 25 minutes

Level medium

1 Puree the strawberries with the sugar syrup and lemon juice and refrigerate.

2 Transfer the mixture to an ice cream maker and process for 10 minutes. Lightly beat the egg white with a fork and add it to the sorbet while the machine is running.

3 When the sorbet is creamy and thick, place a piece of waxed paper over the top of the sorbet and freeze until serving.

4 Serve the strawberry sorbet with chocolate sauce.

Pastry Chef's Tip

To make the sorbet without using an ice cream maker, refrigerate the strawberry puree and then add the beaten egg white. Transfer the mixture to a medium-sized rectangular pan. Place in the coldest part of the freezer and leave for 1 ½ hours. After this time, the sorbet should have formed a frozen crust over the top and along the sides. Blend the sorbet or mix with an electric mixer and return to pan and freeze for 1 ½ hours. Repeat 3 times. After the final blending freeze for 1 hour before serving.

Mixed Berry Sorbet

Serves 4

Sorbet

8 oz (220 g) mixed berries (raspberries, blackberries, currants and blueberries)

1/2 cup plus 1 Tbsp (140 ml) sugar syrup

juice of 1 lemon

Preparation time 20 minutes

Level easy

1 Wash the fruit carefully and drain. Puree the berries with the sugar syrup and lemon juice.

2 Strain the mixture to remove the seeds and transfer to an ice cream maker. Process until the sorbet is thick and creamy.

3 Transfer the sorbet to a bowl, cover with wax paper and freeze until serving.

Pastry Chef's Tip

Straining the pureed berries gives the sorbet an extra-smooth and creamy texture.

Kiwi Sorbet

Serves 4

Sorbet

7 Tbsps (100 ml) water

2 Tbsps apple juice concentrate

4 ripe kiwis, peeled and diced

3 Tbsps whipping cream

Decoration

1 kiwi, peeled and sliced

Preparation time 15 minutes
Cooking time 2 minutes
Level easy

1 Heat the water with the apple juice concentrate in a small saucepan.

2 Add the kiwi pieces and cook for 2 minutes. Remove from the heat and let cool.

3 Puree the fruit and cooking liquid together with the whipping cream and pour into a bowl.

4 Freeze until nearly solid and blend just before serving. Decorate the sorbet with kiwi slices.

PASTRY CHEF'S TIP

Another refreshing sorbet recipe: Clean and hull 9 oz (250 g) of strawberries. Puree and strain them. Make a sugar syrup by boiling 1/2 cup (120 ml) of water, 1 cup minus 1 Tbsp (6 ½ oz or 180 g) of raw sugar for 5 minutes. Add the sugar syrup to the puree and transfer to small glasses. Freeze for a few hours before serving.

Green Tea and Apple Sorbet

Serves 2

Sorbet

4 Tbsps water

3 green tea bags

1/2 cup (120 ml) sugar syrup

2 medium Granny Smith apples

juice of 1 lemon

Preparation time 25 minutes
Cooking time 25 minutes
Level easy

1. Bring the water to a boil and add the tea bags. Let infuse for 6 minutes and cool completely.

2. Heat the sugar syrup. Meanwhile peel, core and thinly slice the apples. Add the slices to the simmering sugar syrup and cook for 5 minutes or until tender. Remove from the heat and let cool for at least 15 minutes.

3. Transfer the apple mixture to the blender and puree with the lemon juice and green tea. Refrigerate until cold and process the sorbet in an ice cream maker until thick and creamy (see p. 306 for instructions for making the sorbet without an ice-cream maker).

4. Freeze until serving. Serve the sorbet with fresh fruit if desired.

Melon Sorbet with Poppy Seeds

Serves 4

Sorbet

1 ¼ cups (300 ml) water

3/4 cup plus 1 ½ Tbsps
(5 ½ oz or 160 g) sugar

10 oz (300 g) peeled
and deseeded melon

1 Tbsp Port wine

3 Tbsps dextrose syrup

Decoration

3 Tbsps poppy seeds

mint leaves

Preparation time 10 minutes
Cooking time 10 minutes
Level easy

1 Bring the water and sugar to a boil in a saucepan and cook for 7-8 minutes, until syrupy.

2 Dice the melon and puree with the port wine. Add the hot sugar syrup and then the dextrose. Let cool and process in an ice cream maker following the manufacturers' instructions.

3 Serve the melon sorbet sprinkled with poppy seeds and garnished with mint leaves.

PASTRY CHEF'S TIP

Melon has a very balanced flavor and for this reason it is frequently used in both sweet and savory dishes. In this recipe, the poppy seeds add a distinct flavor and texture to the sorbet.

Pumpkin and Amaretto Sorbet

Serves 4

Sorbet

7 oz (200 g) peeled, deseeded and diced pumpkin

3 Tbsps sugar

4 amaretto cookies

1 pat of butter

3/4 cup plus 1 Tbsp (200 ml) water

2 Tbsps Disarrono or other amaretto liqueur

Preparation time 20 minutes
Cooking time 15 minutes
Level medium

PASTRY CHEF'S TIP

This unusual sorbet may served drizzled with a few drops of aged balsamic vinegar or can be paired with young cheeses. For a distinctive contrast of sweet and spicy flavors, try serving the pumpkin sorbet with a spoonful of minced Cremona mostarda (spicy preserved fruit).

1 Melt the butter in a frying pan and add the pumpkin. Cook for 3 minutes over medium heat. Add the sugar and lower the heat. Let the sugar caramelize slowly and then add the amaretto liqueur and the water.

2 Cover and cook for 10 minutes or until the pumpkin is very soft. Remove from the heat and let cool completely.

3 Crumble the amaretto cookies over the pumpkin mixture and mix well. Transfer to the freezer. Once the mixture has frozen, remove from the freezer and break up the frozen mass. Transfer to an ice cream maker and process until thick and creamy. Serve immediately.

Lemon Sorbet

Serves 4

Sorbet

3/4 cup plus 2 Tbsps
(6 oz or 170 g) sugar

3 ½ cups (850 ml) water

juice and zest of
2 organic lemons

3 ⅓ cups (7 oz or 200 g)
whipped cream

Preparation time 20 minutes
Cooking time 10 minutes
Level easy

1 Heat the sugar and water in a saucepan until the sugar has dissolved. Continue cooking, stirring with a wooden spoon until the liquid has a syrupy consistency.

2 Cook for another 2-3 minutes and then add the lemon zest and juice. Stir and cook over low heat for 15 minutes.

3 Remove from the heat, transfer to a bowl and let cool completely.

4 When the syrup has cooled, fold it into the whipped cream. Freeze the mixture for 5-6 hours.

5 Remove from the freezer and let sit for 10 minutes. Puree the sorbet, pour into small glasses and serve. For a more fluid sorbet, add 2/3 cup (150 ml) of sparkling water before blending.

PASTRY CHEF'S TIP

Serve this lemon sorbet garnished with a sprig of rosemary or a few peppermint leaves.

Wild Strawberry Jelly

Serves 4

Sorbet

3/4 cup plus 1 Tbsp (200 ml) water

2 Tbsps sugar

juice and peel of 1 organic lemon

1 basket of wild strawberries

1/2 tsp agar agar

3 tsps strawberry-flavored vodka

Decoration

1 green apple, sliced

1/2 cup (2 oz or 50 g) lemon sorbet

Preparation time 30 minutes

Cooking time 10 minutes

Level easy

1 Bring the water, sugar, lemon juice and a piece of lemon peel to a boil.

2 Add the wild strawberries and cook for 10 minutes. Pass the mixture through a sieve and add the agar agar.

3 Stir to dissolve. Add the vodka, pour the mixture into glasses and refrigerate.

4 Decorate each glass with apple slices and a scoop of lemon sorbet.

White Chocolate
and Ginger Sorbet

Serves 4
Sorbet

3/4 cup plus 2 Tbsps
(6 oz or 175 g) sugar

2 cups (500 ml) water

5 ½ oz (150 g) white
chocolate, chopped

1 Tbsp freshly grated ginger

Decoration

red currant sprigs

fresh ginger, julienned

Preparation time 20 minutes
Cooking time 15 minutes
Level medium

1 Heat the sugar and water in a saucepan. When the syrup begins to boil, remove from the heat. Add the chocolate and ginger, beating well with a whisk to obtain a smooth cream.

2 Return to the heat, stirring constantly, until the mixture comes to a simmer. Place the saucepan in an ice-water bath to cool quickly. Pour into an ice cream maker and mix briefly (see procedure on p. 306 to make the sorbet without an ice cream maker).

3 Transfer the container to the freezer and leave overnight. Serve the sorbet with strips of julienned ginger and red currants, if desired.

Pastry Chef's Tip

For a better sorbet consistency, substitute 1/4 cup (2 oz or 50 g) of sugar with 3 Tbsps of glucose syrup. Try decorating the sorbet with slices of candied ginger; dip very thin slices of fresh ginger in beaten egg white, sprinkle with confectioners' sugar and bake at 180°F (80°C) for 1 hour.

Frozen Mandarin Cream Cake
with Coffee Glaze

by **Stefano De Pietri**

Serves 6

Mousse

3 gelatin sheets

2 cups (600 ml) milk

1 ½ lb (750 g) coffee-flavored chocolate couverture

4 cups (1 l) whipping cream

Chocolate Sponge Cake

7 egg yolks (4 oz or 115 g in total)

1 cup plus 2 Tbsps (8 oz or 225 g) sugar

6 egg whites (6 ½ oz or 190 g in total)

7 Tbsps raw sugar

1 cup (2 ½ oz or 75 g) cocoa powder

2/3 cup (2 ½ oz or 75 g) all-purpose flour

Mandarin Cream

1 gelatin sheet

1 ¼ cups (300 ml) mandarin juice and pulp

4 eggs plus 10 egg yolks

1 cup (7 oz or 200 g) sugar

3/4 cup (7 oz or 200 g) butter

Coffee Glaze

7 Tbsps (100 ml) whipping cream

3 ½ Tbsps strong coffee

1 gelatin sheet

9 oz (250 g) white chocolate, chopped

Preparation time 1 hour
Cooking time 40 minutes
Level difficult

1 Make the mousse: Soak the gelatin in cold water, drain and squeeze out. Bring the milk to a boil and add the gelatin. Melt the couverture and drizzle over the hot milk. Whisk until smooth. Beat the whipping cream to stiff peaks and fold into the mousse. Refrigerate.

2 Preheat the oven to 350°F (180°C or Gas Mark 4). Make the sponge cake: Beat the yolks and sugar until thick and foamy. Beat the egg whites with the raw sugar to stiff peaks. Fold the egg whites into the yolk mixture and sift in the cocoa powder and flour. Pour the batter into a cake pan lined with parchment paper. Bake for 15-18 minutes.

3 Make the mandarin cream: Soak the gelatin in cold water, drain and squeeze out. Mix the mandarin juice and pulp, yolks, eggs, sugar and gelatin in a small saucepan and cook over low heat, stirring constantly, until it reaches 150°F (65°C). Remove from the heat, let cool to 95°F (35°C) and add the butter.

4 Cut out a 7-inch (18 cm) round of the sponge cake. Place the round in a 7-inch (18 cm) diameter and 2-inch (5 cm) high spring-form pan. Pour over the mandarin cream leaving a 1/2-inch (1 cm) border at the top of the pan. Freeze until hard. Remove the cake from the freezer and unmold it. Place the cake in a 10-inch (24 cm) round spring-form pan and place on a baking sheet. Spread the mousse over the top and sides of the cake and freeze again.

5 Make the glaze: Bring the cream and coffee to a boil. Soak the gelatin in cold water, drain and squeeze out. Add the gelatin to the hot cream. Pour over the white chocolate and stir until smooth. Pour over the cake and freeze until hardened.

Sabayon Semifreddo
with Strawberry Coulis

by **Piero Rainone**

Serves 6

Semifreddo

4 eggs, separated

2 egg yolks

1/2 cup (3 ½ oz or 100 g) sugar

2 Tbsps raw sugar

2 Tbsps glucose syrup

2/3 cup (150 ml)
Moscato d'Asti wine
(or another dessert wine)

3 gelatin sheets

1 ¾ cups (400 ml)
whipping cream

Strawberry Coulis

7 oz (200 g) strawberries

3/4 cup (175 ml) water

1/4 cup (2 oz or 50 g) sugar

Preparation time 20 minutes
Cooking time 20 minutes
Level easy

1. Beat the 6 egg yolks with the two kinds of sugar and glucose over a double boiler. Whisk in the Moscato and cook, whisking constantly, until the mixture reaches 122°F (50°C). Soak the gelatin in a little cold water, drain, squeeze out the excess water and add it to the sabayon.

2. Beat the whipping cream to stiff peaks and fold it into the sabayon. Beat the 4 egg whites to stiff peaks and fold them into the sabayon. Line 6 individual aluminum ramekins with plastic wrap and fill with the sabayon semifreddo. Freeze for at least 4 hours.

3. Meanwhile, prepare the coulis: Wash and hull the strawberries. Cut them into small pieces and place in a small saucepan with the water and sugar. Bring to a boil, remove from the heat and puree. Return the strawberry puree to the saucepan and cook until it reaches a medium density.

4. Unmold the semifreddos and serve with the strawberry coulis.

PASTRY CHEF'S TIP

Try adding 5 ½ oz (150 g) of crushed amaretto cookies mixed with 2 ½ oz (75 g) of chocolate shavings to the semifreddo after folding in the whipped cream.

Layered Gianduia, Hazelnut
and Sabayon Semifreddo Cake

by **Francesco Elmi**

Serves 6
Base
2 chocolate sponge cake rounds
(about 1/4 lb or 250 g in total)
3 Tbsps finely chopped hazelnuts

Gianduia Semifreddo
3/4 cup (200 ml) water
1 cup (7 oz or 200 g) sugar
2 Tbsps glucose syrup
1 ¾ cups (4 ½ oz or 130 g)
cocoa powder
1 ½ oz (40 g) extra-dark
chocolate couverture
1 oz (30 g) hazelnut paste
1 ½ oz (40 g) sabayon sauce
3 ⅓ cups (7 oz or 200 g)
whipped cream

Sabayon Sauce
6 egg yolks (3 ½ oz or 100 g in total)
3/4 cup (5 ½ oz or 150 g) sugar
7 Tbsps (100 ml) dry Marsala wine

Sabayon Semifreddo
2 ½ oz (70 g) sabayon sauce
3 ⅓ cups (7 oz or 200 g)
whipped cream

Hazelnut Semifreddo
2 oz (60 g) hazelnut paste
5 ½ oz (150 g) sabayon sauce
3 ⅓ cups (7 oz or 200 g)
whipped cream

Preparation time 40 minutes
Cooking time 20 minutes
Level difficult

1 Make a chocolate paste for the gianduia semifreddo: Bring the water to a boil with the sugar, glucose syrup and cocoa powder. When the mixture comes to a boil remove from the heat, add the couverture and stir to combine.

2 Make the sabayon sauce: Beat the egg yolks together with the sugar and place over a double boiler. Whisk in the Marsala and cook, whisking constantly for 5 minutes. Make the sabayon semifreddo: Fold 2 ½ oz (70 g) of the sabayon sauce into the whipped cream and freeze until semi-solid.

3 Make the hazelnut semifreddo: Fold the hazelnut paste into 5 ½ oz (150 g) of the sabayon sauce. Fold in the whipped cream and freeze until semi-solid. Make the gianduia semifreddo: Fold the hazelnut and chocolate pastes into the remaining sabayon sauce. Carefully fold in the whipped cream and freeze until semi-solid.

4 Place 1 sponge cake round in the bottom of a spring-form pan. Pour in the gianduia semifreddo and sprinkle with hazelnuts. Top with a layer of hazelnut semifreddo and freeze until semi-solid. Remove from the freezer and lay over the remaining sponge cake round. Top with the sabayon semifreddo and freeze for at least 4 hours before serving. Unmold the semifreddo cake and serve with chocolate sauce if desired.

Sabayon Semifreddo
with Strawberry Coulis

by **Piero Rainone**

Serves 6
Semifreddo
4 eggs, separated
2 egg yolks
1/2 cup (3 ½ oz or 100 g) sugar
2 Tbsps raw sugar
2 Tbsps glucose syrup
2/3 cup (150 ml)
Moscato d'Asti wine
(or another dessert wine)
3 gelatin sheets
1 ¾ cups (400 ml)
whipping cream
Strawberry Coulis
7 oz (200 g) strawberries
3/4 cup (175 ml) water
1/4 cup (2 oz or 50 g) sugar

Preparation time 20 minutes
Cooking time 20 minutes
Level easy

1 Beat the 6 egg yolks with the two kinds of sugar and glucose over a double boiler. Whisk in the Moscato and cook, whisking constantly, until the mixture reaches 122°F (50°C). Soak the gelatin in a little cold water, drain, squeeze out the excess water and add it to the sabayon.

2 Beat the whipping cream to stiff peaks and fold it into the sabayon. Beat the 4 egg whites to stiff peaks and fold them into the sabayon. Line 6 individual aluminum ramekins with plastic wrap and fill with the sabayon semifreddo. Freeze for at least 4 hours.

3 Meanwhile, prepare the coulis: Wash and hull the strawberries. Cut them into small pieces and place in a small saucepan with the water and sugar. Bring to a boil, remove from the heat and puree. Return the strawberry puree to the saucepan and cook until it reaches a medium density.

4 Unmold the semifreddos and serve with the strawberry coulis.

PASTRY CHEF'S TIP
Try adding 5 ½ oz (150 g) of crushed amaretto cookies mixed with 2 ½ oz (75 g) of chocolate shavings to the semifreddo after folding in the whipped cream.

Vanilla Semifreddo
with Mixed Berries

by **Piero Rainone**

Serves 6

Semifreddo

4 eggs, separated

1/2 cup (3 ½ oz or 100 g) sugar

3 ⅓ cups (7 oz or 200 g) whipped cream

1/2 vanilla bean, halved lengthwise and seeds scraped out

1 gelatin sheet

1 cup (3 ½ oz or 100 g) raspberries

4 blackberries

1 cup (3 ½ oz or 100 g) red currants, stems removed (if desired)

Meringue

1-2 egg whites (2 oz or 50 g in total)

1/2 cup (3 ½ oz or 100 g) sugar

Preparation time 40 minutes
Cooking time 1 hour
Level medium

1 Preheat the oven to 210°F (100°C or Gas Mark 1/4). Make the meringue: Beat the egg white with the sugar to form stiff peaks. Drop spoonfuls of the mixture onto a baking sheet lined with parchment paper, making about 20 meringues, and bake for 1 hour.

2 Make the semifreddo: Beat the egg yolks with the sugar until thick and foamy. Fold in the whipped cream and the seeds from the vanilla bean. Soak the gelatin in a little cold water, drain, squeeze out the excess liquid and dissolve in a little hot water. Fold the gelatin into the semifreddo base, crumble in 2 meringues and add the red currants, raspberries and blackberries. Carefully mix together.

3 Place 6 round cookie cutters of about the same size as the meringues on a baking sheet. Place a meringue in each one. Spread the semifreddo mixture over the meringue and top with another meringue. Add another layer of the semifreddo mixture and top with a meringue. Freeze the semifreddos for at least 4 hours before serving.

Chocolate and Vanilla Cups

by **Paolo Staccoli**

Serves 8

Sponge Cake

6 eggs

1 cup (7 oz or 200 g) sugar

1 ⅓ cups (6 oz or 170 g)
all-purpose flour

1/3 cup plus 1 Tbsp (1 oz or 30 g)
cocoa powder

Semifreddo

1 cup (250 ml) milk

1/2 vanilla bean, halved lengthwise

5 gelatin sheets

15 egg yolks (9 oz or 250 g in total)

1 ¼ cups (9 oz or 250 g) sugar

2 cups (500 ml)
semi-whipped cream

Chocolate Mousse

12 oz (350 g) crème anglaise
(see p. 98)

10 ½ oz (300 g) extra-dark
chocolate couverture

2 cups (500 ml) semi-stiff
whipped cream

Preparation time 40 minutes
Cooking time 20 minutes
Level difficult

1 Preheat the oven to 400°F (200°C or Gas Mark 6). Make the sponge cake: Beat the eggs and the sugar over a double boiler over low heat. Sift in the flour and cocoa powder and mix in using bottom to top folding motions. Remove from the heat and pour into a buttered cake pan. Bake for 20 minutes, remove from the oven and let cool completely. Cut out small rounds using a cookie cutter.

2 Make the semifreddo: Bring the milk to a boil with the vanilla bean. Soak the gelatin in a little cold water, drain and squeeze out the excess liquid. Beat the egg yolks and the sugar in a mixing bowl. Remove the vanilla bean and whisk the hot milk into the egg mixture. Return to the saucepan and cook over low heat until the mixture reaches 185°F (85°C). Remove from the heat and mix in the gelatin. When the cream has cooled to 82°F (28°C) add the semi-whipped cream.

3 Make the mousse: Heat the crème anglaise to 82°F (28°C) and add the melted chocolate and cream. Mix well. Using a pastry bag, fill 8 small glasses a quarter full with the vanilla semifreddo and freeze until the semifreddo is semi-solid. Top with a sponge cake round and complete with the chocolate mousse. Decorate with chocolate curls and serve.

Frozen Strawberry Mousse
in Chocolate Cups

by **Paolo Staccoli**

Serves 6

Chocolate Cups

3 oz (90 g) dark chocolate couverture

Strawberry Mousse

3 ⅔ cups (900 ml) whipping cream

1/3 cup plus 1 Tbsp (90 ml) milk

1/2 cup minus 1 Tbsp (3 oz or 90 g) sugar

6 gelatin sheets

1 basket of strawberries, cleaned and hulled

Gelatin

1 package of gelatin glaze for desserts

Preparation time 35 minutes
Cooking time 10 minutes
Level medium

1 Make the chocolate cups: Melt and temper the chocolate couverture (see p. 21) and then pour it into small fluted chocolate molds. Let harden for a few seconds and then flip the molds over to eliminate any excess chocolate. Refrigerate until cool and unmold.

2 Make the mousse: Heat the cream over low heat with the milk and sugar until it reaches 140°F (60°C). Soak the gelatin in a little cold water, drain, squeeze out the excess liquid and dissolve into the hot cream, stirring to combine. Transfer the cream to a bowl and refrigerate.

3 Puree the strawberries. Whip the chilled cream mixture and fold in the strawberry puree. Transfer to a pastry bag fitted with a smooth tip, and fill the chocolate cups with the strawberry mousse. Freeze the filled chocolate cups for a few hours. Just before serving, brush the strawberry mousse with the gelatin glaze and decorate with chocolate sauce if desired.

techniques&recipes

Risen Breads
and Fried Sweets

Brioche, muffins, plum cake for a rich and flavorful
breakfast. Chiacchiere, fritters and crêpes are crispy
and delicious fried desserts.

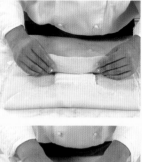

1 Dissolve the yeast in the lukewarm milk and pour the mixture into the flour. Add the sugar, egg and a generous pinch of salt. Mix to form a smooth dough.

2 Wrap the butter in a piece of parchment paper and roll it with a rolling pin to soften.

3-4 Roll the dough into a 1/5-inch (3-4 mm) thick sheet and place the butter in the center. Fold the dough over the butter so that the outside edges meet in the center. Use a rolling pin to flatten the out the dough.

5 Fold the dough into thirds; turn clockwise 180°.

Makes 20 croissants

2 ⅔ **tsps** active dry yeast

4 ¾ cups plus 1 Tbsp (1 lb 2 oz or 600 g) all-purpose flour

1 cup (250 g) milk

1/2 cup (3 ½ oz or 100 g) sugar

1 cup plus 2 ½ Tbsps (9 oz or 250 g) butter

1 egg

salt

6 Roll out the dough again, fold into thirds and turn 180°. Repeat the rolling and folding 2 more times, refrigerating after each turn.

7 Roll out the dough after the final refrigeration and cut it into triangles.

8 Roll the triangles up starting at the base and rolling towards the tip to form croissants. Place the croissants on a baking sheet lined with parchment paper and let rise for 45 minutes or until the doubled in size.

CROISSANT DOUGH

PASTRY CHEF'S TIP
Bake the croissants at 325°F
(170°C or Gas Mark 3) for
35 minutes. Glaze the baked
croissants with a boiling
sugar syrup or sprinkle
with confectioners' sugar.

2 Transfer the dough to a floured work surface and knead vigorously to form a thick and shiny dough. Let rise for 4 hours at room temperature, about 68°F (20°C).

1 Mix together all of the ingredients in a large bowl to form a soft and sticky dough.

3 Preheat the oven to 325°F (170°C or Gas Mark 3). Interrupt the rising by rolling the dough into a thick sheet using a rolling pin. Fold the dough into thirds to form a rectangle and let sit for 30 minutes. Repeat 3 times. Shape the dough into a loaf and place it in a buttered and floured loaf pan. Cover and let rise for a final 20 minutes. Bake for 40 minutes.

Serves 6

3 ⅔ cups (1 lb or 450 g) all-purpose flour

3 eggs

1/2 cup (110 ml) milk

1/2 cup (4 oz or 110 g) butter

6 ½ Tbsps sugar

2 ⅔ tsps active dry yeast

2 tsps salt

BRIOCHE BREAD

Recipe on p. 350

PASTRY CHEF'S TIP

To see if the brioche is cooked, insert a toothpick into the center of the loaf. If the toothpick comes out clean and dry, turn off the oven and let the brioche rest in the oven for another 5 minutes before removing.

1 Mound the flour on a work surface and make a well at the center.

2 Add the corn oil, grappa, egg, orange zest, salt and white wine and mix to form a smooth dough. Let rest for about 30 minutes.

3 Roll out the dough into a very thin sheet and cut into 1-inch (2.5 cm) wide and 4-inch (10 cm) long strips using a serrated rolling cutter.

4 Make an incision in the center of each strip using the serrated cutter.

5 Pull one end of each strip through the incision to form a loop.

6 Heat abundant sunflower oil to 400°F (200°C) and fry the fritters until golden-brown. Drain and dry on paper towels. Sprinkle with confectioners' sugar and serve hot.

Serves 6
4 cups (1 lb 2 oz or 500 g) all-purpose flour
1 Tbsp corn oil
4 Tbsps grappa
1 egg
zest of **1/2** organic orange
salt
3 Tbsps sweet white wine
sunflower oil for frying
confectioners' sugar

CHIACCHIERE (Italian Fritters)

PASTRY CHEF'S TIP
For lighter and puffier fritters, add 2/3 tsp of active dry yeast, dissolved in a little water, to the dough.

1 Beat the egg with the flour and mix to combine.

2 Whisk in the milk and continue whisking until a smooth batter forms.

3 Butter a small non-stick frying pan and place over medium heat. Once hot, pour over a small ladleful of the batter and turn the pan in a circular motion to spread the batter in a thin, even layer.

4 Using a thin spatula, lift one edge of the crêpe and use the fingers to flip the crêpe. Let cook for about a minute or until golden-brown and remove from the pan. Continue making crêpes until the batter is finished.

Serves 4
1 egg
2/3 cup (2 ½ oz or 75 g) all-purpose flour
1 cup (250 ml) milk
butter

CRÊPES

PASTRY CHEF'S TIP
To make a smooth batter without any lumps, it is important that all of the ingredients are at the same temperature and that the egg and flour be mixed for a long time before adding the milk.

Recipe on p. 358

Brioche
with Marinated Cherries and Yogurt

Serves 6

Brioche

1 cup (250 ml) red wine

3 Tbsps sugar

1 star anise

30-40 large cherries, pitted

1 loaf of brioche bread
(see p. 344), thickly sliced

1 cup (9 oz or 250 g)
sweetened plain yogurt

Preparation time 10 minutes
Cooking time 15 minutes
Level easy

1 Heat the red wine in a saucepan with the sugar and star anise.

2 Reduce to half the original volume and remove from the heat. Add the cherries and let sit for 30 minutes.

3 Toast the brioche slices and place them in shallow bowls.

4 Top with the cherries and yogurt. Serve immediately.

Apricot Pastries

Serves 8
Pastries
croissant dough (see p. 342)
1 jar of apricot jam

Preparation time 1 hour
Cooking time 10 minutes
Level medium

1 Roll out the dough and cut out 4-inch (10 cm) squares. Place a generous tablespoon of jam in the center of each square and fold two corners into the center to seal.

2 Place the croissants on a baking sheet lined with parchment paper and let rise for 2 hours in a warm place.

3 Preheat the oven to 350°F (180°C or Gas Mark 4). Bake for about 10 minutes. Let cool and serve sprinkled with confectioners' sugar if desired.

PASTRY CHEF'S TIP
The apricot jam may be substituted with flavored pastry cream if desired.

Chocolate-Hazelnut Cupcakes
with White Chocolate Glaze

Makes 12 cupcakes

Cupcakes

1 ½ cups (7 oz or 200 g) blanched hazelnuts

13 Tbsps (6 ½ oz or 180 g) butter

6 egg whites

1 ¼ cups (5 ½ oz or 155 g) all-purpose flour

1/3 cup (1 oz or 30 g) cocoa powder

2 cups (9 oz or 250 g) confectioners' sugar

Glaze

3 oz (80 g) white chocolate

Preparation time 20 minutes
Cooking time 30 minutes
Level easy

1. Preheat the oven to 400°F (200°C or Gas Mark 6). Finely chop the hazelnuts in a food processor. Melt the butter in a small saucepan, letting it brown slightly, for about 4 minutes. Let cool. Beat the egg whites to stiff peaks.

2. Sift together the flour, cocoa powder and confectioners' sugar. Add the hazelnuts and stir to combine. Fold in the egg whites and then the melted butter. Mix well and transfer to 12 miniature muffin tins, filling each tin half full. Bake for 20-25 minutes. Insert a toothpick make sure the cake is cooked through. Remove from the oven and let cool completely.

3. Melt the white chocolate over a double boiler over low heat. When the first pieces begin to melt, remove from the heat and stir until liquid. Transfer the white chocolate to a pastry bag fitted with a small tip and decorate the cupcakes. Let the glaze set before serving.

PASTRY CHEF'S TIP
In alternative to a pastry bag, make a cone out of parchment paper, fill it with the glaze and cut a small hole in the tip.

Milk Chocolate Cupcakes

Serves 6

Cupcakes

7 Tbsps (3 ½ oz or 100 g) butter

3 eggs, separated

1/2 cup (3 ½ oz or 100 g) sugar

1 tsp vanilla extract

1/2 cup (1 ½ oz or 40 g) crushed graham crackers

1/3 cup (1 ½ oz or 40 g) breadcrumbs

3 Tbsps white rum

1 pinch of salt

1 Tbsp honey

1/2 cup (2 oz or 50 g) shelled pistachios, finely chopped

Frosting

9 oz (250 g) milk chocolate, chopped

salt

Preparation time 30 minutes
Cooking time 40 minutes
Level medium

1 Preheat the oven to 350°F (180°C or Gas Mark 4). Melt the butter and let cool. Beat the egg yolks and the sugar with the vanilla until thick and pale yellow. Whisk in the cooled butter. Add the graham crackers, breadcrumbs and rum and mix well.

2 Beat the egg whites and salt into stiff peaks and fold into the batter. Add the honey and chopped pistachios and stir to combine. Butter and flour 6 aluminum ramekins or muffin tins and fill them two-thirds full with the batter. Bake for 25 minutes, remove from the oven and let cool on a wire rack.

3 Meanwhile, temper the chocolate with the salt (see p. 21). Spread the frosting on the cupcakes and let sit on a wire rack until hardened.

White Chocolate Cupcakes

Serves 4

Cupcakes

9 Tbsps (4 ½ oz or 125 g) butter

1 cup minus 1 Tbsp (6 ½ oz or 180 g) sugar

1 tsp vanilla extract, 2 eggs

2 cups (9 oz or 250 g) self-rising flour

1/2 cup (110 ml) whipping cream

9 oz (250 g) white chocolate, shaved

Frosting

3 ½ oz (100 g) cream cheese

2 ½ Tbsps confectioners' sugar

2 oz (50 g) white chocolate

2 Tbsps whipping cream

Preparation time 30 minutes
Cooking time 20 minutes
Level easy

PASTRY CHEF'S TIP

For a different variation, substitute the white chocolate in the frosting with the same quantity of milk or dark chocolate.

1 Preheat the oven to 325°F (170°C or Gas Mark 3). Cream the butter and sugar together with an electric beater. Add the eggs one at a time and then the vanilla.

2 Sift in the flour, stirring with a spatula, and then add the whipping cream. Mix in the chocolate shavings. Fill miniature muffin tins with the batter until half full. Bake for 20 minutes. Let cool, then unmold.

3 Beat the cream cheese with the confectioners' sugar. Melt the chocolate with the whipping cream and add to the cream cheese mixture. Frost the cupcakes with the white chocolate frosting and let sit for 10 minutes before serving.

Semolina Crêpes
with Honey

Serves 4

Crêpes

1 ⅔ tsps active dry yeast

1 Tbsp sugar

2 ¾ cups (12 ½ oz or 350 g)
all-purpose flour

3/4 cup (5 ½ oz or 150 g)
semolina flour

1 cup (250 ml) water

1 cup (250 ml) milk

3 eggs

4 Tbsps (2 oz or 50 g)
butter, melted

salt

sunflower oil

Decoration

acacia honey

Preparation time 10 minutes
Cooking time 5 minutes
Level easy

1 Dissolve the yeast in a little warm water with the sugar. Sift the flour into a bowl and add the semolina.

2 Pour over the yeast mixture and add the water, milk, eggs, melted butter and a pinch of salt. Mix well to form a smooth batter. Cover and let rest for about 1 hour 30 minutes.

3 Heat a little sunflower oil in a small non-stick frying pan and pour a ladleful of batter into the pan. Move the pan in a circular motion to evenly distribute the batter and cook for a few seconds. Lift up one edge and then flip the crêpe using a spatula or with the fingertips.

4 Let cook briefly and remove from the pan. Continue making crêpes until all of the batter is finished. Serve the crêpes warm, drizzled with honey.

PASTRY CHEF'S TIP

Sprinkle the crêpes with a few chopped nuts before serving for a tasty variation.

Blueberry Crêpes

Serves 4

Crêpes

2/3 cup (2 ½ oz or 75 g) all-purpose flour

2 eggs

1 cup (250 ml) milk

salt

butter

Decoration

1/2 cup (5 ½ oz or 150 g) blueberry jam

confectioners' sugar

Preparation time 10 minutes
Cooking time 10 minutes
Level medium

1 Sift the flour into a bowl and add the eggs, milk and a pinch of salt. Whisk to form a smooth and fluid batter.

2 Heat a little butter in a cast-iron pan and when the butter begins to foam pour in enough of the batter to form a thin layer of the bottom of the pan. Move the pan in a circular motion to evenly distribute the batter.

3 Cook until browned on both sides and remove from the pan. Continue making crêpes until the batter is finished. Spread a thick layer of jam over each crêpe and roll up. Sprinkle with confectioners' sugar and serve.

PASTRY CHEF'S TIP

The crêpes may be filled with other flavors of jam or fresh fruit: we suggest mixing orange marmalade and a few drops of Grand Marnier.

Crumpets

with Blueberries and Red Currants

Serves 4

Crumpets

1 tsp active dry yeast

1 ¼ cups (300 ml) warm water

2 cups (9 oz or 250 g)
all-purpose flour

1/2 tsp baking powder

7 Tbsps (100 ml) milk

2 tsps sugar

butter

Decoration

1 basket of blueberries

1 basket of red currants,
stems removed
(if desired)

2 Tbsps sugar

Preparation time 15 minutes

Cooking time 20 minutes

Level easy

1 Dissolve the yeast in the warm water and let sit for 10 minutes. Pour the flour, baking powder, milk and sugar into a bowl and add the yeast mixture. Stir to form a smooth batter.

2 Heat a non-stick frying pan and add a little butter. Place a buttered, stainless-steel cookie cutter in the center of the frying pan and pour 2 tablespoons of the batter into the cookie cutter. Let cook for 2 minutes, remove the cookie cutter, flip and cook for another 3 minutes. Continue making crumpets until the batter is finished.

3 Toss the blueberries and the red currants with the sugar. Serve the crumpets with the berries.

PASTRY CHEF'S TIP

Savory crumpets can are a great accompaniment to cured meats and cheeses. Follow the above recipe, eliminating the sugar.

Pancakes with Strawberries

Serves 4

Pancakes

1 ⅓ cup (6 oz or 170 g) all-purpose flour

1 tsp baking powder

1/3 cup (2 oz or 60 g) sugar

salt

7 Tbsps (3 ½ oz or 100 g) butter

1 cup (250 ml) milk

2 eggs

14 oz (400 g) strawberries

ground cinnamon

Decoration

confectioners' sugar

mint leaves

Preparation time 15 minutes

Cooking time 30 minutes

Level easy

1 Sift the flour into a mixing bowl and add the baking powder, 2 teaspoons of sugar and a pinch of salt. In a separate bowl, melt 5 tablespoons (3 oz or 80 g) of butter and whisk in the milk and eggs. Pour the liquid into the flour and stir to form a smooth batter. Let rest for 20 minutes.

2 Meanwhile, hull the strawberries, cut them in half and set aside. Mix together the remaining sugar and a pinch of ground cinnamon in a wide bowl.

3 Heat the remaining butter in a frying pan and pour in ladlefuls of the batter. Cook the pancakes until golden-brown on both sides. Transfer the cooked pancakes to the bowl with the sugar and cinnamon and toss each pancake to coat. Serve the pancakes with the strawberries and a few mint leaves and sprinkle with confectioners' sugar.

Coconut Pancakes
with Caramelized Bananas

Serves 4

Pancakes

1 cup minus 1 Tbsp (4 oz or 115 g) whole-wheat flour

2 Tbsps baking powder

2 Tbsps sugar

1 cup (3 ½ oz or 100 g) shredded coconut

4 eggs, separated

1 lb (500 g) ricotta

1 ¾ cups (400 ml) milk

2 bananas

1 Tbsp raw sugar

2 Tbsps (1 oz or 20 g) butter

2 Tbsps rum

1 Tbsp extra-virgin olive oil

Decoration

confectioners' sugar

Preparation time 10 minutes
Cooking time 10 minutes
Level easy

1. Sift the flour and baking powder into a mixing bowl and add the sugar and coconut. Add the egg yolks, 12 ½ oz (350 g) of ricotta and the milk and mix to form a smooth batter.

2. Beat the egg whites to stiff peaks and fold them into the batter. Heat a non-stick frying pan over medium heat. Add enough oil to coat the pan, and pour a small ladleful of batter into the pan. Cook for 2 minutes per side. Continue making the pancakes until the batter is finished.

3. Meanwhile, slice the bananas and cook them in a non-stick pan with a little butter and the raw sugar. When the bananas begin to caramelize, pour over the rum and cook off the alcohol. Place three pancakes on each plate and top with the remaining ricotta and caramelized bananas. Sprinkle with confectioners' sugar and serve.

Fried Cream

Serves 4

Cream

3 egg yolks

2/3 cup (4 ½ oz or 125 g) sugar

1 ⅔ cups (7 oz or 200 g)
all-purpose flour

4 cups (1 l) milk

zest of 1 organic lemon

1 egg

5 Tbsps breadcrumbs

sunflower oil for frying

Decoration

confectioners' sugar

Preparation time 25 minutes
Cooking time 30 minutes
Level easy

Pastry Chef's Tip

Serve the fried cream topped with
a little ground cinnamon or with a
dark chocolate sauce if desired.

1 Beat the 3 egg yolks with the sugar. Sift in the flour and stir to combine. Drizzle in the milk, add the lemon zest and whisk until smooth. Transfer the mixture to a saucepan and cook over low heat, stirring constantly until the cream is thick. Do not let the cream boil.

2 Remove from the heat when the cream coats the back of a spoon. Pour into a baking dish and cool completely. Once cool, cut the cream into small diamond shapes. Lightly beat the egg and pour the breadcrumbs onto a plate. Dip the cream into the egg and then roll in the breadcrumbs.

3 Heat abundant sunflower oil in a saucepan and fry the breaded cream diamonds until golden-brown on all sides. Remove from the oil using a slotted spoon and drain on paper towels. Sprinkle with confectioners' sugar and serve hot.

Castagnole Fritters

Serves 8

Castagnole

7 Tbsps (3 1/2 oz or 100 g) butter

3 cups plus 3 Tbsps (14 oz or 400 g) all-purpose flour

4 Tbsps sugar

4 eggs

1/4 cup (60 ml) rum

zest of 1 organic lemon

salt

sunflower oil for frying

confectioners' sugar

Preparation time 20 minutes
Cooking time 5 minutes
Level easy

1 Clarify the butter in a double boiler and then transfer to a bowl. Sift the flour into the butter and then add the sugar, eggs, rum, lemon zest and a pinch of salt. Mix well.

2 Roll the dough into chestnut-sized balls. Heat the sunflower oil. Fry the dough until golden-brown and puffy.

3 Drain on paper towels and sprinkle with confectioners' sugar. Serve hot.

PASTRY CHEF'S TIP

Enrich these fritters by adding a few tablespoons of rum-soaked raisins to the batter.

Ricotta Cannoli

Serves 4

Cannoli

2 ⅓ cups plus 1 Tbsp (10 ½ oz or 300 g) all-purpose flour

1 tsp baking powder

1 egg, separated

2 Tbsps sugar

2 Tbsps (1 oz or 30 g) butter, melted

salt

dry Marsala wine

sunflower oil for frying

lard for frying

Filling

14 oz (400 g) sheep's milk ricotta

1 ⅔ cups (7 oz or 200 g) confectioners' sugar

3 ½ oz (100 g) candied orange and citron, diced

2 oz (50 g) dark chocolate, chopped

1/4 cup (1 oz or 30 g) pistachios, chopped

Decoration

dark chocolate shavings

vanilla-flavored confectioners' sugar

Preparation time 50 minutes
Cooking time 30 minutes
Level difficult

1 Mix together the flour with the baking powder, egg yolk, sugar, melted butter and a pinch of salt. Add enough Marsala to form a smooth dough. Cover and let rest for 2 hours. Pass the ricotta through a sieve and stir in the confectioners' sugar. Stir until the mixture is soft and creamy. Add the candied fruit, pistachios and chocolate and mix well.

2 Roll out the dough into a thin sheet. Cut into 4-5 inch (10-12 cm) squares. Brush each square with a little beaten egg white and wrap the dough squares around stainless-steel cannoli molds.

3 Heat abundant sunflower oil in a saucepan with a little lard. When the oil is very hot, immerse the cannoli one by one, keeping them on the molds. Once the dough is golden-brown, remove from the oil and let cool on paper towels. Slide the cooled cannoli off of the molds and fill with the ricotta cream. Sprinkle with vanilla-flavored confectioners' sugar, chocolate shavings and candied orange rind, if desired, and serve.

Sweet Ricotta Fritters

Serves 4

Fritters

1 egg plus 1 egg yolk

1 tsp vanilla extract

1/2 cup (3 ½ oz or 100 g) sugar

2 Tbsps all-purpose flour

zest of 1 organic lemon

1 Tbsp milk

12 ½ oz (350 g) ricotta

sunflower oil for frying

Decoration

confectioners' sugar

Preparation time 20 minutes

Cooking time 10 minutes

Level easy

1 Mix together the egg, egg yolk, vanilla and sugar in a bowl.

2 Add the flour and lemon zest and stir to form a creamy batter, adding a little milk if the batter seems too thick or dry. Add the ricotta and mix well.

3 Heat the sunflower oil in a frying pan and drop spoonfuls of the batter into the pan. Fry until golden-brown on both sides.

4 Remove from the pan using a slotted spoon and let the fritters dry on a paper towel. Sprinkle with confectioners' sugar and serve hot.

PASTRY CHEF'S TIP

If desired, the fritters can be glazed with chestnut honey or cinnamon-infused honey.

Rice Fritters

Serves 4

Fritters

2 cups (500 ml) milk

peel of 1/2 organic lemon

2 Tbsps sugar

salt

1/2 cup (3 ½ oz or 100 g)
Carnaroli rice
(or short-grain risotto rice)

3 Tbsps rum

3 eggs, separated

6 ½ Tbsps all-purpose flour

1/4 cup (1 oz or 30 g) pine nuts

1/3 cup plus 1 Tbsp (2 oz
or 50 g) raisins

sunflower oil for frying

Decoration

confectioners' sugar

Preparation time 30 minutes
Cooking time 30 minutes
Level medium

1 Heat the milk, lemon peel, sugar and a pinch of salt in a large saucepan. Add the rice and cook over medium heat for 15 minutes or until all of the liquid has been absorbed.

2 Let the rice cool, remove the lemon peel and add the rum, egg yolks, flour, pine nuts and raisins. Stir to incorporate all of the ingredients and let rest for a few hours.

3 Beat the egg whites to stiff peaks and fold into the batter. Heat abundant sunflower oil in a deep frying pan. Drop in a few spoonfuls of batter and fry until golden-brown, turning the fritters a few times.

4 Drain on paper towels and continue cooking the fritters until the batter is finished. Serve the fritters hot, sprinkled with confectioners' sugar.

Zeppole Fritters

Serves 4

Zeppole

1 cup (250 ml) water

4 Tbsps (2 oz or 50 g) butter

salt

1 cup plus 3 Tbsps (5 1/2 oz or 150 g) all-purpose flour

6 ½ Tbsps cornstarch

2 eggs

2 Alchermes liqueur or sweet Marsala wine

1/2 tsp baking powder

sunflower oil for frying

Preparation time 20 minutes
Cooking time 5 minutes
Level easy

1 Bring the water to a boil with the butter and a pinch of salt. Remove from the heat and sift in the flour and cornstarch. Stir with a wooden spoon until the dough is thick and forms a ball. Return to heat and cook for 1 more minute, stirring constantly.

2 Transfer the dough to a warm bowl and add the eggs, one at a time, stirring constantly. When the eggs are incorporated, stir in the Alchermes or Marsala. Let the dough cool. Sift in the baking powder and stir, then transfer the dough to a pastry bag with a ridged tip.

3 Heat abundant sunflower oil in a large saucepan. Pipe small strips of dough directly into the oil. Fry until golden-brown and drain on paper towels. Serve the fritters sprinkled with sugar, if desired.

PASTRY CHEF'S TIP

The zeppole dough can also be rolled by hand into doughnuts and fried.

Tiny Honey Dumplings

Serves 8

Dumplings

3 cups plus 3 Tbsps (14 oz or 400 g) all-purpose flour

4 eggs plus 2 egg yolks

2 Tbsps dark rum

zest of 1 organic lemon

zest of 1 organic orange

salt

3/4 cup (5 oz or 140 g) sugar

6 Tbsps (3 oz or 90 g) butter

sunflower oil for frying

3/4 cup (10 oz or 280 g) light honey

3 ½ oz (100 g) candied orange and citron, chopped

Preparation time 30 minutes
Cooking time 20 minutes
Level medium

1. Mix together the flour, eggs and egg yolks with the rum, citrus zest, a pinch of salt and 2 tablespoons of sugar. Roll the dough into a ball and wrap in plastic wrap. Refrigerate for 45 minutes.

2. Break off bits of dough and roll them between the hands or on a work surface to form long ropes. Cut each rope into small pieces and roll into tiny balls. Toss the balls in a little flour and fry in abundant hot sunflower oil until they begin to color. Drain on paper towels.

3. Place the remaining sugar, honey and 4 tablespoons of water in a saucepan and cook until amber-brown. Add two-thirds of the candied citrus and the fried dumplings to the pan. Mix carefully to coat and pour onto a piece of parchment paper. Using a spoon, break off small spoonfuls of the mixture.

4. With wet hands, shape each spoonful into a pyramid. Decorate with the remaining candied citrus or colored sugar if desired.

Chocolate-Chestnut Fritters

Serves 4

Dough

3 ⅔ cups (1 lb or 450 g)
all-purpose flour

2 eggs

6 Tbsps (3 oz or 80 g)
butter, softened

3/4 cup (5 ½ oz or 150 g) sugar

milk, salt

1 Tbsp baking soda

extra-virgin olive oil for frying

lard or shortening for frying

Filling

9 oz (250 g) chestnuts,
boiled and peeled

3 ½ oz (100 g) dark chocolate,
chopped

1/3 cup (2 oz or 50 g)
almonds, chopped

2 oz (50 g) candied fruit, diced

zest of 1 organic lemon

Decoration

confectioners' sugar

Preparation time 40 minutes
Cooking time 20 minutes
Level easy

1 Mix together the flour, eggs, softened butter, sugar and a pinch of salt. Add enough milk to form a smooth dough. Let the dough rest for 1 hour. Dilute the baking soda in a little warm milk and add it to the dough.

2 Puree the chestnuts and place in a bowl. Add the chopped chocolate, almonds, candied fruit and lemon zest. Mix to incorporate. The filling should be fairly dense. Roll out the dough into a very thin sheet. Using a round cookie cutter, cut out as many rounds as possible. Place a teaspoonful of filling on each round and fold it into a half moon shape. Pinch the edges to seal.

3 Heat equal parts of olive oil and lard in a saucepan and deep-fry the fritters until golden-brown. Drain on paper towels, sprinkle with confectioners' sugar and serve immediately.

Apple Fritters

Serves 6

Fritters

5 apples, peeled and cored

4 Tbsps grappa

1/3 cup (2 ½ oz or 75 g) sugar

1 tsp ground cinnamon

2 eggs, separated

4 Tbsps milk

salt

1 cup (4 ½ oz or 130 g)
all-purpose flour

2 tsps baking powder

sunflower oil for frying

Decoration

confectioners' sugar

Preparation time 40 minutes
Cooking time 20 minutes
Level medium

1. Slice the apples into 1/4-inch (1/2 cm) thick wedges. Toss with 2 tablespoons of grappa, stir in the sugar and cinnamon and let rest.

2. Meanwhile, beat the egg yolks with the milk and add the remaining grappa and a pinch of salt. Sift in the flour and baking powder and stir to combine. Beat the egg whites to stiff peaks and fold into the batter. The batter should be fluid and smooth.

3. Dip the apple slices into the batter and fry in abundant hot sunflower oil. Cook until both sides are golden-brown. Remove from the oil using a slotted spoon and sprinkle with confectioners' sugar before serving.

PASTRY CHEF'S TIP

Serve the fried apples with a
strawberry or blueberry compote.

Orange Crêpes Filled
with Apples and Strawberry Coulis

by **Piero Rainone**

Serves 4

Crêpes

1 egg

1/4 cup (2 oz or 50 g) sugar

zest of 1 organic orange

1 Tbsp Cointreau

1/2 tsp baking powder

2/3 cup (2 ½ oz or 75 g)
all-purpose flour

1 cup (250 ml) milk

butter

Filling

4 Tbsps (2 oz or 50 g) butter

1/2 cup (3 ½ oz or 100 g)
raw sugar

2 Golden Delicious apples,
peeled, cored and quartered

1/4 cup (60 ml) brandy

ground cinnamon

Coulis

3/4 cup (175 ml) water

1/4 cup (2 oz or 50 g) sugar

7 oz (200 g) strawberries

Decoration

9 oz (250 g) brioche bread
(see p. 344)

confectioners' sugar

Preparation time 30 minutes
Cooking time 20 minutes
Level medium

1 Make the crêpes: Beat the egg with the sugar and add the orange zest, Cointreau, baking powder and flour. Whisk to combine. Add the milk little by little and refrigerate for 15 minutes.

2 Butter a 13-inch (32 cm) non-stick crêpe pan. Pour in a ladleful of batter and move the pan in a circular motion to evenly distribute the batter. Cook until the surface of the crêpe is covered with little bubbles and then flip using a spatula or fingertips. Cook for a few more minutes and continue making crêpes until the batter is finished.

3 Heat the butter and sugar for the filling in a saucepan until it begins to caramelize. Add the apple quarters and pour over the brandy. Let the alcohol cook off and remove from the heat. Add a pinch of ground cinnamon.

4 Prepare the coulis by bringing the water, sugar and strawberries to a boil. Remove from the heat and puree. Return the puree to the pan and cook until the sauce is thick. Using a cookie cutter, cut out 4 rounds of brioche bread. Place 1 round on a crêpe and top with 2 apple quarters and a little sauce. Fold up the crêpe and top with a little strawberry coulis. Sprinkle with confectioners' sugar before serving.

techniques&recipes

Decorations

Suggestions and advice for making decorations with sugar and chocolate. Quick and easy ideas and recipes for garnishing with fruit and sauces.

1 Melt the white chocolate over a double boiler or in the microwave.

2 Melt the dark chocolate over a double boiler or in the microwave.

3 Fold a piece of parchment paper into a triangle and cut along the diagonal with a knife.

4-5 Roll the triangle into a cone, overlapping the edges, and stick the paper together with tape or by folding over the corners.

6 Pour the melted dark chocolate into the cone.

7 Make zig-zag designs on a piece of parchment paper and freeze until hardened.

8 To make a chocolate base for a dessert, spread the melted chocolate onto a serving plate using the back of a spoon.

9 Pour the white chocolate into a parchment paper cone and make a spiral design over the chocolate round.

CHOCOLATE DECORATIONS

10 Starting from the inner most part of the spiral, use a toothpick to pull alternating lines of the spiral towards the outside of the plate or towards the center of the spiral.

11 Spread the melted chocolate on a piece of parchment paper and sprinkle with finely chopped nuts; freeze until hard.

12 Spread the melted chocolate on a piece of parchment paper and decorate each round with a little melted white chocolate.

13 Wash and dry some fresh herb leaves. Paint one side of each leaf with the melted tempered chocolate. Freeze for 5-6 minutes or until hardened.

14 Remove the leaves from the chocolate.

15 Heat a baking sheet in a warm oven. Spread a thin layer of melted chocolate over the warm baking sheet and let chill in the refrigerator for a few minutes. The chocolate should be soft to touch.

16 Using a metal spatula, scrape along the chocolate to form curls.

17 Use the same technique to form chocolate curls of various sizes.

1 Bring the water, sugar and glucose syrup to a boil and cook until the liquid reaches 284°F (140°C). Add the citric acid and cook to 305°F (152°C).

2 Remove from the heat and immerse the pan in an ice-water bath, cooling the liquid to 140°C.

3 Lightly oil a stainless-steel dome mold and place it on a piece of parchment paper. Using a ladle, drizzle thin streams of the hot liquid over the mold.

4 Create a web or basket design with the hot liquid and let cool before unmolding.

Ingredients

2 ½ cups (1 lb 2 oz or 500 g) sugar

3/4 cup plus 1 Tbsp (200 ml) glucose syrup

1 ¼ cups (300 ml) water

1 tsp citric acid

SUGAR-THREAD DOME

PASTRY CHEF'S TIP
Do not stir the sugar syrup
while cooking as it may
cause the sugar to crystallize
and the temperature of the
syrup to drop.

Recipe on p. 312

1 Bring the sugar, water and glucose syrup to a boil. Cook until the mixture reaches 248°F (120°C). Dip a fork into the liquid and move it around to form long, very thin threads of sugar.

2 Place a sheet of parchment paper mat on a work surface. Use a whisk to transfer the hot sugar threads to the parchment paper. Form the sugar into the desired shape.

3 Return the sugar mixture to heat and cook until it reaches 230°F (110°C). Drop a few hazelnuts into the mixture and stir to coat.

4 Place each hazelnut on the parchment paper and pull the sugar to form a long string or ribbon. Let cool completely.

Ingredients
2 ½ cups (1 lb 2 oz or 500 g) sugar
1 ¼ cup (300 ml) water
3/4 cup plus 1 Tbsp (200 ml) glucose

CARAMEL DECORATIONS

Recipe on p. 153

PASTRY CHEF'S TIP

To preserve the sugar
decorations, store them in
a container with silica gel.
Place the gel in the bottom
of an airtight container,
cover with parchment paper
and then place the sugar
decorations in the container.
The silica gel with eliminate
the humidity.

1 Blend the almonds into a fine powder and transfer to a mixing bowl. Add the confectioners' sugar and honey and stir well.

2 Beat the egg white to stiff peaks and fold into the almond mixture.

3 Mix well to obtain a smooth dough.

4 Cut off a piece of the dough and roll it into a very thin sheet.

5 Use a round cookie cutter to make marzipan rounds.

Ingredients
2 lb (900 g) almonds

4 cups plus 2 Tbsps (1 lb 2 oz or 500 g) confectioners' sugar

1/2 egg white

1/4 cup plus 1 Tbsp (3 ½ oz or 100 g) honey

MARZIPAN ROSES

6 Form each round into a rose, sprinkle with confectioners' sugar and let dry for 8 hours.

Dessert 385

1 Cut out a small circle in the rind at the center of the whole watermelon, reserving the rind as it will be used for the center of the flower decoration.

2 Use a paring knife to cut out "petals" around the circle.

3-4 Cut out enough of the watermelon rind so that the red color of the fruit shows through, making pink petals.

5 Cut the watermelon in half horizontally and separate the top and a bottom halves.

WATERMELON FLOWER

6 Use a small knife to cut out a zig-zag pattern around the edge of the bottom half of the watermelon.

1-2 Cut the melon in half making a zig-zag design.

3 Use a melon baller to make a hole in the rind at the "navel" on one half of the melon. Reserve the removed pulp.

4-5 Use a paring knife to decorate the area around the hole made at the center, creating petals around the center of the flower.

6 Peel away some of the rind around the flower petals to make a green border.

7-8 Carefully cut away another circle of petals around the green border.

9 Remove the seeds from the uncarved half of the melon and then scoop out many balls.

CANTALOUPE MELON FLOWER

10 Fill the uncarved half of the melon with the melon balls.

1 Use a paring knife to score a line around the circumference of the orange.

2 Score a line perpendicular to the other line to form a triangle.

3 Carefully remove the peel and the pulp from the triangle keeping the pulp intact.

4 Remove the peel and pulp from the corresponding triangle, keeping the pulp and peel intact, to form a cut out in the shape of a half moon.

5 Set aside the removed orange wedges.

6 Cut along the initial score to form a zig-zag design around the circumference of the orange.

ORANGE BASKET

7 Make another perpendicular cut on the other side of the orange to form a triangle, leaving a strip of peel along the center to make the handle of the basket. Remove the peel and pulp. Repeat the cut and remove the peel and pulp so that only the handle remains. Cut the reserved orange pulp into small pieces and fill the "basket" with the orange.

1-2 Use a paring knife to score the circumference of the apricot with a zig-zag design. Take care not to break the apricot.

3 Cut the apricot in half, maintaining the zig-zag design.

1 Cut out several very thin vertical slices from the nectarine.

2-3 Cut out a few thicker slices horizontal slices to form ledges for the thin slices.

APRICOTS AND NECTARINES

4 Fill the ledges with the slices of nectarine.

1 Cut the pineapple half and slice each half lengthwise into 3-4 wedges.

2 Remove the tough core from the center of each pineapple wedge. Slice through the pineapple where the flesh meets the rind so that the wedge is no longer attached to the rind.

3 Cut each wedge horizontally into many 1/2-inch (1 cm) thick slices.

PINEAPPLE BOAT

4 Use the pineapple wedges in a mixed fruit composition.

Almond-Pistachio Brittle

Serves 4

Brittle

2 ¾ cups (9 oz or 250 g) sliced almonds

1 Tbsp peanut oil

2/3 cup (4 oz or 120 g) sugar

3 ½ Tbsps water

3/4 cup (3 ½ oz or 100 g) pistachios, minced

Preparation time 15 minutes
Cooking time 15 minutes
Level easy

1 Preheat the oven to 400°F (200°C or Gas Mark 6). Toast the sliced almonds until they begin to color. Oil a large sheet of parchment paper with the peanut oil and place on a work surface.

2 Heat the sugar and water in a saucepan and let caramelize over low heat. When the caramel is a light-brown color, add half of the toasted almonds. Pour the mixture onto the oiled parchment paper and quickly spread the mixture. Top immediately with the remaining almonds and the pistachios.

3 Cover with a second sheet of parchment paper and press down evenly to form a thin layer. Let cool completely and cut into squares. Store the brittle in a tightly sealed container.

Walnut Brittle

Serves 4

Brittle

1 ¼ cups (9 oz or 250 g) walnut halves

1 ⅓ cups plus 2 Tbsps (10 oz or 280 g) sugar

2 Tbsps water

1 Tbsp lemon juice

Preparation time 10 minutes
Cooking time 5 minutes
Level easy

1 Toast the walnuts briefly and rub them with a clean kitchen towel to remove the skin.

2 Heat the sugar and water in a heavy-bottomed saucepan over low heat. After the sugar has completely dissolved, stir frequently to ensure even cooking. Let cook until the caramel is an amber-brown color. Add lemon juice to the caramel and then the walnuts.

3 Pour the mixture onto a baking sheet lined with parchment paper and spread the brittle into an even layer with an oiled spatula. Let cool and break into pieces.

Pastry Chef's Tip
Walnuts can be substituted with chopped hazelnuts.

Honey Torrone

Serves 8

Torrone

1 cup (4 ½ oz or 130 g) almonds or hazelnuts

1/2 cup (6 oz or 160 g) honey

1 cup (7 oz or 200 g) sugar

1/2 cup (120 ml) glucose syrup

salt

5 Tbsps water

2 egg whites

5 Tbsps (2 ½ oz or 70 g) butter at room temperature

Preparation time 20 minutes
Cooking time 10 minutes
Level medium

1 Preheat the oven to 350°F (180°C or Gas Mark 4). Toast the almonds in the oven until they have colored and smell toasted. Remove from the oven and let cool completely.
Place the honey, sugar, glucose syrup, a pinch of salt and the water in a saucepan. Cook over low heat, stirring constantly with a wooden spoon, until the mixture caramelizes.

2 Meanwhile, beat the egg whites to soft peaks using an electric whisk. Drizzle half of the caramel mixture into the egg whites while the mixer is running, and continue beating until the caramel has been incorporated and the mixture is shiny and smooth. Slowly drizzle in the remaining caramel and beat until the mixture is firm. Fold in the room temperature butter and the almonds or hazelnuts.

3 Butter a sheet of parchment paper and pour the torrone mixture onto the paper. Let cool for 5 minutes. Roll the parchment paper around the torrone and close the two ends like a candy, twisting to close tightly. Refrigerate until firm and serve slices into rounds or cubes.

Chocolate-Covered Strawberries
with Mint

Serves 6

Strawberries

5 ½ oz (150 g) mint-flavored dark chocolate, chopped

20 strawberries

Decoration

mint leaves, minced (optional)

Preparation time 20 minutes
Cooking time 10 minutes
Level easy

1 Melt two-thirds of the chocolate over a double boiler or in the microwave at the lowest setting, taking care not to overcook it.

2 Remove from heat and add the remaining chocolate. Stir until melted.

3 Dip the strawberries in the melted chocolate. Let any excess chocolate drip off, then place them on a baking sheet lined with parchment paper.

4 Sprinkle the strawberries with the chopped mint leaves if desired and refrigerate until set. Serve chilled.

Pastry Chef's Tip

For an elegant variation and a stunning visual effect, stick an edible gold leaf to each strawberry instead of the mint leaves.

Peppered Chocolate Cherries

Serves 4

Cherries

9 oz (250 g) pepper-flavored chocolate

1 Tbsp sunflower oil

20 cherries, stems attached

1/3 cup (1 oz or 30 g) ground hazelnuts

Preparation time 10 minutes
Cooking time 5 minutes
Level easy

1 Melt the chocolate with the sunflower oil over a double boiler, stirring frequently.

2 Place 20 paper baking cups or cylindrical silicon molds on a baking tray. Pour a spoonful of melted chocolate into each cup.

3 Place 1 cherry in the center of each cup, pushing down so that the chocolate nearly covers the cherry.

4 Sprinkle with ground hazelnuts and refrigerate until hard. Remove the cherries from the cups before serving. These cherries are ideal to serve at the end of a meal, accompanied by a cherry liqueur.

PASTRY CHEF'S TIP

If peppered chocolate is unavailable, it can be prepared by melting excellent quality dark chocolate with 1/2 tsp of freshly ground white pepper. Use this same technique to prepare other types of flavored chocolate, such as chili pepper or mint.

Raspberry Vanilla Coulis

Serves 4

Coulis

2 Tbsps sugar

7 Tbsps (100 ml) water

1 vanilla bean

1 basket of raspberries

Preparation time 20 minutes

Cooking time 15 minutes

Level easy

1 Bring the sugar, water and vanilla bean to a low boil. Reduce heat and simmer for 5 minutes. Remove the vanilla bean and slice it in half lengthwise. Return the bean to the pan and reduce the syrup for another few minutes.

2 Remove from heat and remove the vanilla bean. Scrape out the seeds and return them to the pan. Discard the bean.

3 Puree the raspberries, adding the syrup slowly. Strain the puree to remove the seeds, if desired. Serve the coulis with ice cream or cheesecake.

Hazelnut Crème Anglaise

Serves 4

Crème anglaise

3/4 cup plus 1 Tbsp
(200 ml) milk

1 ¼ cups (300 ml)
whipping cream

1 tsp hazelnut paste

4 egg yolks

2/3 cup (4 oz or 120 g) sugar

salt

Preparation time 10 minutes
Cooking time 15 minutes
Level medium

1. Heat the milk and the cream in a saucepan. Add the hazelnut paste and stir to dissolve completely.

2. Beat the egg yolks, sugar and a pinch of salt together in a mixing bowl until thick and pale yellow. Drizzle in the hot milk mixture, whisking constantly.

3. Return the mixture to the saucepan and cook over medium heat or a double boiler, whisking constantly until the cream has thickened and coats the back of a spoon. Remove from the heat and immerse in an ice-water bath to stop the cooking immediately.

PASTRY CHEF'S TIP

Serve the hazelnut crème anglaise with soft cookies. The hazelnut paste may be made by grinding 1/2 cup (2 oz or 60 g) of hazelnuts to form a paste.

Sweet Basil Cream

Serves 4

Cream

2 cups (500 ml) whole milk

6 fresh basil leaves

2 egg yolks

1 Tbsp sugar

3 Tbsps cornstarch

3 Tbsps sweetened condensed milk

Preparation time 20 minutes

Cooking time 15 minutes

Level medium

1 Heat the milk, add the basil leaves and remove from the heat. Let infuse for at least 2 hours. Strain the milk and reheat it.

2 Beat the egg yolks with the sugar until thick. Sift in the cornstarch. Drizzle in the hot milk, whisking constantly, and add the sweetened condensed milk.

3 Return the mixture to the saucepan and bring to a simmer over medium heat, whisking constantly. Let cook for 2 minutes and remove from the heat. Transfer the cream to a bowl and let cool completely.

4 Refrigerate until use and serve chilled with fruit-based desserts.

Spiced Hot Chocolate Sauce

Serves 4

Sauce

7 Tbsps (100 ml) milk

1 Tbsp sugar

1 dried red chili pepper

1 cinnamon stick, broken into pieces

1 clove

7 Tbsps (100 ml) whipping cream

3 ½ oz (100 g) extra-dark chocolate, chopped

Preparation time 25 minutes

Cooking time 15 minutes

Level easy

1 Heat the milk together with the sugar, chili pepper, cinnamon and clove. Let infuse for 3-4 hours and then strain the mixture.

2 Heat the infused milk with the whipping cream. Add the chocolate and let melt completely, stirring until smooth.

3 Let cool slightly and serve in small glasses or ceramic cups as hot chocolate or as a sauce to accompany chocolate desserts.

PASTRY CHEF'S TIP

This hot chocolate may also be used as a sauce for ice cream.

White Chocolate-Coffee Sauce

Serves 4

Sauce

3 Tbsps milk

1 Tbsp Arabica coffee beans

7 Tbsps (100 ml)
whipping cream

3 oz (80 g) white chocolate

Preparation time 20 minutes
Cooking time 5 minutes
Level easy

1 Heat the milk in a small saucepan, remove from the heat and cool slightly. Pour the milk into a bowl with the coffee beans and let sit long enough for the flavors to infuse but not to color the milk. Remove and discard the coffee beans and refrigerate for 8 hours.

2 Heat the cream and the milk together. Add the white chocolate and whisk until the chocolate is melted and the sauce is smooth and fluid.

3 Let cool completely and use to accompany semifreddos or dark chocolate desserts.

Pastry Chef's Tip

This sauce pairs well with cakes like pandoro and panettone or any type of sponge cake.